"WE TO INFORM YOU…"

Stories of Former Prisoners of War

William F. Rutkowski

Revised Edition

American Ex-Prisoners of War
Maryland North Chapter

First Edition 2001

Revised Edition 2006

ISBN Number 1-59971-708-5

Published by:
Aardvark Global Publishing Company, LLC

Printed by:
Linemark Digital, Inc.
1220 Caraway Court
Largo, MD 20774-5338
United States of America

Contents

Acknowledgements

First and foremost, my grateful thanks to the men of the Maryland North Chapter of the American Ex-Prisoners of War who have taken the time and trouble to share with us the stories that have been locked in their memories for so long. Above all, thanks to my wife Imogene, the commander in chief of this undertaking, for all her support and incredible skills in managing the project to its fruition and my son Bill who came through when his help was so desperately needed. Words will never be enough.

I also thank Eleanor Huson for her invaluable assistance in coordinating the interviews, providing information and for support from afar.

Special thanks to Herndon Inge, Jr. and Thomas R. Johnson, Jr. for allowing me to quote excerpts from their vivid accounts of the battle of Orscholz published in the 94th Infantry Division Association's Commemorative History.

My gratitude to John B. Berg, Jr. who provided a copy of the actual longhand Diary of the 2nd Battalion, 28th Infantry Regiment, 8th Infantry Division from June 26, 1944 to December 31, 1944.

I also extend my appreciation to the librarian at the 8th Air Force Museum near Savannah, Georgia for her friendly assistance in securing and copying documents during my research there.

Finally, what would I have done without the keen eyes and special editing talents of our friend Phyllis Nordgren, whose cheerful involvement enhanced the quality of this work.

To all the people above, I am forever indebted.

Introduction

This project began more than five years ago when the American Ex-Prisoners of War, Department of Maryland Commander Jack Meyers began advocating that members document the stories of their imprisonment to preserve their legacy. I had recently completed writing my brother's memoirs and he shared my work with the group. They were impressed and inquired if I was willing to chronicle their stories. I was honored by the invitation and willingly accepted their offer. I have always had so much admiration for the men and women of this era and their heroic deeds and I welcomed the opportunity to get to know them personally and learn first hand of their experiences.

Twelve men, including my brother Charles, agreed to participate in the project and resulted in publishing the first edition of *We Regret to Inform You*. The stories reveal not only the appalling conditions these men had to endure but also tell of the pain and anxiety parents and wives experienced when notified that their loved one was "missing in action" and not knowing whether he was dead or alive for many months. The stories are about faith and hope and hopelessness and reveal the strength that many took from their trust in God.

The results were beyond expectations. Congressman Robert L. Ehrlich Jr., 2nd District, Maryland and now the Governor of Maryland recognized these efforts to document the stories of former prisoners of war and his kind words were an embodiment of the many accolades received. He wrote, "The stories allowed individuals who had never experienced combat a glimpse of the horrific conditions and emotions these soldiers were forced to endure. One can only imagine the psychological tortures these young men overcame. They represent the very best characteristics which our great nation is founded upon." He continued, "Your book is more than a collection of stories and memories, it is a tribute to the courage and spirit these young men embodied. By telling their stories, your book provides current and future generations valuable life and leadership insights and learning, which I hope they take to heart."

The first printing sold out. The Maryland North Chapter considered a second printing; however, several other members requested that their stories be included in a new edition. I agreed to revise the book, add five new stories to the existing twelve and modify existing stories as requested. The number of pages in this new edition has increased by sixty percent. This effort became more arduous than anticipated, but with all the encouragement and support I received, I was able to finish this work and provide copies of this revised edition to all participants. They are still my heroes.

Throughout our Nation's history, the men and women of America's Armed Forces have preserved our freedom, protected our security, and upheld our democratic values. Through out history, our men and women in uniform have stood proudly in defense of the United States and our cause of liberty. In the two centuries since our Nation's birth, more than one-half million Americans were captured and interned as prisoners of war. It is neither dishonorable nor heroic to be a prisoner of war. Often capture comes as a complete surprise and is frequently accompanied by injury. Internment is a physical and emotional ordeal. American prisoners of war have suffered and died from starvation, disease, exposure, and lack of medical care, forced marches, and outright murder. Some have experienced the prisoner of war ordeal for only a few days, others for years. All have experienced the loss of freedom.

Presented are the stories of seventeen men – all heroes – all members of the Maryland North Chapter of the American Ex-Prisoners of War. They all suffered the prisoner of war ordeal. Their stories are stories of ordinary men of extraordinary valor. They were abused mentally and physically, subjected to the wrath of German citizens – shot at and spat upon. Their focus was kept their on their next meal because they were systematically starved and rendered too weak to attempt escape. They experienced one of the great atrocities ever perpetrated against American prisoners of war, the march across Germany, an event unknown by most living Americans but never forgotten by those who lived through it.

Their stories are stories of death and destruction, deprivation and sacrifice, courage and comradeship, human feelings and inhuman acts, and a fight to survive and retain sanity.

Their stories celebrate the qualities of the hero, and just to survive on a day-to-day basis, every man had to be just that.

It is their stories we humbly attempt to present in this book so they may be passed on to their children and their children's children, and shared with all freedom loving men and women everywhere. Their history should be preserved so that we all can better understand the loss of freedom and cherish it even more.

In the first edition, we indicated that ninety percent of living former prisoners of war were World War II veterans and we are losing them at an accelerating rate.

Before the first edition of this book was completed, we lost William P. Booth on September 27, 2000. Bill was a terrific storyteller and his insights into prison life contributed greatly to the success of this work.

On September 9, 2002, Richard V. Mulcahy died. Dick was the youngest of the men whose stories are chronicled herein to serve his country. He enlisted when he was only seventeen years old. He fought in Normandy and became a prisoner of war shortly after his nineteenth birthday.

On May 26, 2005, Daniel D. Dudek, Jr. left us at age 81. Dan was a tail gunner on a B-24 and following a midair collision with another American bomber, he was captured and became a prisoner of war. A devoted family man, Dan was quiet, kind and respected by all who knew him.

My beloved brother Charles Milton Rutkowski went to his peace on October 6, 2005 at age 85. He had served with the 28th Infantry Regiment during World War II, fought in Normandy and was captured during the battle of Brest. He was an active member of the American Ex-POW organization and a member of the Maryland North Chapter's speaker bureau. He enjoyed assisting other veterans by sharing his vast knowledge of veteran's benefits and helping them obtain the benefits they had earned.

William Mitchell's story is not included in this book. Failing health prevented his needed active participation. Nevertheless, he deserves special recognition. He enlisted in early September 1942, and because the American armed forces were so desperate for men, he was shipped to North Africa with only the minimum of training. Assigned to the 168th Infantry Regiment he entered combat in Tunisia in early 1943, and became a prisoner at the Kasserine Pass on February 18, 1943. He spent more time as a prisoner of war then any of the other men who participated in this book. He described being a captive of the German government as a "two-year sentence at hard labor." He was one of the many thousands of American prisoners who were forced to march across Germany between February and April 1945. Bill Mitchell died on September 24, 2005.

In Memoriam

Rest easy, sleep well my brothers
Know the line has held, your job is done.
Rest easy, sleep well,
Others have taken up where you fell; the line has held
Peace, peace, and farewell.

Author Unknown

Edwin S. "Bud" Huson

EDWIN STERLING HUSON

*"We paid a terrible price for serving our country but
I have never regretted it."*

BETWEEN JANUARY 1, 1942 and June 1943, the Army Air Forces (AAF) experienced their greatest period of growth and added more than 1.8 million men and women to their ranks. They offered all types of incentives to entice you to enlist. My recruiter explained that the AAF had bases throughout the country and implied that following basic training, I would be sent to the base of my choice. Olmstead Field, outside Harrisburg, Pennsylvania was an easy commute to my home, northeast of Baltimore. The deal sounded pretty good to an eighteen-year-old who had never been much farther away from home, so on October 28, 1942, I enlisted in the Army Air Forces.

After swearing in, our group walked from the Emerson Hotel to the Camden Station in Baltimore and boarded a train for Camp Lee, Virginia. The next few days were spent processing – being issued uniforms, getting a GI haircut, taking aptitude tests, receiving the dreaded shots, and learning the army way – hurry up and wait.

The Air Forces remained true to their word. From Camp Lee, I was sent to Olmstead Field – for two days! The next stop was Kellogg Field, Michigan where I pulled guard duty until a week before Christmas. Basic training was at Keesler Field, Mississippi and we arrived by train on Christmas Eve.

Following basic training, I stayed on at Keesler to attend Airplane Mechanic School, a twenty-seven week training course. My technical training concluded at Ford Motor Company's half-mile-long aircraft assembly line at Willow Run, Michigan. We called it "Willit Run?" Here, assembly workers produced a B-24 Liberator every two hours.

My first ride in an airplane was in a single engine AT-6 piloted by Lt. Allison from York, Pennsylvania, during Gunnery School at Harlingen, Texas. When firing for record at a towed target with a .30-inch caliber Browning machine-gun, I qualified as "expert marksman." I was always rather proud of that. At graduation, I received corporal stripes and my aerial gunner wings.

Following a seven-day delay en route furlough that allowed me to return home for the first time since my enlistment, I reported to Salt Lake City, Utah and was assigned to a B-17 aircrew. We flew to Dalhart Air Force Base in Texas, to begin Air Combat Crew Training. Shortly after arriving, I was hospitalized for more than a month with scarlet fever, and as a result, in January 1944, I was reassigned to Lt. Durwood Marshall's B-17 aircrew and remained with that crew until our plane went down over Germany on May 12, 1944.

After completing combat crew training in April, we were assigned to a new B-17 Flying Fortress at Kearney, Nebraska. We loaded our gear on board in the bomb bay and drew fifty rounds of .50-inch caliber ammunition for each gun, checked the fuel and oil, had chow and turned in early, in order to leave before sunrise the next day. It really rattled my cage when I awoke and it was broad daylight. I thought that they had left without me, but it turned out that sometime during the night officials grounded all the planes because of a brake problem. So we unloaded all our gear and waited for new orders. The next day, while boarding a train to Camp Kilmer, New Jersey, Sgt. Richard Schmutte, our tail gunner and the crew clown, mislead us into believing we were on the wrong train, so we all started to get off. This got us into a whole lot of trouble with the Transportation Officer, and we had our butts chewed out. He was infuriated! From Camp Kilmer, we were transported to New York City, and boarded the English Ship, *Mauretania*, for our voyage to England.

Following arrival in South Hampton, England, we moved to a place called the "Wash," a big long beach where planes could make emergency landings. There we had gunnery practice with .50-inch caliber machine-guns mounted on posts that we fired out over the ocean. After a day or two, we moved to a large town (name of which I can't remember). On the first night in this town, there was an air raid and we could hear the bombs going off in the distance. Everyone started going to the shelters, but not me. I stayed in the sack. Suddenly, there was a thunderous bang. The light bulb, hanging on a two-foot cord, flew up against the ceiling and dust and glass flew, and in about two seconds, I was out of the bunk and headed for the shelter!

In mid-April, we transferred to Podington Air Base, near North Hampton, and assigned to the 92nd Bomb Group, *Fame's Favored Few* and the 327th Bomb Squadron. Initially, we flew around the area to become familiar with the terrain and local landmarks, and slow-timed repaired flak-damaged planes to assure they were again ready for combat.

Our first potential combat flight was on May 10, 1944. The targets were in northwest Germany. Including three spares, thirty-three aircraft were airborne. We flew spare; meaning we would replace an aircraft that had to head back. None of the planes aborted, so halfway over the channel, the spares turned back and returned to the base, but the next day we became air combat veterans. Our target was the rail yards at Lille, France. We encountered some flak, but no damage and we all returned to the base safely.

The following day, May 12, would be different. Our target was a ball bearing factory in Merseburg, deep in the heart of Germany. Just after daylight, we pushed the props through and pulled our pre-flight checks, and loaded about eight cases of ammo aboard. We did all this work in our long john underwear to keep from sweating, otherwise once we reached high altitudes our clothes would freeze. Sgt. Richard Schmutte and I were in our long johns when we started boxing around like the old-time fighters used to do. Our co-pilot Lt. Norman Peck chewed us out. He wanted to know if we understood that this was serious business, and what might happen. Hours later, we learned how right he was. It was very serious business.

We had trouble getting the right in-board engine started. It was belching out old bluish-black smoke and missing. During mag check, I noticed a significant drop in rpm's, so I notified the pilot, Lt. Durwood Marshall, of the situation. He acknowledged my concern but said we were going anyway. We taxied out to the runway and pulled up as close as we could to the plane in front of us. When our turn came to take off, we were at full-throttle, but due to a heavy load of eighteen 300-pound general-purpose bombs and ammunition, and one engine not functioning properly, we used up every foot of runway to get off. I kept saying to myself, "Come on, you SOB, get up!" We barely cleared the trees at the end of the runway. There were twenty-one planes airborne and when we got out over the English Channel, no one turned back, and I knew then why the pilot said we were going despite our malfunctioning engine. It was one of those missions – if you got the plane off the ground, you flew. You made a showing despite the additional risks.

A mission is a long-drawn-out ordeal. Airmen spend many miserable hours jammed into a cramped duty station and are weighed down with sixty pounds of gear. Our electrically heated flying suits allowed us to function in minus-forty degree temperatures that are the norm when flying at 25,000 feet. Discomfort accompanied grinding tedium. This was the longest flight for our crew and we were well into France when our right waist gunner, Jack Browder, and I were about to get chewed out this time. Jack liked to do minstrel show skits and he was quite good at it. As we neared the target, we began to experience flak, which was heavy but not too accurate. Jack got on the intercom.

He asked, "Mr. Bones, why do a cannon roar?"

I replied, "I don't know, Mr. Interlocutor. Why do a cannon roar?"

"Mr. Bones, you would roar too if you had your balls shot off!" Yuk. Yuk.

A voice boomed over the intercom, "KNOCK IT OFF BACK THERE!"

The exciting part of a raid is when you approach the Initial Point (IP) and begin to make the turn for the run up to the target. Everyone jumps into action. At this point, the bombardier controls the plane, flying on autopilot, until the bombs are released. The pilot holds a preset heading, altitude and airspeed for a considerable period. The plane must remain steady and level, and flown in a parade-like formation. No evasive actions can be taken. This made us more vulnerable to the German flak gunners.

About twenty-five miles from the target, the troubled right inboard engine completely quit and we dragged behind the formation. As we approached the IP, visibility was excellent, but with only three engines

15

functioning, we were like ducks in a shooting gallery. The German answer to the bombers was flak, exploding shells fired from a wide-range of anti-aircraft equipment. As the flak became very heavy and more accurate, we took a hit and lost a second engine. Now, the plane began to lose altitude and we had to drop out of the formation. When we were hit again and lost a third engine, leaving us flying with only one engine, the pilot called for fighter escort. An escort party came but they did not hang around long because other planes were under attack. The last functioning engine started acting up and the pilot ordered a bailout. The "serious business" had begun.

I frantically checked my parachute harness. Sgt. Schmutte went out the hatch in the rear. The rest of us tried to go out the waist door but the hinge pin cable broke off and the pins stuck in the hinges, so we all went out the bomb bay. As I floated down, I watched our plane make a large circle and go down into the woods and burst into flames.

Lt. Durwood Marshall, Sgt. James Brown, our ball turret gunner, and Sgt. Richard Schmutte were killed that afternoon. Civilians or German troops most likely killed both Lt. Marshall and Sgt. Brown. Sgt. Schmutte's parachute did not blossom out – it just streamed. Lt. Norman O. Peck, co-pilot; Lt. Harry J. Pachesky, navigator; Lt. James B. Kealey, bombardier; S/Sgt. Victor L. Knesz, top turret gunner and flight engineer; S/Sgt. Will J. Cleere, radioman; Sgt. Jack L. Browder, waist gunner; and I were all captured that day and became prisoners of war.

This was my first jump, ever. Floating down, I could see Krauts waiting for me to land and, because I came in backwards, my feet caught on the top of a small fruit tree causing me to land on my butt. It felt like my backbone went through the top of my head. My tongue and mouth became very numb. A farmer with a pitchfork tried to stick me, but other civilians took control and headed me toward town. When we reached the edge of town and started down the street, a crowd gathered and one of the on-lookers struck me behind the ear with a fist and knocked me to the ground. The civilians, who had brought me that far, pulled them away and we started again. A woman came up, spat in my face and said several choice words in her native tongue, which I did not understand, but I got the meaning of her tirade. We walked a couple of blocks farther to the local jail.

The jailer became infuriated because I would not give him my dog tags. When I told him my watch was government-issued, he let me keep it, but he took my rings. After a while I heard someone hollering "Essen" in the next cell. It was Vic Knesz, our flight engineer. The Krauts must have thought I was the one calling for food because they came in and took me from the cell to an office in another building. They tried to question me in German but I had no idea what they were saying. They believed that I did understand them but just would not answer. A guard in front of me struck in the face several times while another one in back kept pushing me forward like a punching bag. They bloodied my nose and busted my mouth, but finally they motioned for me to go out the door. As I started down the stairs, the guard kicked my feet out from under me and I landed at the bottom of the stairwell.

The next day, German soldiers came for Sgt. Knesz and me for a trip to the Dulag Luft Interrogation Center located near Frankfurt, where all captured airmen were taken for initial questioning. Along the way, angry mobs of civilians tried to get at us twice – once on a streetcar and another time on the train. We were both truly scared. When the soldiers cocked their burp guns, everyone backed off fast. We made it to the center where we were questioned some more. They provided food but I had no appetite and I was placed in solitary confinement. The Germans believed that isolation loosened the tongue, and during the night, they took me from my cell and questioned me again. This time they presented my pilot's I.D. card and asked me who he was. I told them I'd never seen him before and they said, no matter, he was dead and soon I would be, too. They pronounced that I would be hanged because I was a "Luft Gangster" or 'Terrorflieger.' Most airmen were told at one time or another that they would be hanged before the war was over and I learned, toward the end of the war, it was not uncommon for crews to be lynched by civilians and, occasionally, murdered in cold blood by the military. When they finished the interrogation, I returned to the cell. Actually, from this interrogation, it became apparent to me that the Germans knew more than I did about my bomb group. They wanted their wards to think that they had all the answers.

Several days later, I was taken from my cell to a distribution center where I was loaded onto a boxcar with other airmen who had been incarcerated at Dulag Luft. For the first time since my capture, I saw two other crewmembers, Jack Browder and Will Cleere. The boxcars were about the same size as the First World War *Forty and Eight* (forty men or eight horses) but almost sixty men were jammed into my car. No food or water was provided. A bucket was available for body waste but only those up close could use it. The rest of us had to relieve ourselves where we were standing. All of us were fearful our own planes would strafe us while on the journey to the prison camp.

The trip took two full days and nights, and after we reached the rail stop at Keifheide in Northeastern Germany (now Poland) we were marched about two and one-half miles to a new prison camp designated Stalag

Luft IV. I was assigned to Compound A. There were only about 400 prisoners in the camp when I arrived. The number would soon swell to more than 10,000 airmen. Because I was so quiet, Will Cleere dubbed me "Silent Yokum." After I became acquainted with the gang, the name was soon forgotten. Sgt. Frank Paules, the ranking NCO for the entire camp, held the title "man of confidence" and had authority to approve whatever we wanted to do within the camp. His tests were – Was it feasible? Could it hurt others? Was it good for the camp?

Stalag Luft IV

A little history of the camp: Stalag Luft IV was situated at Grosstychow, in the German region of Pomerania (now Poland). The camp was activated in April 1944, but despite German efforts, it was never actually completed due to the pressure of war. It was cut into a forest, whose dense foliage and underbrush served as an added barrier to prevent escape. There were two barbed-wire fences each ten feet high, completely surrounding the camp. Rumor had it that the outer fence was electrically charged, but we could not verify that and had no desire to test it.

Between the two fences was another fence of rolled barbed wire four feet high. An area two hundred feet deep from the fence to the edge of the forest was left clear, making it necessary for anyone attempting to escape to traverse this area in full view of the guards. A warning wire was fifty feet inside the barbed wire. A prisoner could expect to be shot first then questioned if he stepped over this wire. At close intervals around the camp were towers with powerful spotlights and machine-guns. It was enough to deter anyone from attempting escape this way.

There were four compounds: Lagers A, B, C, and D, with ten barracks of ten rooms each – a kitchen, an outside hand-pump for water, and a building used for the latrine. Each had a shed for storage of potatoes, carrots, and the like. The kitchen had a couple of large steam-type boilers used to cook potatoes, barley, carrots, cabbage and broth. Each lager looked the same from what we could see. Outside the lagers were German administrative buildings, equipment storage, offices, barracks, and a barracks used as a hospital for POWs who were very ill. I was assigned to Lager B, Barracks 3, Room 10. There were only eight triple bunks to accommodate twenty-seven men. The three who did not have a bunk slept on the floor.

A bunk had six slats (3 feet long by 3 inches wide), and a burlap mattress partially filled with grass or straw. We had a table, two benches, and two stools, along with a stove and few coals or rubbish to burn in it. During the cold winter, we would get five lumps of coal per day.

Stalag Luft IV was a camp for non-commissioned officers, and the Germans respected our rank. We were mostly airmen with the rank of sergeant. Before entering a lager, a POW had his picture taken and assigned a camp number printed on a piece of tin with the camp designation on each end. I arrived at the Stalag before they started taking pictures. My camp number, 1452, was printed on a small piece of cardboard instead of tin. One of our two American dog tags had been taken from us earlier in the capture; the tin ID's were to serve as a replacement.

Food, or the lack of it, was our biggest problem. During the first month, we were near starvation. We received no food until the third day when then they fed us a single slice of bread and a cup of coffee. It is hard to describe how hunger affects you; it deprives you of sleep and makes you think of nothing but food. Your stomach must shrink, because after a while, I did not mind the empty gut so much. In June, the food situation began to improve somewhat, but I was always hungry. When available, we had ersatz coffee and a piece of bread for breakfast. Loaves of bread were about 8 inches long and 3 inches high. Eight men shared a loaf of bread per day.

The bread was supposedly made of one scoop of rye flour and two scoops of ground tree flour (sawdust) minced leaves and straw. We also saw bits of glass and sand; someone was not following the recipe. For lunch, we had a cup of boiled dehydrated cabbage and horsemeat, cut in very small pieces. Occasionally, we could even see a piece of the meat. For supper we had soup and one boiled potato not much bigger than a golf ball. One day a wagon came into the compound and all we saw were four black legs sticking up above the edge of the wagon. I do not know how long this horse had been dead; he was bloated and stiff as a board. We had meat in our soup that evening.

Camp life was mostly boring and dull during the nine months I spent at Stalag Luft IV. Our work was primarily cleaning up after ourselves and pulling K.P. We kept busy doing whatever we wanted to do, playing cards, writing, reading, playing ball, walking or jogging around the compound.

Poker was the game of choice and the stakes were cigarettes that were included in the Red Cross parcels we occasionally received. Some of us made yo-yos and sailboats out of bits of board. We floated the boats on the fire pond in front of the mess hall/cook shack. Every time a new guy arrived in our room we gave him a bowl and sent him to the mess hall for a bowl of mustard or ketchup. When he returned, we asked why the bowl was empty and what the cook had said. It was pretty funny, then.

Every morning and evening we had headcount. They eventually discontinued roll call because too many of us were answering "here" at the same time, which really irked them. At times we would shift our feet and move around causing them to lose count and they had to start the roll call all over again. We would do anything to disrupt their train of thought, but once the snow began falling, it became too cold for us to play with them. We did not have any heavy clothes.

Most of the guards were older men and reasonable, but others were down right mean. The one most despised was a fifty-five year old giant of man called "Big Stoop." He was at least six feet six inches tall and weighed close to two hundred pounds. He had extremely large hands that seemed out of proportion to those of the average person. His peculiarity was he used those huge hands to cuff men in the ears with an open-hand sideways movement. This would cause pressure on the eardrums and sometimes puncture them. I had my first and only encounter with Big Stoop in mid-summer 1944. Apparently, I did not get out of his way fast enough and I suffered the consequences. Using his special technique, he palmed my ears with those massive hands, rupturing my eardrum. To this day, I can still see his ugly face and vividly remember that blow to my head.

On December 16, 1944, I received an overcoat and a pair of gloves from the Red Cross. The weather was getting colder and it had snowed the previous night so the overcoat and gloves really helped. I was always cold and hungry. That night the water pump froze, not that it made much difference. We all were so lousy with body lice that bathing would not help. If lice were one cent a dozen back then, I'd be a rich man today!

After the evening headcount, the guards routinely locked us in our barracks and shutters were placed over the windows. However, on Christmas Eve and New Year's Eve they allowed us out until midnight – which was really a treat. On Christmas day I had barley soup for breakfast and turkey from our Red Cross parcel for dinner. There was a nice show in the Recreation Hall, band and all, but it was too crowded for me to get in. Standing outside and hearing the men sing *Silent Night* and other Christmas carols is something I will never forget. It was a pretty good Christmas, but I wished I were home.

March Across Germany

In late January, as the Russian army approached from the east, we could see the distant flash of artillery fire. This meant their advancing front, and hopefully our liberation, was not far away. Then, with only a short notice, we learned we were being evacuated to another prison camp. The sick and wounded prisoners went first by train, and more men followed by rail a few days later. Finally, on February 6, 1945, those of us remaining set out on foot. No one knows for sure, but we probably numbered about 10,000 men. We left in three groups: A, C, and D compounds. Compounds B and D were combined. I marched with compound C.

The guards divided us into groups of 250 to 300, not all of which traveled the same route or at the same pace. The result was a diverging, converging living river of men that flowed slowly but predictably west. This odyssey occurred during one of the coldest winters ever in northeast Germany.

During the day, we marched four or five abreast in bitter cold, freezing rain, snow, sleet and mud. At night, we were herded into nearby barns, if we were lucky enough to find one. When we did, it was usually impossible for all the men to find room to lie down, so many had to sleep standing up or sleep all night in barn filth. With luck, a bed consisted of straw on a barn floor. We were so filthy and covered with lice the German farmers would withhold clean straw, saying the men would contaminate it and make it unfit for their animals.

We never had a change of clothes, and did not dare take our shoes off because our feet were so swollen from frostbite, that we would not have been able to get them back on.

Our daily meal was a slice of bread, a cup of ersatz coffee, a small potato, and whatever else we could find in the fields. Some days there was no food. Sources of water were unsanitary surface water, melted snow, dirty or not, and water from ditches that others may have used as latrines. We scrounged the fields for whatever we could find, and the firewood to cook it, often finding no more than a potato or turnip root to boil or eat raw when necessary.

On the rare occasions when Red Cross parcels arrived, we would trade cigarettes, soap or anything else we had with the guards and civilians for basics such as bread and spuds. My government-issued watch brought three loaves of bread and one-half pound of bacon. Some men resorted to stealing from pigs the feed that had been thrown to them, and to grazing like cows on roadside grass. A handful of stolen grain, eaten while marching, provided many a mid-day meal. There were times we marched all day with little food, water or rest. I recall one day when it was windy and raining very hard as we stood in line for our issue of bread, but it ran out just as I was to receive mine. I thought to myself that my T. S. Card would be fully punched by the time I got back home – if I lasted that long.

Adding to our misery was the bitter cold. Snow piled knee-deep at times, and temperatures plunged well below zero. Under these conditions, virtually all the marchers grew gaunt and weak, and hundreds of us suffered from malnutrition, trench foot, dysentery, exhaustion and other diseases. We formed into small groups and relied on each other for survival. I was so sick and weak from dysentery I began passing blood. I didn't think I had a muscle left in my legs or back. Once we went down, we needed help getting back on our feet.

As we marched, we would pass slave-labor people – French, Russian, Polish and Jewish working in the fields and in compounds. Their clothing was made of burlap and their shoes were either wooden "Dutch" shoes or tire treads tied to their feet with rags. I will never forget the sunken eyes of the children and the look of despair on the faces of the adults. We were not the only ones on the road. The roads became crowded with German people escaping from the advancing Russians. Some had carts harnessed to their horses or cows, and they often ran the animals to their death.

After walking for fifty-two days and about six hundred kilometers, we reached Stalag XI B on March 30, 1945. This camp, located at Fallingbostel southwest of Bremen, was some kind of staging area containing people of all races, and from all nations. The camp's sights and smells set up a weird situation. The POWs inside the camp wanted out and we wanted desperately to get in, and for a time we did, taking our first shower in more than six months as a part of their delousing regimen. After putting on our filthy clothes, we were dusted with DDT. For a few days, we slept in tents, one hundred men to a tent, and given some hot brew, a cup of soup and one-sixth of a loaf of bread with liverwurst.

The camp was too crowded to accommodate all of us so we stayed less than a week. On April 6, 1945, we began marching again and once again had to scrounge for food. Like manna from heaven, Red Cross parcels started to arrive; usually one parcel was divided among four men. Soon, we began receiving both American and Canadian Red Cross parcels - one per man. The Krauts were still afraid that we might attempt to escape so they punched holes in all the cans before they gave us the parcels, making it impractical for us to save anything due to potential food spoilage. All empty cans were turned in before we received our next issue.

On April 10, we walked 25 kilometers to a small town. The heavies were over that day and their escorts gave us a short burst that raised some dust in the rafters of the barn we were in. I tried to hide under the straw. After it was over, I felt stupid but we all had a good laugh about it. When he made his next run, he came up the other side of the road and blasted the woods to pieces across from the barn. There was a Jerry motor pool in there and our planes worked it over pretty well. On his last pass, he dipped his wings and left.

As we continued on our march, a German farmer gave us a can of milk, two small calves and two small pigs. We made a beef and pork soup that filled the gut that day. On April 30, I slept outside on the ground and blanketed myself with straw. It was a good thing because we were covered with an inch of snow the next morning.

On May 2, 1945, a British officer and soldiers came into our area. The Krauts threw their rifles down and put their hands behind their heads. All of us were laughing, crying, cursing or thanking God all at the same time. It is impossible to explain our feelings. We had survived!

The Officer told us to head for the rear, and we took off like cut cats. We walked a short distance when British soldiers driving GI trucks picked us up. We crossed the Elbe River and headed west for Luneburg where we were deloused and issued new clothing by the British. I had worn the same clothes since I left Stalag Luft IV. All that was left of my underwear was the waistband; I had no toes and heels in my socks, and my clothing was covered with human excrement and manure. After wearing the same clothes for 85 days, it felt fantastic to be free of parasites and wear clean clothes.

We now slept in a heated building for the first time since we left Stalag Luft IV on February 6, 1945. On the march we had slept in cattle runs, barns, and fields. It did not make a difference if it was snowing, raining, sleeting or freezing weather; we just curled up on the ground and went to sleep.

The British fed us gradually. When I entered the Air Forces, I weighed approximately one hundred and sixty pounds. I now weighed ninety-five pounds. On May 4, we moved by truck to a camp about thirty miles southwest of Luneburg. From there, we were to be flown to Brussels, but several days of bad weather kept us in the sack for most of the time as we waited for our flight. On May 8, we boarded a train in Brussels and were on our way. I was still wearing a British uniform as we traveled to Namur, Belgium. There were all kinds of goodies to eat and they made me sick but I still ate them. Some POWs died by gorging themselves because we were only supposed to have one tablespoon of food at a time. We received new clothing, paid twenty dollars, and then taken by hospital train to Camp Lucky Strike near Le Havre, France. There we received physical exams and the usual checks and questions.

We had one more journey to make. We were now ready to hit the road one more time – and head for home. I returned to the U.S.A. on the ship *U.S.S. Explorer* in June 1945.

Personal Message

I, along with many others, faithfully served my country during World War II, suffered imprisonment and inhumane cruelty at the hands of my captors. All of which was in violation of the Geneva Convention, which conferred a protected status on prisoners of war. We persevered and recovered from these indignities, defied our captors again and again during life-threatening times.

We paid a terrible price for serving our country, but I have never regretted it. I proudly served in the Armed Forces as I believed, and still believe; we must live up to our obligations in order to ensure freedom for our country.

With God's help I survived the torture and difficult conditions, especially the eighty-five day forced march then referred to as the Black Death March. Many made the ultimate sacrifice and did not return home. They deserve never to be forgotten. Let us hope and pray that future generations will never have to face the ordeal of being a prisoner of war and that we will work to keep the peace.

I thank the Lord I made it through the war and returned home to my parents and sisters. Also, that I am still here to share my life with Eleanor, my wife of fifty-six years who still bears with me the brunt of my captivity, yet always has a smile for me without a harsh retort. I am also grateful for my son Stephen, daughter-in-law Andrea, and grandsons Matthew and Jonathan.

Edwin S. "Bud" Huson received his honorable discharge at Andrews Air Force Base on November 8, 1945 at the rank of Staff Sergeant. He was twenty-one years old. He was awarded the Air Medal; POW Medal; World War II Victory Medal; European, African, Middle-Eastern Campaign Medal with a Battle Star; American Theatre Medal; Good Conduct Medal; and a Presidential Distinguished Unit Citation. His military career included three years active duty, twenty-seven years as a full-time Technician with the Maryland Army National Guard and five years with the State of Maryland Military Department.

Bud Huson (2nd from top left) &
a few of Fame's Favored Few

Eleanor and Bud Huson, 1999

29

Howard Hartman, July 1945

HOWARD N. HARTMAN

*"We shouted and applauded in delight. Nazi Germany
was dead and we helped kill it."*

HOWARD HARTMAN grew up in Shelby, Ohio,
a small town located midway between
Columbus and Cleveland. He had recently
graduated from Shelby High School and found
employment as a lathe operator at Wright Field when the
war began. In April 1942, he enlisted in the Army Air
Corps. Howard tells his story:

I reported for duty in October 1942 and sent to the
Classification and Pre-Flight Center at Nashville,
Tennessee. We took a battery of general education and
physio-motor tests and a physical exam to determine for
which specialty we best qualified. Naturally, everyone
wanted to be a fighter pilot and those of us who did not
'wash out' reached cadet status and transferred to
Maxwell Field in Montgomery, Alabama for two months
of pre-flight training.

Following successful completion of this program,
we were next sent to various primary flying schools
located throughout the south. I went to Charlstrom Field
in Arcadia, Florida. It had been a private flying school
before the war and the quarters were splendid. It was like
living at a resort with a swimming pool and tennis courts
and other amenities not usually found at an Air Corps
facility.

We flew PT-17s open-cockpit biplanes with forward
and aft cockpits. The instructor sat in the rear seat. The
landing wheels on this craft were very close together

which caused the plane to ground loop upon landing. Two of these and you were out. You had to be proficient in landing techniques and recover from stalls and spins. We began the solo phase after six hours of dual time and had to solo before ten hours. My roommate heard my instructor say, "There goes Hartman. Yesterday he successfully soloed by the grace of God."

Those of us who survived were sent to Bainbridge, Georgia for basic flying training and after 60-hours of basic flying, we went to Valdosta, Georgia for advanced flying training. We flew twin engine AT-10s and the instructor sat beside us. By now, we could fly quite well and we learned formation flying and navigation. My class graduated and we were awarded silver pilot's wings on August 30, 1943 and commissioned as 2nd lieutenants. Fifteen of us were assigned to the 15th Air force, 456th Bomb Group at Mountain Home, Idaho as co-pilots. For the next several months, we were welded into fighting teams and received extensive training in formation flying, gunnery, and practiced bombing runs (dropping flour bags). Eventually, we picked up a new B-24 in San Francisco and flew to the East Coast, then to Brazil and across the Atlantic to Africa. We arrived at our base in Cerignola, Italy on February 1, 1944.

At Navigator Milton Halberstadt's suggestion, the crew named the aircraft *Boojum* after a character in the Lewis Carroll story *"Hunting the Snark."* Anyone who looked upon the mythical monster Boojum evaporated. The crew of the *Boojum* flew a score of missions from the German submarine pens at Toulon to the rail yards at Budapest and Bucharest including forays into enemy strongholds at Anzio and Monte Cassino. Since February 17, 1944, we had flown nine missions. The target for our tenth and what was to be my final mission was the marshaling yards at Budapest, Hungary.

Monday morning April 3, 1944 was cloudy and overcast. We were up before daybreak, dressed quickly, downed as much breakfast as our jittery stomachs could take, and headed for the briefing room. The mission map was unveiled and the length of yarn stretched from Italy to Budapest. The weather outlook, the proper approach to take, the kind of flak and fighter opposition expected were all covered. We climbed into our planes with all our gear and the pilot and I ran through a long pre-flight checklist. The bombers lined up on the taxiways and 30 seconds apart thundered from the runway and struggled into the air. When every plane was in position, and squadrons, groups, and wings had joined forces, the formation headed for the rendezvous with the fighter escorts.

I had an uneasy feeling about this flight. We were not flying *Boojum* but were using a plane name *Texas Ranger* named by the pilot who flew her. He was from Texas and had a mouth of equal size. He arrived at our base in Italy a month late claiming that he had had engine trouble. Following arrival, he made nine starts on missions and aborted each one. Until this day, the plane had never seen combat. Tex blamed it on various malfunctions and not his lack of courage. We were given the plane to prove to him and his crew that the craft was all right but he was not.

We crossed the coastline of Yugoslavia and had reached an altitude of 10,000 feet and climbing. As was our practice, our pilot Jeff Laszewski turned the controls over to me when we noticed flak bursts breaking around the ships ahead. The unexpected flak was being fired from an anti-aircraft gun mounted on a railway car in the city of Mostar. The Germans moved these guns up and down the coast anticipating where we would cross.

Suddenly, there was an explosion behind the nose turret. The ship seemed to lift a few feet and at that moment all the instrument readings toppled back to zero. I looked out the window and saw a gaping hole in the number 2 engine. The pilot tried to feather the engine that had been pierced by flak but had no success. The only working instrument was our compass and since there was no doubt that we would have to abort, I turned the direction setting the course for home. Despite the pilot's efforts the damaged engine continued to windmill, slowly dragging the plane down. Bombardier Ed Bonham called on the intercom to say that the navigator was seriously wounded.

As we headed back toward the Adriatic Sea, we were the lone target and flak was breaking all around us. We were able to get out of the range of ground fire without taking another hit but as we neared the coastline, we realized that we were losing altitude too rapidly to make it back to base. The pilot ordered us to throw out everything possible and the bombs jettisoned. The bomb bay doors would not open and the bombs were dropped on them tearing the doors partially off. The guns, ammunition and all else followed. Despite these efforts, we continued to lose altitude and had fallen below 6,000 feet. We knew that if we attempted to ditch in the sea, the ship would break up because of the missing bomb bay doors. We turned back inland and the pilot ordered the crew to prepare to jump.

Bonham notified us that Halberstadt was too badly injured to jump. He had lost several fingers and his leg wound exposed the bone. Our engineer, George Dancisak, went down to the nose to see if we could bandage his wound and throw him out of the plane if we opened his parachute. Our hope was that that the Germans would find him and treat his wounds. George called and advised that Hal was too wounded to be tossed out. The pilot ordered me to start jumping the crew. We fell to about 2,000 feet and began maintaining altitude when Jeff told me to jump. I went back to the catwalk and dropped into the slipstream. As soon as I had cleared the ship, I pulled the ripcord and there was a terrific snap as the white silk blossomed and checked my descent. The ground was racing toward me. For a moment it appeared that I would drift into a mountain village, but I was falling too fast. I was going to land on a mountain peak with sharp, jagged rocks. The village disappeared behind the peak as I landed unhurt on the flat side of a huge boulder.

Suddenly, the pulsating roar of an airplane split the air. It was the *Texas Ranger*. I recognized our plane by the missing bomb bay doors and it was maintaining altitude. Without my 200 pounds plus equipment, it was now flying level and headed for home. Hal now had a chance to survive his injuries if the plane could make it back to base.

I hid my parachute under some rocks and hurried away from the village but no matter which way I turned, I ended up looking down into the valley and houses. I could see people on the path that connected the houses. As I turned, I came face to face with a small boy. He had to be more surprised than I was as he let out a piercing yell and hurried down the mountain. In my haste to get away, I fell cutting my hand in several places. As I got to .my feet, I saw a civilian covering me with a rifle. His shout brought others who began to search me for weapons. They were disappointed when they did not find any. My captors seemed friendly and for a moment, I thought partisans might have captured me. "Ruskie?" one asked. "American," I replied. I pulled out my escape kit that held maps of the territory over which we were flying. I pointed to Greece with an expression that cried for help. They began to laugh and shook their heads pointing to Germany on the map.

It took about thirty minutes to descend the mountain and reach the edge of the village where six German soldiers awaited us. Villagers began to gather as word spread of my capture. The word "Americano" passed from lip to lip. The soldiers motioned that I should come along with them and we followed a path to a stone wall. Dry blood covered the path and wall. They stood me facing the wall and I was sure that they intended to execute me. The soldiers walked back several steps and stopped. A sharp command was given followed by the sound shells being loaded into their gun chambers. I was afraid that I would faint before my execution. Then a guttural German voice split in my ear as a hand firmly gripped my shoulder and swung me around, and pushed me back against the wall. The soldiers were removing the cartridges from their weapons when a new order was shouted. The shells were reloaded and the rifles all pointed at my chest. All I can remember is that I prayed as I had never prayed before. Suddenly, the soldiers all broke into laughter and I realized that they had been playing with me.

They allowed me to sit and it was then that my legs began to tremble and my stomach began to quiet. I did not want to empty in front of the German soldiers. The civilians who had followed along came forward and began touching me. They repeated the name "Nick" and pointed back down the path. In a while, an elderly gentleman appeared who greeted me in English. Nick had once lived in Cleveland and returned to Yugoslavia to please his parents. He told me not to be afraid, that the soldiers would not harm me, and indicated that another crewmember named Thompson had landed in a tree and had been captured. He explained that the Germans had control of the area and that I could not escape and he did not know what would happen to me. I offered some pocket candy to Nick and the children who had gathered, and answered questions about the United States. One little boy had his eyes on my fur-lined flying boots. I pulled them off and gave them to him. His eyes widened and he was gone before the soldiers could catch him. Eventually, the rest of the search parties returned without any prisoners. There were twenty-three soldiers and we began down the path toward the valley. Nick could not keep up and he said goodbye and fell behind.

My ankle began to swell and by the time we were half way down the mountain, it was twice its size. I managed to make it to the road where an old dilapidated truck picked some of us up. We had not traveled very far when we reached a mountain outpost. I could make out a farm-like building before the Germans blindfolded me. After being helped off the truck bed, I was searched. My pen, sunglasses, comb, gloves, handkerchief, escape kit and an extra pair of socks were taken from me. However, they overlooked my watch, which I had pushed to my elbow, and my pilot wings worn since I had left the States.

Following the search, they led me to a straw stack. I sat down and shortly fell asleep. After I awoke, I noticed that I could see out of the bottom of my blindfold and about fifty feet in front of me sat our tail gunner, Thompson. He too was blindfolded. I decided to let him know that I was there, so in a loud voice I called out asking for water. Thompson turned his head and I was sure that he had recognized my voice. That trick got me a kick in the ribs and I knew not to speak out again. About an hour later, a truck arrived and I was pulled to my feet. There appeared to be a lot of confusion as many pairs of feet shuffled onto the truck. I recognized some of the "Ohs" and "Ahs" as the voices of my crew. Apparently, the lesson I had learned previously, taught with a kick to the ribs, did not stick as I again cried out, "Who is here?" A gun butt smashed into my ribs as four voices rang out, followed by blows and shouts from the guards. There were three men from the tail section – Thompson, Abner and Fischler and the top gunner, Ed Dement. Neither the bombardier nor the nose gunner was among us. A year later, I learned that the nose gunner never jumped.

About an hour later, we stopped and the bombardier, Ed Bonham, was put on board. I spoke to him, expecting another kick and when none came, I asked more questions of the crew. None of us had been seriously injured in our landings nor had we been abused physically by the soldiers. Shortly afterward, we stopped and another American flyer was put on the truck. I could see his nametag and I called him by name. He wanted to know who we were and, of course, we would not tell him.

We finally arrived at Mostar, Yugoslavia. They removed our blindfolds and we climbed down from the truck. The soldiers marched us to the city jail and here we were separated. They put me into a cell with the flyer that was not part of our crew. I suspected he was not American and each of us thought the other had been placed in the cell by the Germans to extract information.

The cell was bare except for a one long, narrow bench and when the doors banged shut, we were in semi darkness. Thin streams of light slithered through a window near the ceiling. I leaned the bench against the wall and, with my cellmate holding the bottom, shimmied up to look out. The window was barred on the outside and we were on the third floor. About fifty feet back, a road ran parallel with the building and beyond that was an airfield that held only a few training planes. After awhile, a guard brought us a half loaf of black bread that was bitter and tasted of mold. I spat it out.

After a sleepless night, my cellmate and I began communicating with each other. He told me how their plane had been shot down and he parachuted at a low altitude as I had. His ship had crashed in the valley and was on fire. As he descended, he kept drifting toward it and as he told the story, I could visualize the fear he must have had, thinking he would drift into the flames.

Later in the morning, a guard threw open the cell door and motioned us to follow him to another room where the rest of the crew had gathered. We had so much to say to each other but were afraid that the room was wired to pick up our conversations. I told the crew that I had seen the *Texas Ranger* flying toward the Adriatic Sea. It was the first that any of them knew of the fate of our plane. The guard brought some ersatz coffee and more black bread. At the time, I thought it was impossible to eat stale bread and drink that awful imitation coffee but eventually I would act differently.

My cellmate and I were removed from this group and taken to a small railroad station to an awaiting train. The train's cars were crowded with troops going northward and some had to stand. In our car, there were three other American prisoners and their guards. One of the prisoners had a bandage covering his face. The train left the station shortly after noon and arrived at Sarajevo about seven o'clock that evening, a distance of approximately fifty miles. We were removed from the train and along with the other American prisoners were marched through the streets to the city jail. In the jail, we were placed in one large room. There were steel beds with boards across that served as mattresses. This basic accommodation was better than sleeping on the floor. Through a large crack in the wall, we could see some Russian prisoners in the adjoining room. I recall one grinning Russian soldier holding up three fingers and saying, "Stalin, Roosevelt and Churchill" as he pointed to each finger.

Early the next morning we boarded another crowded train accompanied by our guards who were to escort us as far as Belgrade. We traveled only during the day and understood why when we saw derailed trains at the bottom of an embankment. The partisans were active in this area and they were continually blowing up bridges and trains. Through the magic of sign language we learned that our guards were going home on furlough and they said repeatedly, "For you, the war is over!" We got the impression that they would have been happy to exchange places with us. True, we were alive, albeit prisoners, but what we did not know that we were now in a different kind of war – a fight for survival.

As we traveled during the day, we had to open our compartment window to allow some air to come in. Our guards allowed us to stand and look out the window. I noticed that when the train turned in a direction opposite my side of the track, a person leaving the train would be quickly out of view. I began to formulate an escape plan but my fellow prisoner wanted no part of it. He was glad to be alive and wanted to stay that way. I asked the guard for permission to use the toilet that was on our side of the train. On previous visits, he made me leave the door open but this time I pretended not to understand and closed the door. Quickly I opened the window and stuck my head out. In the cars ahead, the soldiers had their heads out but no one was paying attention to me. From the car behind, someone called my name and there in the open window next to mine was my guard.

Later, that same day, my guard was escorting me again to the toilet room when the train screeched to a stop at some small town. German soldiers, anxious to get off came between us and my guard was pushed across the aisle. He could not see me so I ducked my head and pretended that I had entered the toilet room and closed the door. Instead, I joined the crowd of soldiers filing past and walked off the train. Their uniforms were so diverse that I was able to pass through unnoticed. I made it through the station without a single challenge and walked along nonchalantly, outwardly calm.

When I entered the first side street, I quickened my pace. I heard shouts from people on the street I had just left and running feet coming toward me. I stepped into a recessed doorway and pressed against the door. A moment later, a soldier, weapon in hand, flashed by. In a minute he returned and this time he saw me. At the point of a rifle, I was marched back to the train.

Early next morning, we were out of the mountains and I knew that my chances of escape were growing slimmer. When our guards opened the tiny suitcases they carried and began to eat black bread and cheese, I became hungry. So I opened the paper bag the Germans had provided at our departure. It contained a loaf of inedible bread and moldy cheese. It tasted awful, and my guard laughed when I put it back under my seat. He offered me two boiled eggs and a withered apple. I devoured the apple, core and all along with the eggs. I was grateful but it awakened my stomach to the fact that food existed and I was hungry from that day on.

At about ten o'clock that evening, we reached the outskirts of Brod. Bombers had been over recently and blown the marshaling yards into turmoil. As the train crept along, the three other American prisoners were placed in our compartment. The guards were taking no chances of us walking off the train this time. The bombing had been pinpoint perfect and the wreckage strewn around was fascinating. Tracks and railroad cars were scattered all over the area. Buildings and homes near the tracks had been struck, some were completely destroyed. A number of homes were still smoldering and in the glow, I could see men, women and children carrying away the few items they could salvage as they evacuated the ruins.

When our train finally stopped, one of the guards leaned out the window and called to the hapless civilians. "American terrorfliegers," he shouted, pointing to us. The people began screaming and shaking their fists and moved toward our car and began beating on it. They begged the guards to release us to them. We tried to move back from the windows but the guards not only blocked our way but also pushed us to an open window. An enraged civilian caught the sleeve of one of the prisoners and nearly pulled him out of the train. Fortunately, the train started and began moving down the tracks away from the enraged mob. We dropped into our seats exhausted from fear.

The train stopped about a mile down the tracks and we had to walk in a drizzling rain back toward town. We were separated from the other Americans and my friend and I were forced to shoulder the heavy packs of our guards. The main bridge across the river had been destroyed and we had to walk miles to reach another. The streets were nearly deserted as we stumbled along. It was after midnight when we finally reached a private jail. The civilian owner protested vehemently; he did not want the responsibility of keeping us. The Germans won the argument and we were put into a dungeon below the jail. The room was cold and damp. Several cinder blocks and two old doors served as our bed that night. Throughout the night, we could hear rats moving about and occasionally crawled across our legs. My cellmate and I huddled together for warmth, and to ward off the rodents.

The next morning the jailer brought his wife and children down to see us. He knew a few English words and was much more congenial now that the Germans were not present. He led us from the dungeon to a courtyard behind the jail where we drank water from a clean cup and splashed cold water on our faces. The jailer's wife handed us a towel.

Suddenly, a warning was shouted and we were hustled back to the cell. Moments later, our two guards appeared and marched us across town to another jail. There, we were placed into a similar dungeon that held the three Americans who were on our train the night before.

That afternoon we were on the move again and after two days of travel, we arrived in Belgrade on the morning of April 8, 1944. During the ride that day, my guard made it known that he would be leaving in Belgrade. He reached into his bag and extracted a bottle of schnapps. He offered me a drink, which I accepted. At the time, I thought of him as a rather decent fellow.

In Belgrade, we were again separated from the three other airmen. Our guards ordered us to carry their heavy packs on our backs and another large one between us as they paraded us through the streets of Belgrade. One of the guards kept shouting "American terrorfliegers!" Although crowds gathered around, there was no attempt of violence. We suspected that the pack we carried between us contained bottles of schnapps so as we were climbing a flight of stone steps, I told my partner to lower the pack and let it smash into the next step. This happened several times when my guard became furious and began shouting, "schnapps" "schnapps." We shrugged our shoulders pretending not to comprehend, took another step and again let the pack bang against the next riser. With that, my guard angrily retrieved the pack and shouldered it himself. If looks could kill, two American airmen would have died that day on a long flight of steps somewhere in Belgrade.

Our journey through Belgrade carried us past the American Embassy. It appeared to be vacant and our guards mocked us with taunting laughter. Along the way, a little boy ran up to me, slipped something into my hand and darted away. Although I did not smoke, I was now five cigarettes richer and had something to barter. It was comforting to know that many Serbs considered us their friends.

Once again, we were on a train but our journey was short. Six miles outside of Belgrade, we once again disembarked from the train and were taken to a building where captured American and British airmen were collected until they had enough to transport them to the Dulag Luft Interrogation Center in Frankfurt.

The rooms in this jail were clean and straw mattresses were on the cots. We were fed black bread and ersatz coffee and this time the bread was edible or perhaps my hunger overcame my taste buds. After eating, we stretched out on the cots and slept for twelve hours. In the morning, a German officer brought us shaving equipment. He spoke English and indicated that officers, even enemy captives, should not appear unkempt. Later that morning, thirty-seven POWs were placed on a bus and returned to Belgrade where we boarded a boxcar. It was an old "forty and eight" – meaning it held forty men or eight horses. Not too bad, except we had to share the car with ten German guards and they got half the car and the thirty-seven prisoners got the other half. The journey was a trip never to be forgotten nor fully remembered. Days and nights ran together. All of us were tired, dirty and hungry. With so many men crowded into the half-section of the car, it was impossible to lie down and sleep. Our toilet facility was a bucket. We had no food. Each man suspected the other might be a German plant so we bounced along mostly in silence.

When we reached Munich, the railroad station had been bombed and severely damaged. We had to leave the train and walk through the station. The roof was just a twisted frame. When the civilians recognized us as American airmen, they came at us menacingly. Our ten guards did their best to protect us but the sheer number of the enraged crowd overwhelmed them. They succeeded in pulling one of the prisoners away from our ranks. They tied him to some upended railroad ties and doused him with what appeared to be gasoline. We could hear his screams as we ran down a flight of steps toward an air raid shelter. We sat in silence in the shelter for a long time. I wondered if the event in the station was staged to control us by fear or if that airman was actually put to the torch. If it was a ruse to frighten us, it worked. We left the shelter and returned to our train that somehow made it through the station and departed from Munich.

Eventually we arrived at the Dulag Luft Interrogation Center in Frankfurt. There, we stripped and they searched our clothing and belongings. They took my watch and wings and when they tried to remove my dog tags, I protested. After some bickering, we agreed that they could take one to send to the Red Cross in Switzerland and I would keep the other. After they copied the information on the tag, they allowed me to dress and placed me in a solitary cell. The cell contained a single board bed with a straw mattress and a table and chair. On one wall, bars reflected through a frosted pane window. The room was six paces long and two paces wide. Food was slipped in through a flap in the door. We received two slices of bread with a dab of butter for breakfast, soup for lunch and two slices of bread for supper.

To pass the time away, I paced the floor, recited as many poems as I could remember, and counted the number of nails in the walls and cracks in the floor. I removed some straw from my mattress and created weird designs on the floor. I did everything I could not to think of the predicament that I was in. If we had to use the toilet facilities, we turned a small knob on the wall that dropped an arm on the outside wall. When a guard was in that part of the corridor, he would unlock the door and guide the way.

After several attempts to open my window, I became frustrated by my lack of success. The challenge turned into an obsession. Using my lieutenant's bars as a screwdriver, I was able to remove several screws and pry the window open enough to see out. I only saw German soldiers walking around the compound. I tested the bars and finding them solid, I closed the window.

One time, I was singing to myself when I heard a pounding from the next cell. It was another American airman and he had been in his cell for fourteen days. He believed he was being held for an inordinate length of time because the Germans did not have any information about him and they were trying to break him down. He said I was in a lucky cell and that I had been the third person in that cell since his incarceration. He advised how the interrogation would proceed and suggested that I say nothing. The more information you share, the longer they keep you hoping to elicit more.

It was late afternoon when a German colonel interrogated me. He was quite elderly and his age made me question if he was really a soldier? After I refused a cigarette, he tossed a piece of gum toward me. When I did not pick it up, he began asking questions about Italy, our target on the day we went down, and other military inquiries. I gave the name, rank and serial number routine. He ignored my response and began asking about America. He indicated that he liked our country and asked if I had ever been to California. I remained silent and he said, with more time he would have me talking but it was not necessary. He summoned a female soldier and spoke to her in German. She left the room and returned quickly with what appeared to be a photo album.

Across the front were the numbers 456 in bold. This was my bomb group. He thumbed through the pages and began to read:

Howard Neal Hartman, residence 11 Oak Street, Shelby, Ohio.
Born December 8, 1920 at Minneapolis, Minnesota
Father, John Willis Hartman.

He looked up and asked, "Why are you fighting the fatherland?" I told him my ancestors were Swedes as well as German but more important I was an American. There was something in my response that he found humorous and he threw back his head and laughed. Returning to the book, he cited nearly all the fields where I had trained and even had a clipping from my hometown newspaper describing my commission as an officer and a pilot. He knew the history of the bomb group, the names of the officers and practically all there was to know of my life. He asked if I wanted to know the status of anyone from the group who had been identified as "missing in action."

That afternoon my wings and watchband were returned to me; they kept the watch. I was released into a large compound where several hundred other Americans were held but before my release from solitary, I opened my window and let it stand ajar. I spent the next two days in the compound and since all of us had just been released from solitary, we talked our heads off. I made several friends who became my roommates at Stalag Luft I.

We traveled by boxcar to Luft I, located north of Barth, Germany on the Baltic Sea approximately 100 miles north of Berlin. The railroad station was in the center of town and the town people were there to greet us. We lined four abreast and marched through town when some women attacked us with broomsticks and rakes screaming "Terrorfliegers." No one was seriously hurt as we made our way to the camp that was about a mile away. Upon entering the compound, we stripped and while our clothes were deloused, we showered and shaved, then marched into the prison compound.

When I arrived at Stalag Luft I on April 16, 1944, it was composed of two compounds housing about 4,000 war prisoners from nearly every Allied nation but mostly British and Americans. By the end of the war the 0.following year, the camp had swelled to four compounds and nearly 10,000 prisoners. Each compound was a prison within itself separated from the others by barbed wire and had its own guards and guard towers.

Our housing was long low barracks that were divided into rooms holding two to sixteen men. As the largest numbers of men were lieutenants, we were assigned to the fourteen and sixteen man rooms. Our room contained the bare essentials for living quarters - two tables, two benches, a stove and bunks. Our bunks were double decked with straw-filled burlap for mattresses and a pillow on top of board slats. We had a mattress cover, pillowslip, one sheet and two blankets.

The camp was originally a Hitler Youth Camp and the weather was tolerable except in the winter when temperatures dipped below freezing. The barracks had no heat so we went to bed fully clothed. We called ourselves "Kriegies" an abbreviation of the German word for prisoners of war "Kriegsgefagen." Our life style was quite simple. Boredom was the greatest threat to our sanity. The Red Cross sent food and medical supplies and the Canadian YMCA sent books and sports equipment. Weather permitting, we played ball or walked around the compound or played cards, read, studied, or simply talked to keep ourselves occupied.

During June, July and August, the days were warm and we spent most of our time outdoors. We were in excellent spirits because we were aware that Allied Forces had made a successful landing on the continent and were racing across France. The YMCA had sent musical instruments and each compound had its own band. Our band, named the "Round the Benders," played three times a week at the mess hall during our suppers in the summer. Red Cross parcels were combined with the German rations and served there. A group presented plays on a makeshift stage with men, out of necessity, playing the rolls of women. One of the first musicals presented a small fellow with a tenor voice dressed like a female.

The audience went wild. They stamped their feet and beat on the tables for more. The fellow came back on stage, took off his homemade wig and said, "Look fellows, don't get carried away. Remember, I am just one of the boys!" He put his wig back on and sang a few more songs.

Every morning and evening, we lined up in groups of sixty for headcount. Dogs were turned loose in the barracks to ensure that all the Kriegies fell out to be counted when the bugle sounded. Shortly after my arrival, during an evening count, I noticed a fellow who looked like a boyhood friend of mine named Reggie Smith. Before the war, he lived on the street behind mine and I knew him most of my life. Before the U.S. entered the war, Reggie had joined the Canadian Air Force and was sent to England. I had lost contact with him, and after roll call I raced to his barracks. When he saw me, he could not believe his eyes and was speechless for a moment. It was wonderful to be together again and we knew our parents would be equally excited when they learned the news. It took about three months before they received our letters.

Twice that summer, the Germans took about 200 of us for a nude swim in the cold Baltic Sea and three movies from Switzerland were brought in. They even dusted off Max Schmeling, the former heavyweight champ and brought him into camp. German or no, we were excited to meet him. Our spirits were running high and we would devise various tricks to play on our guards. We had more cigarettes than our guards so one of our favorites was to tie a string to a lighted cigarette and toss it out the window at night when we saw a guard coming. He would hurry toward the butt and just as he leaned down to snipe the butt, we would pull it out from under his nose. I could not speak German but I understood profanity when I heard it.

The Germans thought a good way to collect information was to have a man dressed in dark clothing creep under our barracks floor, which was several feet off the ground and listen to our conversations. We called him the "ferret." What the Germans did not know was that we had a watch system and always knew when a ferret was under our barracks. Usually we would jump up and down to send dust down on him. One night, in another barracks Kriegies poured a bucket of hot water through a crack in the floor when they thought he was in that location. However, it was not as much of a joke as intended. The ferret opened fire shooting through the floor. One bullet went through the bucket a prisoner was holding. That was the last time we used water on the ferret.

We had our own methods of collecting information and kept current of the progress of the war from several sources. Information was "purchased" from a guard who would sell anything for cigarettes; also, there was a crystal set hidden in a barracks in the south compound. A German guard provided it as a gift for not telling his commander that he had fallen asleep in the guard tower.

It was used only fifteen minutes a day to pick up BBC broadcasts. A Catholic priest carried the abbreviated news from compound to compound.

I helped with the publication of a secret newspaper edited by Lowell Bennet, an International News Service correspondent who was captured while covering a bombing raid. We named it *Pow Wow* – Prisoners of War Waiting on Winning. One copy was issued to each barracks where it was passed from room to room, read and then destroyed. The Germans knew we had a radio and a newspaper, but in search after search they never did locate the radio but did find some copies of our newspaper.

Besides working on the newspaper, I managed to get a job in the library, helping to hand out books and keep track of them. Jobs were so few and the takers so many, it was a feat to get one. I bribed the head librarian by promising to inform him of any hot news that came in. Besides having something to do, I could get better books and kept my roommates and friends in all the books they could read. I personally read 225 books that year.

When I arrived at Stalag Luft I, the soldiers guarding us were very professional. Later, as the Russian front was proving to be a disaster for the Germans, these soldiers were replaced by inexperienced soldiers and finally by the home guard, whom we were very apprehensive about. Some guards would steal what little food we had managed to hoard from our Red Cross parcels or parcels from home. It became so blatant that the commandant issued orders that any guard caught stealing prisoners' property would be sent to the Russian front.

We knew of this order and used it to trap one nasty, arrogant guard. A prisoner in our barracks stayed in his room during roll call pretending to be ill. When the guard came through to count the number of sick prisoners, our man offered the guard several packs of cigarettes if he would not report that he was not ill. As soon as he was outside, the prisoner shouted out the window that the guard had stolen his cigarettes. When the guard was searched, they found the cigarettes and we never saw him again.

Everyone talked about escape and making it back to our lines but it was virtually impossible. A great many tunnels were dug but no one ever made an escape through them. The Germans had buried seismographs in the ground outside the fence and they would permit digging until it neared the fence when they would cave it in. Each compound had an escape committee that would lend support to anyone willing to attempt escape. Several prisoners had managed to get outside the camp but they could not get off the peninsula. It was sixty miles by water to Sweden in one direction and the town of Barth was at the end of the peninsula blocking the way to the continent.

Lowell Bennet, the news correspondent, was proficient in German and French, and one night he led an attempted mass escape. We were able to purchase a German officer's uniform piece by piece. After roll call one evening, Bennet dressed in the officer's uniform marched twenty prisoners to the main gate and gave the password that we purchased for a pack of cigarettes. The password had changed when the night guards came on duty. When informed that the password he had given was yesterday's, he calmly turned the men around and marched them back to our compound. The uniform was burned in several different places and by the time the search began, all evidence had disappeared. The guards did not find anything related and no one was put into solitary confinement for attempted escape.

After the breakthrough in Normandy, Allied forces raced across France and outran their supplies as they reached the West Wall or Siegfried Line as Americans liked to call it. During the fall of 1944, our food and fuel supplies began to run desperately low and when the Germans opened their counter offensive in the Ardennes just before Christmas, our morale sank to its lowest ebb. We were fearful what the home guards would do to us now that the war had switched favorably to them. Eventually, the tide of war turned back to our favor and the unrelenting pounding the Germans were getting day and night had virtually destroyed their transportation and economic system.

The country was in disarray and our food supplies of Red Cross parcels were exhausted. We were told that civilians in nearby towns looted the trains carrying food to our camp, which had now grown to 10,000 men. Then our mess hall burned down which was no great loss, as there was no food in it. When food became scarce, it was no longer pooled and cooked in the mess hall. What food we had was allocated to each prisoner. One day in March, two huge Red Cross trucks arrived from Barth. We shouted with joy, danced and patted each on the back but our joy was short lived. The trucks were not carrying food but toilet paper! We had so little food that it had been months since we needed toilet paper.

We existed on what few rations the Germans gave us usually thirteen spoonfuls of dehydrated turnip soup a day. An old horse was killed in an air raid and the Germans gave it to the camp. One dried up old horse did not go far among ten thousand men. We got the bones that were passed from room to room. We boiled them and drank the water. We all began to lose weight at a dramatic rate. British doctors, captured at Dunkirk in 1940, advised us to stay in our bunks and conserve whatever energy we had. Some men began going "around the bend." Some talked incessantly, others would not talk at all. Some cried uncontrollably while others walked or ran around the compound continually. Several attempted suicide by cutting their wrists. We did our best to help those who had "flipped" but in our weakened condition, we easily became exhausted. We resumed card games and held quiz contests, anything to keep our minds active.

The lack of food was a major concern but not our only one. With the war going badly against the Germans, the Nazis ordered all Jewish prisoners to be collected and placed in one building. One hundred and thirty men were moved. My bunkmate was a Russian Jew. Shortly before the war's end, an order supposedly came from Berlin to execute all Jewish prisoners. Knowing how the war was going, the Germans in charge of our camp refused to carry out the order.

I will always remember April 30, 1945 as a great day in my life. On that day the war in Europe ended for the prisoners at Stalag Luft I. Early that morning we heard rumors that the Germans were evacuating the camp. We were aware that the Russian army had crossed the Oder River, ten days before. Although the river was sixty miles east, a terrific bombardment that preceded the crossing rocked us out of our bunks. We knew it was just a matter of time.

The Germans were uncertain if the Russians knew that our facility was a prisoner of war camp, so they granted us permission to dig slit trenches. We dug with cans, boards, and iron rods that appeared from nowhere, and with our bare hands. When we reached a depth of three feet, we were exhausted and called it a day. At the same time, the Germans began to blow up the nearby flak school with all its equipment, and destroy the airfield two miles west. One blast blew out the windows of a guard tower and knocked the door off the latrine. Debris began to rain down on us. Later, another blast at the flak school opened the door to some Red Cross supplies that the Germans had hidden from us.

Our commanding officer, Colonel Zemke, received permission to send men to the flak school and secure the food. It was late afternoon when we formed ranks of one hundred men and marched out the gate toward the warehouse. As we marched down the path toward the school, civilians and soldiers glared at us with hatred in their eyes. We were afraid that some fanatic might take a pot shot at us. We returned with 4400 parcels and stored them in the open where the mess hall had been.

Our guards began packing and shouldering what they could carry. Some were taking the opportunity to get drunk. Even though these men would probably kill us at the slightest provocation, there was a feeling of compassion in my heart. Their homes had been destroyed, families scattered and their country was suffering the worst military defeat in history. Now, these vanquished few were taking whatever they could carry destined to reach the American or British lines before their greatest enemy arrived. As soon as the German guards were gone, pre-prepared plans went into effect. Within moments our men were in the towers and surrounding grounds keeping vigil. We were fearful that civilians may seek revenge and although the guards had left some weapons behind, it was not enough to drive off an attack by a group of armed, enraged civilians.

The next day, a small blue car that had been liberated from the Germans left camp flying a white flag and an American flag on each fender. It carried Colonel Zemke who set out to meet the Russian forces. Numerous British and American prisoners took possession of the abandoned airfield. They located the system the Germans had used to pipe in propaganda over loud speakers into each barracks. Before, we had been subjected to German newscasts such as Lord Haw Haw and Axis Sally. Now, we tuned in the BBC and heard General Eisenhower order all prisoners to "stand by." We were listening to the "Hit Parade" when word spread that Russian soldiers had entered the camp. They were from an advance spearhead that had just reached Barth. We were officially liberated.

The next day, a Russian colonel drove into camp and a prisoner who spoke Russian served as his interpreter. He was disappointed that we were not showing more enthusiasm about our liberation. He ordered us to go from compound to compound, and boisterously demonstrate to our fellow prisoners and the Russian troops how grateful we were to be free. He next questioned why we were still behind barbed wire and ordered that we take the fences down. Colonel Zemke who was concerned about maintaining discipline tried to convince him otherwise but the Russian officer was beyond reasoning with. The situation quickly became hectic as gates were torn from their hinges, fences pulled down and guard towers were toppled over. Kriegies began pouring through the broken fences and flooded the road to Barth. Our newfound freedom was short lived when it was announced that within six hours we were to organize into groups and march thirty miles to the railroad station at Demmin where we were to board trains for Russia and then to a repatriation center in Odessa. Colonel Zemke stood firm and said firmly that we will not go and he persuaded the drunken Russian to call off the movement. This may have been the only successful sit-down strike in Russia. The Russian officer relented and Reggie Smith and I and many others visited Barth that evening.

Kriegies were everywhere. We stood on the sidewalk and watched the Soviet army roll by in American jeeps, tanks and trucks. Much of their army consisted of horse-drawn wagons filled with Mongolian soldiers and their women. Huge glass jugs of vodka hung on the side of the wagons. We wandered down to the railroad station and watched horses being unloaded. We were able to communicate with the Russians and their camp followers. American cigarettes did the talking. A Major offered us some vodka, which of course we could not refuse. He filled several teacups from a five-gallon jug. It burned all the way down. They gave us bread, canned sardines and fresh fish. We disposed of the fish behind a hedgerow as soon as we were out of sight.

A pretty German girl darted out of one house and into another across the street. She paused on the doorstep when we called to her. She hesitated at first but after we explained that we were Americans and had been prisoners at the camp, she invited us inside. It was a small row house. We met her mother, father, grandmother, husband and four other people who were refugees from East Pomerania. Suddenly, an armed Russian soldier and Polish civilian entered the house and demanded to know why we were there. They suspected we might be German soldiers in disguise. We were fearful that we could be shot. With much difficulty, we were able to explain that we were Americans from the prison camp, and had just happened to wander into this house. After we convinced them, they allowed us to leave and we quickly departed.

For the most part, our Russian liberators treated us well. They asked what we wanted most and we told them food. They confiscated everything edible they could fine. Hogs and cattle were driven into the camp for butchering. Truckloads of potatoes and sugar beets were brought in. They literally stripped the countryside around Barth for food. The Red Cross parcels that we had removed from the flak school were divided among the prisoners the night before the Russians arrived, as our officers were fearful that the Russians might confiscate the parcels. Nearly every one became ill from overeating. All during the night you could hear the sounds of men jumping out of their bunks and running for the latrine. The barracks began to smell foul because many did not make it in time. It was incredible to recall that only several days before, I witnessed men devour rotten cabbage, potato peelings and dead birds.

On May 2nd the Russians posted their

Military District Regulations

Effective Wednesday, 2 May 1945, this district is under martial law as established by the Senior Russian Officer, Colonel Zchervynick. All personnel will comply with these district regulations. Failure to do so may result in being shot without trial.

A. *Ninety (90) men from this camp are permitted in the Barth area between the hours of 1000 and 2100.*

B. *No man is permitted outside this camp without a Pass, obtainable only at wing headquarters.*

C. *All passes previously issued are rescinded.*

D. *The official language with Russians is Russian.*

E. *Personnel will obey all orders issued by Russians.*

F. *All outgoing messages will be transmitted through the Russian Commander.*

The Russians attempted to enforce these rules by posting guards on the roads and bridges leading to Barth. Many of the Kriegies, frustrated by the Russians' treatment began to make packs and set out across country toward the American lines. I was part of a group that had acquired a rather large boat and we were going to attempt to sail to Sweden but our navigator backed out. Besides, we had heard the broadcasts wherein Eisenhower had ordered us to stay put. The Allies knew of the camp location and they were coming for us. He warned about becoming lost in the mass movement of humanity taking place all over Europe.

During the waiting period, two senior Russian officers visited our camp. Marshall Pokotofski and General Borisoff were checking to see how everything was going for us. At that time, I was assigned to a group whose task was to interview prisoners and document incidents where prisoners were deliberately mistreated in any manner. We compiled evidence that showed clearly that some men were needlessly tortured. Shortly before the war's ending, several thousand emaciated enlisted men were brought into our camp from Eastern Germany. Their condition was deplorable and stories of their march across Germany described horrific conditions and an incessant struggle for survival. Tents were erected at the end of our barracks to accommodate them and they began receiving the nourishment and medical attention they desperately needed.

The night the war in Europe ended, May 8, 1945, we turned out at midnight and had a huge bonfire in the center of our compound. The guard towers, fence posts, gates and shutters were fuel for the fire. Colonel Ross Greening, who had been on the first raid over Tokyo, the Doolittle Raid, gave a brief speech. He told us that the war in Europe was officially over and our contributions and sacrifices helped defeat the Nazi aggression. Now millions of people throughout the Continent were free from tyranny and captivity. As he spoke, he held a bust of Herman Goering in his hand. This, he proclaimed, represented the Third Reich and he tossed it into the fire. We shouted and applauded in delight. Nazi Germany was dead and we helped kill it. As the flames crackled, we stood at attention and sang our nations' anthem – *The Star Spangled Banner*. I was never so proud to be an American.

The next morning I joined an official party and hiked to the flying field. It brought back so many memories. We had so often watched German planes take off from this field. A year earlier, we watched as our own P-51s strafed this field on two occasions and RAF fighters before that. Once we watched a RAF Mosquito shoot down an enemy FW 190 over the bay north of Barth.

During the summer of 1944, the 8th Air Force would fly over our camp at high altitudes on missions deep into Germany. We would rush out into the open compound and literally jump with joy. The Germans put a halt to this by sounding an alert and we were required to remain in our barracks until the all clear sounded We were told we would be shot if we dared venture out during an alert. We did not believe they would actually shoot us but no one was willing to test their resolve, so we all stayed inside. Except on one occasion, the alert had been on for an unordinary length of time and a prisoner, we believe forgot the alert was still on, ventured out and was immediately shot by a trigger-happy guard. I have pictures of his casket and funeral.

Our Wing Commander, Colonel Byerly, was so irate over this incident that he warned the camp commander that following the war, he would personally hunt down and kill any Kraut who murdered a prisoner of war. No one else was killed but we watched the bombing runs from our windows after that. On two different occasions we witnessed men bailing out of returning crippled planes near our camp.

Colonel Byerly was a tough officer and often pushed the Germans to their limits. I remember on June 15, 1944, he told us not to get into formation for the evening count. I am not sure why he took that position. We went into the compound and began milling around. The Germans ordered us to line up but we refused. It was a huge test of wills. The Germans brought in armed combat troops and placed machine-guns on the outside of the barbed wire. They told us to line up in formation for the evening count or they would open fire. In view of the consequences, we lined up. Colonel Byerly was sent to solitary confinement. There were other occasions when the Colonel would confront the Camp Commandant and each time he wound up in solitary.

When we visited the airfield, most but not all of the German planes were gone. There was considerable activity as American engineers worked to remove mines from the landing strips to allow our planes to land there. We were to be flown from this field once the Russians gave their okay. They kept busy making "passports" for us. They were paranoid about Germans getting away. Despite their efforts, we brought out two Germans who had assisted us considerably with news and information during our confinement.

By the end of April 1945, the Allied Air Forces task of destroying the German military and industrial might had ended. The 8th Air Force and the RAF now began the task of ferrying home prisoners released from German prisoner of war camps. The British prisoners were evacuated first from our camp. On the afternoon of May 12, 1945, several squadrons of B-17s poked their noses out of the clouds and landed at the Barth airfield. They departed at 5:00pm with their joyous cargoes and headed for England. Most British soldiers and airmen had been imprisoned at our camp longer than the average American so it was only proper that they would leave first. As we stood watching the planes fly into the setting sun, we knew that in a few hours they would be home. How we envied them.

We began the first leg of our journey home the next day, Sunday, May 13, 1945, which was Mothers' Day. It seemed fitting. Early that morning, we formed in ranks of thirty (a full planeload) and marched to the airfield through the town of Barth. As we passed through town, we began singing songs we had marched to during Cadet training. My mind wandered back thirteen months earlier when I passed through Barth on the way to the prisoner of war camp. How different it was now. Before, they had poked at us with rakes and brooms and shook menacing fists in our faces. Now they stood meekly in their doorways waving goodbye. The vanquished were now the victors.

We took off at 8:30am and flew west and south over cities such as Rostock, Hamburg, Bremen, Dusseldorf, Cologne and Aachen. I was glued to the window, mesmerized by the sights of terrible destruction one thousand feet below. The cities were in ruin, bridges blown away and everything looked flattened for mile after mile. Cologne was the saddest looking of all. I had the impression that the standing factory chimneys were now sentries standing guard over the ruble below. In the center of town, the renowned Cologne Cathedral stood intact as a monument to the 12th century craftsmen who built it.

Following our landing at Laon, France, we traveled in army trucks to a huge tent city where we ate a hot army meal. We were then transported to Reims where we boarded a hospital train and departed for Saint-Valery on the English Channel. German prisoners of war were everywhere, doing manual labor jobs. The railroad cars were equipped with bunks and we stretched out in comfort while G.I. medics passed up and down the aisle with hot chocolate and sandwiches. We arrived at Saint-Valery the next afternoon. Camp Lucky Strike was an enormous tent city capable of handling sixty thousand military personnel. Before it had been turned into a camp for recovered allied military personnel (RAMP) it had been the last stop for troops going to the front. We delighted in a hot shower, were issued new uniforms and that night crawled between clean sheets to enjoy a peaceful sleep. After our ordeal that had seemed like an eternity, we took comfort in now being back in American hands.

Camp Lucky Strike was a family reunion of old cadet buddies. Each day I met someone I had known in flying school or in combat. It was amazing to learn how many others had survived after their planes were shot down, identified as missing in action and now alive to share their stories. On the third day, I met my radioman, Samuel Fischler. It was the first I had seen any of our crew since that morning in Yugoslavia a year earlier. He told me that the other crewmembers who had parachuted had been with him at Stalag IIIB and all were in good health. I had known that Jeff and the remaining crew aboard had made it safely back to Italy after we had bailed out. Some squadron members who had later been shot down sent word to me that he had made it back and that our seriously wounded navigator would recover fully after losing several fingers. The substitute in the nose turret did not jump and, unknowingly had ridden back to Italy. Our engineer, George Dancisak, was unable to follow me out because his parachute had been blown out of the plane. The four men aboard were awarded for bringing home the crippled ship. Jeff received the Silver Star. Jeff and George assembled a new crew and were soon flying again.

My boyhood friend Reggie and I remained close following our reparation. We visited nearby Le Havre on a day trip but we really wanted to see Paris, which was off limits unless you had a pass and, of course, we did not. We decided to go anyway and made our way. In Paris we went to the International News Service office, trying to locate Lowell Bennett. He was long gone but a reporter there let me use a typewriter to type our own passes, similar to his. It was good enough to get us a hotel for the night but we ducked every MP we saw.

Celebrities galore came to Camp Lucky Strike to entertain us while we waited for a ship to take us home. General Eisenhower appeared and said he was doing everything possible to get us home as fast as possible. He asked if we were willing to rotate bunks, three men to a bunk, eight hours each day. The entire gathering screamed, "Yes!" And that is what we did. Seven thousand three hundred of us left LeHavre on Sunday, June 17, 1945 aboard the USS General Butler and arrived at Camp Patrick Henry, Newport News, Virginia on Saturday June 23, 1945 shortly after daybreak. That evening I was able to make a telephone call home. It was very emotional and I had a difficult time convincing my mother that I had come home without a scratch and that all was well.

The next day we boarded a train for home and at 1:30am the following day, Reggie Smith and I stepped off the train at the Shelby Depot. Despite the hour, many of our families and friends were there to greet us. I was so excited and happy to see them. My legs were already unsteady from all the excitement and when Jeff stepped out of the darkness they nearly gave away. Jeff had been discharged about three weeks earlier and aware that many former prisoners were returning home, he came to Shelby to check on my status. When he learned that I was due to arrive shortly, he stayed to welcome me home. The next few days, our house was in turmoil with people constantly dropping in. I cannot remember too much of those days; I was intoxicated with the joy of being home.

While still in the Air Force, I started college at Ohio State University in September 1945. I was not ready to enter the dorm life so my first year I rented a furnished attic room from the head of the English department at the university. It was at his urging that I wrote this memoir. He encouraged me to write everything I could remember and as it turned out, this work was wonderful therapy for me.

Martha and Howard Hartman, London 1985

Michael Romanelli, prior to shipment overseas, 1944
Company B, 301st Infantry BN, 94th Infantry Division

MICHAEL ROMANELLI

*"I am forever grateful to the German doctors
and nurses for treating and saving my feet."*

MICHAEL ROMANELLI was born in a little coal mining town in eastern Pennsylvania that he affectionately calls "Hometown, USA." The town of Tresckow is a suburb of the mountain city of Hazelton and is located approximately midway between Allentown and Scranton. Although raised during the great depression of the late 1920s and early 1930s when times were hard for all, he grew surrounded by a loving, caring family that included his mom and dad, six brothers and six sisters. To relatives, friends and neighbors each child was considered as just one of the Romanelli family but within the family the children were aware that each of them was unique, important, special, loved, and importantly "no better than another." Life's lessons taught them to accept responsibility willingly and have mutual respect for the others.

On December 7, 1941, the day Japan attacked Pearl Harbor; Michael was the 'best man" at his brother Carmen's wedding. He had not reached his 19th birthday. Shortly following the wedding, Carmen was drafted in 1942 and served in the Pacific Theatre with the 7th AAA in the Ryukyu Islands, a chain of about one hundred islands of which Okinawa is the largest. Following, his sister Christine volunteered for the Army Nurse Corps and she served twenty-nine months as a Lieutenant in field hospitals in the China-Burma-India

Theatre. Next, Louis entered the military and he served with a signal company in Luzon. Then Maurice entered the Army Air Corps and served as a bombardier in a bomber squadron stationed in San Angelo, Texas. Salvador was with the 204th Infantry in Camp Blanding, Florida, and Michael was with the 94th Infantry Division and fought in Europe. James, a cousin, was killed while serving in the Marine Corps. Joseph, the youngest of the Romanelli brothers, served during the Korean War. Another cousin, Louis, a medic, was killed in Vietnam. Clearly, the Romanellis have made significant sacrifices for their country in times of war.

Michael Romanelli was twenty years old when drafted in March 1943. Assigned to the Signal Corps, he received basic training at Camp McCain, Mississippi, and then selected for the Army Specialized Training Program (ASTP) at the University of Florida in Gainesville. Michael points out with pride that the criterion for acceptance into the ASTP was fifteen points higher than for entry into Officers Candidate School. He felt confident that his military experience would be positive. During this period, the war in Africa was over and victory won, but fighting in Italy and the Pacific was raging. Replacements for the many casualties of battle were desperately needed. Therefore, after completing two accelerated semesters with a focus on engineering, the army terminated the specialized training program and the group returned to Camp McCain. Michael was assigned to the 94th Infantry Division, 301st Regiment, 1st Battalion, Company B, 3rd Platoon. They began intense infantry training and they all knew that it would not be long before they became combat infantrymen. Michael recalls that contrary to the usual complaints of many GIs, he found army chow great and he did not mind the required daily physical training, forced marches with full gear and running the obstacle courses.

Soon after, the Division traveled to Camp Shanks, New York, a port of embarkation for the European Theatre. The entire 94th Division sailed from New York Harbor on Sunday morning August 4, 1944 aboard the *Queen Elizabeth.* Despite frequent changes in direction, the unescorted ship reached Glasgow, Scotland in five days. The Division moved quickly to Southampton in southern England and on September 1, 1944, they crossed the English Channel and landed on Utah Beach in Normandy, France.

Their first mission was to contain a contingent of about 60,000 German troops who were guarding an assembly of submarines held in fortified pens at the French ports of Lorient and St. Nazaire, on the southern shore of the Brittany Peninsula. Offshore, the British navy held the submarines in check. The German troops had been cut off from the retreating German army and did not have the equipment or supplies necessary for a breakout. Although the 94th Division had enough troops to contain the Germans, it did not have enough to capture them, so, the two armies played a waiting game. The men of the 94th experienced periodic shelling, and spent their time on patrols and nightly out-post duty in no-man's land. Compared to what was to come this duty was a picnic.

It was during this period that Michael's squad developed into a cohesive unit. Pvt. Jim Covalt, an ammo bearer, once characterized the squad as "one man and eleven boys who were quickly transformed into twelve men." Michael indicates they were truly an All-American group from at least eleven different states. Squad leader Sgt. Bill Heinlein was from Wisconsin; Michael was the squad's B.A.R man and was from Pennsylvania. His ammo bearers were Pvt. Jim Covalt, Indiana, Pvt. Bob Simonds, California; and Pvt. Harold Hiner, Ohio. The other riflemen were Pvt. Guzek,

Massachusetts; Privates Schultz and Alwood Scheler, Texas; Pvt. Butke, West Virginia; Pvt. Ralph DiLellis, New Jersey; Pvt. Smialek, Illinois and Pvt. Mills, Virginia. Ralph DiLellis was the first fatality in the trenches at Orscholz.

On December 16, 1944, Hitler launched a desperate attempt to recapture the port of Antwerp, and cut off and destroy the British and Canadian armies with a last great offensive through the Ardennes Forest. Because it put a "bulge" in the Allies' line, the offensive became known as the "Battle of the Bulge." On Christmas Eve 1944, the 66th Division was crossing the English Channel for assignment to the "Battle of the Bulge" when one of their transport ships was torpedoed and they lost more than 800 men. As a result, the undermanned division replaced the 94th Division in Brittany and the 94th was sent to Patton's 3rd Army. The Division moved to Northern France by rail and then loaded onto army trucks for a grueling sixteen-hour trip to the German border.

Michael Romanelli's nightmare began in mid-January 1945, when the 301st Regiment's 1st Infantry Battalion attacked Orscholz, a fortified village within the Siegfried Line located twenty miles southeast of Luxembourg. The Siegfried Line stretched from Luxembourg to the Swiss border, and it consisted of massive pillboxes and other fortified emplacements, concrete tank barriers called *dragon's teeth*, machinegun bunkers and other firing embrasures, along with strategically placed observation posts. It was covered with neatly placed *schu* mines that blew off the feet of the first to venture close. The Siegfried Line, built in 1938, was considered impregnable. Michael's company, "B" Company, led the attack.

Pfc. Thomas R. Johnson, Jr., rifleman in the 2nd Platoon, B Company, and Lt. Herndon Inge, Jr., forward observer for D Company assigned to B Company, have both written accounts of the battle of Orscholz that were published in the *94th Infantry Division Association's Commemorative History*. To give individuals who have never experienced combat a glimpse of the horrific conditions these soldiers endured, excerpts from PFC Johnson's *Memories* and Lt. Inge's *Perils of a PW,* and *Battlefield Revisited* are provided with permission to compliment Michael Romanelli's vivid story:

Lt. Inge: General George S. Patton had ordered "an attack a day" on a town by each battalion on the front lines to keep pressure on the Germans, and find a break though the Siegfried Line and race to the Rhine River. Our objective was to attack Orscholz.

Pfc. Johnson: A few minutes after midnight on January 20, 1945, the first battalion of the 301st Infantry with some attached engineers left Ober-Tunsdorf in a heavy snowfall with snow already more than a foot deep and thickly crusted in places. We had improvised snow camouflage made from bed sheets and tablecloths.

I will always remember the beauty of that night. I had seen snow for the first time only a few days earlier and I was still amazed by it. The huge evergreens were shrouded with snow. The reflected light from the snow on the ground made everything stand out in silhouette.

Pfc. Romanelli: We trooped through the woods unobserved by the German defenders until we reached an open field. We hesitated. Our leaders ordered us to charge across the field. We knew it was highly likely that the enemy had set mines and the risk was great but soldiers are trained to obey orders and follow our leaders, even into slaughter. B Company and several other platoons made it across but the Germans were now aware of the attack and began to lay down murderous fire. We took refuge in a narrow communication trench and spent the next several nights in trenches surrounded by Germans intent on killing every last one of us.

Lt. Inge: The men of our battalion, with full combat equipment, weapons and ammunition, trudged a thousand yards through snow-covered woods undetected by the Germans. At the edge of the woods was an open field, heavily mined and the German soldiers were dug in on the other side. On orders, we moved out on the double careful to step in the footprints of the man in front. Suddenly, schu mines began to explode behind me and men fell and stained the white snow red. Machine-gun bullets began popping, alerting the Germans who began spraying the area. The head of the column successfully crossed the open field, and we raced toward a thin line of pine trees ahead but artillery and mortar fire prevented the others from advancing. Rifle fire and hand grenades silenced some German resistance as we raced through the woods and grouped behind a log antitank barricade. Here, we received word by radio that only B Company, two platoons from A Company, and a platoon of heavy machine-guns from D Company made it across the open field. Our group of about two hundred fifty men was isolated within the enemy lines.

Pfc. Johnson: I remember passing through the dragon's teeth – parallel rows of concrete piers designed to prevent tanks from penetrating. We then moved into communication trenches that connected the bunkers and other fortifications. The trenches were about shoulder high and no more than two-feet wide and directed toward the village. Our leaders decided to utilize them for our advance. I could do nothing else but play follow-the-leader, following the man ahead of me. During the afternoon, the action picked up. We captured several bunkers and returned to the trenches when the Germans counter-attacked and began lobbing grenades as they lay in the snow followed by machine-gun and mortar fire. Casualties began to mount.

Pfc. Romanelli: Despite the Germans' deadly fire, our Company continued to advance, and later that day captured a German pillbox. We stayed in the trenches that afternoon under machine-gun and mortar fire and later learned that we were surrounded.

Lt. Inge: The Germans, now alerted, closed in around us. We took shelter in some deep zigzag trenches. The Germans began grazing the areas with machine-gun fire and dropping mortar rounds down through the trees. The rounds crashed in on us, sharp deadly shrapnel cutting the limbs off trees causing them to fall down on top of the trench. Throughout the night, we crouched on the icy wet bottom of the trench and remained alert in anticipation of a move by the Germans. We also knew that if we slept we could freeze to death.

Pfc. Romanelli: They dropped mortar rounds all night that would explode in the trees and light up the woods. None of us slept, a number of men were killed and some wounded froze to death. The Germans had no fear of a tank attack on the dragon's teeth of the Siegfried Line. The concrete bunkers, pillboxes and minefields made it easy to defend against infantry and the bad weather grounded air support. The enemy easily repulsed our attack; hence, the disastrous results of the Orscholz debacle. The First Battalion of the 301st Regiment lost 40 men killed or wounded, and 400 missing in action. Though soundly defeated, some of us survived to triumph over the agonies of battle and subsequent inhumane treatment by our captors.

Pfc. Johnson: Shells were bursting directly overhead. We fell to the bottom of the trench and covered our heads with our arms to hold our helmets on. Shrapnel caught me in the elbow shattering it. Within minutes, the medic came and sprinkled sulfa powder on my arm, bandaged it and put it into a sling, but no splint. Strangely, the arm felt numb, but there was no severe pain. The medic took me to a bunker that was being used as a first-aid station. As we were leaving, I noticed that the same shell had killed the man next to me. There were no empty bunks left at the aid station so I had to lie on the floor in a half-inch of water. It was still warmer than in the trenches. They gave me morphine and I hallucinated or drifted into unconsciousness for most of the night.

Pfc. Romanelli: Jim Covalt, my ammunition bearer, crawled around me to get a better look at what was going on in front of us. A "booby-trap" land mine exploded. Jim had so many wounds; I did not know where to begin dressing them. We were trained to give sulfa pills to seriously wounded comrades to prevent infection. When I broke open the packet to give Jim the pills, they fell in the snow. I quickly scooped them up gave him the pills, along with some snow and water from his canteen. Our Sergeant, Bill Heinlein, came back to us and said a medic would be by shortly; we had to move on.

Lt. Inge: After the second night without sleep, we could see some German soldiers over in the open fields to the south of us hauling an artillery piece down a snow-covered road and we knew that it was an 88-mm gun because of its long tapered barrel. Out of the effective range of our rifles, the gun was quickly put in position on the road about six or seven hundred yards away with the barrel pointed toward us. Almost immediately, it went into action and began firing point blank. The rounds crashed in on us, cutting the limbs off trees by the sharp deadly shrapnel that rained down on us. The ground bursts would throw snow, dirt and shrapnel all over us. Many of the men in the trenches, who had survived the freezing night and earlier mortar and artillery barrages, were now being killed or badly wounded as the firing continued incessantly.

The Company Commander of B Company, Captain Herman Straub, passed word down the trench that the battalion had called for artillery and mortars with smoke shells to try to give us a chance to get back to our lines. Soon white phosphorous shells began to land in the open fields covering the areas to the south and east of us with smoke.

Pfc. Romanelli: Following that horrible night in the trenches under constant fire, the next day we tried to break out of the trenches and retreat to the forest but several attempts failed. Word came that we should try to get back on our own. Reasoning that it would be safer under cover of darkness, we determined to wait until nightfall. Just before dusk, we agreed to escort a captured wounded German soldier, who was bleeding profusely from his chin, back to the bunker where he could get treatment from our medics. When we arrived, a sergeant told us that we were completely surrounded and captured and to "lay down our weapons." Those of us who had survived now faced a new kind of fear. Having regularly received the *Stars and Stripes,* we were aware of the recent German massacre of Americans taken prisoner at Malmedy, during the Battle of the Bulge.

Lt. Inge: Captain Straub led the way taking along with him captured German soldiers to lead us around mined areas. We began to move down the trench in the direction of the smoke, stepping over dead and wounded. A direct hit by an 88 shell caused a tree to fall on the trench and blocked our exit. About twelve or fourteen men were now trapped at the end of the trench under heavy fire. We were completely surrounded, our ammunition was gone and I believed we were about to be killed.

75

Realizing that remaining in the trenches would be fatal to all of us, whereas movement would greatly increase our chances of survival, I jumped out of the trench; a feat requiring all the strength I could muster. The men remained huddled in the trench. I shouted for them to follow me. They followed as I ran up the hill toward the bunkers that were about fifty yards from the trench. Racing up the snow-covered hill to its crest and into the safety of the bunkers took about thirty seconds. Moreover, despite the bedlam of exploding shells, crashing branches and machine-gun fire, we all made it over the top without a single man being hit.

Entering a nearby bunker, we found the frozen bodies of several men who had died during the night and others badly wounded lying on the cold concrete floor. Not knowing what was going on beyond our immediate area, we calmly waited for the arrival of medical help to keep the severely wounded from joining their dead comrades lying beside them. All of us who were crowded into the bunker could see that the route we had traveled the day before the attack, our only escape route, was now closed. We watched as German soldiers in the woods began moving toward us. I sat on a box by the steel door of the bunker too exhausted to move, shell-shocked and with the hopeless despair of being trapped inside German lines.

Pfc. Johnson: Dawn came with no visible change in the situation. Some of the men in the bunker began to leave. Two men from my platoon came into the bunker and told me the battalion was getting ready for a breakout and they were going to take me with them. While they were getting me to my feet, an officer asked what they were doing. They told him, and he said they were going to kill themselves and me and it was best to leave me there. Reluctantly, they put me on one of the bunks and left cigarettes, chocolates and water nearby. They left and I never saw them again.

Late in the afternoon of the next day came the most frightening experience of all. Looking out the open door of the bunker, I saw German medics coming toward us. They had vests with red crosses but they were also carrying machine pistols. There were only four of us remaining in the bunker and I was the only one ambulatory. The others begged me to get up and lock the door. I did not know what to do. I was afraid of being shot and yet if I locked the door, they would blow it with some charges. I got to my feet still undecided but then collapsed from loss of blood. The German medics were in the bunker when I regained consciousness. Although they were using Americans for litter bearers, a German soldier pulled me on a child's sleigh to their command post in the village. Following interrogation, they bandaged my arm with white crepe paper and placed it in a splint to restrict movement.

Lt. Inge: It was not long before the Germans saw that most of our men had gotten out of the trench and were in the woods to the east. The firing stopped and a sweet silence descended on the woods. The quiet seemed strange after twenty-four hours of deafening shelling by both sides. After a while, I looked out the door of the bunker and saw some German soldiers, led by a big sergeant in a long leather overcoat, walking toward us and holding a Schmeisser machine pistol or burp gun in his hands.

As he neared the bunker, the German sergeant shouted in perfect English for us to come out with our hands up. I pushed the door open and we went out, a motley group of dirty, unshaven men, on the verge of being overcome by fatigue and hunger. They took us to a farm building where a group of men whom I recognized from the rifle companies were collected.

They were all who remained from Able and Baker companies and they told us that the Germans captured the others soon after their attempt to break through to the forest. The Germans had taken them back toward the rear; leaving only these men to assist several wounded who were lying on some straw on the muddy floor.

Pfc. Romanelli: I spent that entire evening and night with three other Americans and a German Red Cross medic searching for wounded GI's in the field. Upon finding a body lying in the snow, the medic would feel the body's wrist to determine if there was a pulse. If so, we would place the body on a litter and carry it back to the bunker. If not, the medic would drop the hand and move on to the next body.

Lt. Inge: A German sergeant ordered me to take the enlisted men and remaining sleds and go back to the anti-tank barrier outside of Orscholz, and evacuate our wounded to their aid station in town. It was early afternoon of January 21, 1945, our third consecutive day without sleep. Under the guard of several German soldiers, we started back pulling sleds and carrying empty stretchers toward the trenches where we had spent the night before. It took us about an hour to make our way through the snow and woods back to the area around the bunkers and trench. When we arrived on the scene, the sight of so many of our men lying dead and frozen and red blood staining the white snow once again saddened us. It was then that I saw how many of our men had been killed in the trench or frozen to death the night before.

Pfc. Johnson: During the night, They took me to a field hospital in the basement of a house. I remember twenty or thirty of us lying on blankets on straw in the basement. When my turn came to enter the operating room, I begged them not to amputate my arm. A German enlisted corpsman said, "We will do what is necessary."

as he placed an ether cone over my nose. When I regained consciousness, I knew my arm was gone, but that did not prepare me for the shock of seeing crepe paper bandage over the short stump.

During the daylight hours, we reached a hospital in the town of St. Wendel. I was placed in a room with eight beds. There were four other Americans and several German soldiers in the room. We had been at St Wendel for three weeks when the Germans began rushing around, placing everyone on stretchers and moving us to a hospital train. We left hurriedly. I learned later, it was about thirty minutes before American troops entered the town.

Pfc. Romanelli: We, the survivors of the horrible battles, were now prisoners and marched away from the front lines. We walked until about midnight to a German farmhouse where we were placed under guard in the cellar. Tired and exhausted, I took off my cold wet combat boots and fell asleep on the floor. Awakened in the morning by guards, who told us to raus or get out. I tried to put on my boots, but my feet were so swollen that they would not fit into the boots. Several GIs helped me up the steps and took me outside, where our Company Commander, Captain Straub, told the Germans that I needed and should get medical attention.

They transported me to the hospital at St. Wendel with frozen/swollen feet. I had to have been relieved but I remember very little about my stay there. I know I slept in a bottom bunk and listened under blackout to sirens and bombings and the moans and groans of wounded men in pain. I do remember a German nurse or attendant soaking my feet in a liquid solution (it may have been just plain hot and/or cold water) and then wrapping them in paper bandages. I cannot recall having even one meal at the hospital other than what appeared to be a tube of toothpaste or shaving cream. The nurse who gave it to me motioned that I should put it toward my mouth. Upon unscrewing the cap, I found that it was processed cheese. I squeezed it and tasted the ribbon of cheese in my mouth.

I remained in the hospital for about a week or ten days, and then transferred to a small schoolhouse where they were holding other prisoners. After I was liberated and back in the USA, I learned that Tom Johnson from our second platoon, and Jim Covalt, whom I had left lying in the snow, and other wounded from our Company were all in the same hospital. Long after the war, an American airman named Charles W. Hartney told me that many German soldiers at St. Wendel's had limbs missing implying that the hospital may have specialized in amputations. Nonetheless, I am forever grateful to the German doctors and nurses for treating and saving my feet!

At the schoolhouse, we slept on straw on the floor of what must have previously been a classroom. Each morning we stood in formation, were counted, and received our loaf of bread to be divided among eight of us. We had to cut the bread into reasonably equal portions, and arguments followed as to who got the largest or smallest or thickest or thinnest pieces. This was soon resolved by establishing a pecking order. On the day you cut the bread, you had the last choice.

In his memoirs, Tom Johnson describes lunch and dinner. I was never so lucky. Our group had nothing more than one slice of bread per day for more than three months. Some of my fellow prisoners had great will power; they would break their slice of bread into three pieces, eat one piece for breakfast, and retain the other two pieces in their pocket for lunch and dinner. I tried, but by mid-morning, not even a crumb remained in my pocket. We were always hungry and were obsessed with thinking about food. Some guys wrote elaborate descriptions of what food they would eat on their first day at home; what they would have for breakfast, lunch and dinner of that first day, the second day, the third day, and following days.

One day, a young prisoner started crying because someone had stolen his slice of bread. A few NCOs formed a "kangaroo court" which decided, and made known to everyone, that anyone caught stealing another man's bread would be branded on the forehead with the Nazi swastika. It never happened again.

Sometime in the latter half of February, we left the schoolhouse to begin a march that would continue day after day. We would walk in two single files, one file on each side of the road, for about an hour and have a ten-minute break. At dusk, we would sit or lie down in the open fields and later try to sleep. Early the next morning, after head count, we were given our "daily bread" ration and resumed the march until evening. We were always hopeful that we would soon reach a prisoner of war camp. It never happened. We never got to a prisoner of war camp.

My mother, Carmella Romanelli was a very devout woman who went to mass every day. It was her deep faith in God that gave the family strength to face the fact her children were in harm's way all over the world in service to their country. On January 21, 1945 she received a telegram informing her that *her son Michael has been reported missing in action* somewhere in Germany. "Missing in action?" what does that mean. Has he been wounded? Is he dead? Is he alive? What do parents and other loved ones do following receipt of such a telegram? I have been told that they cried and cried and prayed. Every evening the family, along with friends and neighbors, would gather in the Romanelli's living room and prayed for my safe return.

Days turned into weeks and weeks into months and they grieved for ninety-seven days without further details or any additional information. How do you measure heartache? How does one measure the mental anguish of not knowing if your child is dead or alive? The elixir to aspirate anguished hearts is the fervent belief that God will answer the prayers of His people and bring loved ones home safely.

We marched the latter half of February, all of March and most of April, sleeping only in open fields at night in rain, snow and ice during one of the most severe and coldest winters in the history of Germany. It was miserable lying in those wet cold fields with no blankets and no shelter. We never had a roof over our heads and huddled together, shrinking into fetal positions to try to keep warm. To add insult to our misery, during one of the days of the march, our own P47 fighter planes strafed us. Thinking back, I was always hungry, cold, dirty, anxious, scared and miserable. Most of all, I minded being cold. The wind stings your toes and bites your nose. I learned that it is simply astonishing, almost unbelievable what the human body can endure.

I recall once finding a whole potato. I am not sure where it came from. It may have fallen from a cart or it may have been uncovered from the earth. I do know that I closed my eyes and took a bite of that raw potato. It tasted like a banana! The next bite tasted like a juicy apple! And the next bite tasted like a sweet pear! My rusty taste buds were sending false signals to my brain. On another occasion we discovered a "cache" of buried sugar beets that a German farmer probably planned to feed to his animals. I ate and ate, and only suffered mild heartburn and diarrhea as a result. While walking in single file, a GI right in front of me had drawn with indelible pencil on the back of his field jacket a picture of a platter stacked with pancakes, with butter and molasses running down the sides and surrounded with fat link-sausages.

At one time during a ten-minute break during our march, I saw a Russian POW lying in a ditch on the side of the road in a little town. A German woman, in long black skirt, black blouse, and black babushka came out from her house and, from the folds in her skirt, took a piece of bread and placed it in the hand of the Russian. He had difficulty getting the bread to his mouth. He must have been so delirious that he could not find his mouth. On several attempts, the bread hit his eyes, his cheeks, and nose. I know not if he ever succeeded; we had to move on. I was told that Russian POWs did not get even one slice of bread per day, and they survived by eating grass and earthworms.

Every step I took I dreamed of a camp where I could have a roof over my head, a Red Cross package, write a letter home, take a shower, have some clean clothes and some real food. It never happened. One day, we heard rumors that we were going to a camp in Ludwigsburg. Upon arrival, we were disappointed to learn that it was not a camp but a warehouse used to store Red Cross packages and it had been looted and abandoned. So we continued the march and passed the cities of Stuttgart and Augsburg. Finally, on April 27, 1945, somewhere between Augsburg and Munich, not far from the concentration camp at Dachau, an American armored division liberated us. The Germans had taken us to a big, empty farm building. Some of the GI's thought it may have been used for drying tobacco. We heard the rumbling noise of approaching tanks and, sure enough, we recognized them and they recognized us as Americans. The tank crews were throwing all kinds of goodies to us – candy, fruit, cigarettes and C-Rations. I caught a package of Chesterfield cigarettes, lighted one, took two puffs and became very dizzy and light-headed.

I had not had a cigarette in more than three months. I had not had a meal in more than three months. It was truly a happy day.

The first thing I did was to write V-Mail letters home to let my family know I was alive and well. We were taken to an airfield, loaded onto C47 cargo planes, sat on benches against the fuselage walls, and without parachutes flew to Reims, France. We went to Camp Lucky Strike for processing, ate to our heart's content, showered, and new clean clothing was issued to us. It was my first clothes change in more than three months! We then boarded a Liberty ship in LeHavre, France for the voyage home. Before departing, I sent a telegram to my parents letting them know that I was safe and well and on my way back to the good old U.S.A. In retrospect, I believe there exists in each of us, an indomitable, unshakeable desire to live and one does not know his or her capacity to endure until tested. Looking back, I think of Tom Johnson's *Memories*. As I did, he saw the hand of God in his life. In the words of the eminent philosopher, Paul Dalrymple, "I would not have missed it for a million dollars and I would not repeat it for five million dollars."

Among my meager possessions I have a faded, one-page program entitled, *Memorial Service at Sea*. Printed on it in my handwriting is "U.S.S. Santa Maria, May 30, 1945." I must confess that I do not remember the Memorial Service; however, the *Santa Maria* was bringing me home. We arrived in Boston and I telephoned my family to let them know I had arrived and would soon be home on furlough.

My oldest brother, Charlie, met me at a train station about fifty miles from home, and took me to his house where his wife, Dorothy, had prepared a big dinner. I ate contentedly and then we drove to my home where Mom, Dad, sisters and brothers were waiting for me. They had prepared a feast for my homecoming – all my favorites as known by my mom and sisters. Alas, after three months of starvation, I was not hungry. I had just eaten this wonderful dinner an hour ago. Nevertheless, I was happy; they were happy. Their prayers and mine were answered. It was the happiest day of my life. It was so great to see and be with them.

After my furlough, I reported to Asheville, North Carolina, for two weeks of rest and recuperation (R&R). From there, I went to Camp Polk, Louisiana, where I again began advanced infantry training, preparing to be shipped to the Pacific. This was June/July of 1945. Fortunately, Japan surrendered and the war in the Pacific ended in August. I had accrued enough points to be eligible for discharge. I went to Camp Robinson, Arkansas and then to Indiantown Gap, Pennsylvania, where I had been inducted, and was discharged honorably.

I was one of the fortunate ones who experienced the tragedy and cruelty of war and returned to my loved ones relatively unscathed. There were so many, many, many more that did not return. Almost with a sense of guilt I have asked, "Why was I spared?" since I know that many next of kin prayed diligently for their loved ones who did not return. I have concluded there is no earthly answer to my query.

After the war when I again heard from my ammo bearer Jim Covalt, a truly great army buddy, who I had to leave lying cold and wounded in the snow on that fateful January day. He wrote and told me during that night he hallucinated and kept dreaming that "Terry and the Pirates" were coming to rescue him.

I went to school under the GI Bill and earned a Bachelors and Masters Degree in Mathematics. I graduated on a Saturday and started working for the Army the following Monday, where I remained employed for thirty years until I retired. The Army was very good to me. I gave them a few years of service; they gave me an education and a life-long job.

I am grateful that Thomas R. Johnson, Jr. and Herndon Inge, Jr. who so eloquently wrote and published the details of our experiences in the *94th Infantry Division Association's Commemorative History* and permitted excerpts from their memoirs to be included in this book. My relatives all have copies of the written record and associated stories I have told and written. It is my fervent hope that my children, grandchildren and future generations will never have to experience war, and that they will become familiar with and recognize the hardships faced and sacrifices made. May they long remember the valor of those who fought to preserve freedom in the Second World War, especially those who did not return home.

Michael Romanelli received his honorable discharge in November 1945 after almost three years of service at the rank of Corporal. He was twenty-two years old. He was awarded the Purple Heart; Combat Infantryman and Expert Infantryman Badges; Bronze Star Medal; POW Medal; American Campaign Medal; European, African, Middle-Eastern Campaign Medal with Four Battle Stars; WW II Victory Medal; and Good Conduct Medal.

Michael Romanelli
Camp McCain, Mississippi, 1944

Milton O. Price, Rapid City Army Air Forces Base
September 14, 1944, prior to going overseas

MILTON O. PRICE, SR.

*"This journey to hell would be the single worst
experience of my entire life*

F ATE WORKS in strange and wondrous ways.
Milton Price can attest to that. During the war
years, he served in the Naval Reserve, the 29th
Infantry Division and the 8th Air Force. Unquestionably,
his military career path was quite unusual. He joined the
Naval Reserve in 1936 when he was only seventeen
years old. The country was moving out of the Great
Depression, but times were still hard and duty with the
naval reserves provided both opportunities for adventure
and some extra cash as well. Two years of his four-year
tour in the Naval Reserve were on active duty.

Drills were held twice a month and sea duty for two
weeks each summer was required. The first summer
aboard the *U.S.S. Tatnall,* a destroyer that was tossed
around like a rowboat in rough water, training focused
on heavy weapons and submarine warfare. That year,
weekend liberty was in Havana, Cuba. The following
summer, aboard the battleship *Texas,* training
concentrated on firing the 16-inch guns. Boston was
liberty port that year. Living on a battleship is like living
in a small regimented city.

In October 1940, Milton Price had a momentous
decision to make. His enlistment in the Naval Reserve
was up and he had two choices – he could reenlist in the
Navy or take his discharge and face the likelihood of
being drafted. This was more than a year before the
attack on Pearl Harbor and America's entry into the

Second World War. The draft was for a one-year period, while reenlistment in the Navy was for the "duration." No one would attempt to define or estimate the length of the duration. Compounding his decision was the fact that he had fallen in love and planned to marry, so he and his fiancée, Vera Zepp, decided that a one-year tour in the Army was better than being in the Navy for an indefinite term.

Milton was discharged from the Naval Reserve in October 1940, and drafted into the Army in April 1941. The December 7, 1941 attack on Pearl Harbor changed the marriage plans of Vera and Milton because instead of a one-year tour of duty, he was now in the Army for the duration. While on a three-day pass, they married on December 27, 1941, and honeymooned in New York City.

Following basic training at Fort George C. Meade in Maryland, Milton was assigned to the *Blue and Gray* 29th Infantry Division, 175th Infantry Regiment, Company B. The 29th became infamous for the disaster it faced on Omaha Beach on D-Day and other battles throughout Europe. The struggle of those heroic young men has been documented in the epic film *Saving Private Ryan*.

This is Milton's story:
In October 1942, the 29th Division embarked from New York City aboard the *Queen Elizabeth* and sailed to Greenock, Scotland. We trained on the moors of Salisbury Plains in England near Tidworth Barracks. It was always foggy, wet, uncomfortable and disagreeable. Several times a week, we would hike for twenty or twenty-five miles with full field pack. When we were not hiking, we were on the rifle range. Night maneuvers and similar field exercises were common. Early in Autumn 1943, the Division moved to the coastal areas of

Plymouth and St. Ives in Devon, southern England, where we began training for the invasion of France. Every morning we would go out into the English Channel in assault crafts and return in the afternoon. It was amazing to experience the tides in this area. When we left in the morning, we stepped from the pier onto the boat, but when we returned in the afternoon, we had to climb twelve-foot ladders to reach the pier.

During this period, the Army Air Forces were desperately seeking people with the qualifications to become airmen, especially pilots. Every applicant was considered a potential pilot. Formal schooling was not a prerequisite. All applicants were given a qualifying exam; short-answer or multi-choice questions, and if qualified, next underwent a series of general education and physio-motor tests to measure mental acuity and physical coordination. Scores on these and other tests were used to determine the particular phase of flying – pilot, bombardier or navigator – in which candidates could be best trained. If any failed to meet the minimum standards in any category, they became eligible to apply for gunnery school.

Because my IQ was over 110, I was invited to take the exam to determine if I could qualify. It was a no-brainer. When you are in the infantry, you'll do anything to get out, and reassignment to the Air Forces sounded good. After the initial exams, I went to London for more testing. I really did not think I had a chance, but thought, "What the heck, a weekend in London was a break!" To my surprise and delight, I qualified and was reassigned from the 29th Infantry Division to the Army Air Forces and returned to the States for more testing and training. The return voyage was aboard the *Queen Mary*, which also carried a number of German POWs who had been captured during the African Campaign and a group of English brides of American servicemen. The prisoners were quite relaxed and entertained us singing in their native tongue.

From New York, I went to Keesler Field where I failed to qualify on the depth perception test. At that juncture, I knew I was destined to become an aerial gunner. My training began at Las Vegas, Nevada, a very different place from the Las Vegas of today. We received both classroom and aerial training, shooting at targets being towed by aircraft. Next stop was Denver for armored-gunner training and a twenty-week course in the operation and maintenance of aircraft armaments. From there, I proceeded to Lincoln, Nebraska, where our flight crew was formed and was then sent to Rapid City, South Dakota for training. While at Rapid City, my son Buddy, Jr. was born and I was able to get a furlough home.

While I was attending gunnery school, the D-Day invasion occurred, and the 29th Division caught unmerciful hell on Omaha Beach. Of the eleven men in my former squad, six were killed and five others were wounded on D-Day +1. Had I not transferred to the Air Forces, I am sure I would have joined my fallen comrades in death or would have been seriously wounded. I have always thanked God for sparing me. Ironically, the battleship *Texas,* on which I had trained while in the Naval Reserve, was one of three battleships supporting the invading forces on D-Day, firing at German coastal gun emplacements.

Following completion of flight crew training, we flew from Rapid City to Manchester, New Hampshire, and then on to Labrador, on to Iceland and then England. We arrived at our destination, Lavenham, England, on October 7, 1944, and were assigned to the 487th Bomb Group, 839th Bomb Squad. Immediately after arriving in England, we began our bombing runs. We hit the cities of Cologne, Kassel and Merseburg, and provided bombing support to our troops on the front lines in France. Our sixth or seventh mission was over Hamm, Germany, where we encountered extremely heavy flak and our plane was hit. We lost the inner engine on the starboard side. The pilot, Lt. Burr E. Davidson, directed the co-pilot, Lt. Douglas C. Brink, to feather the damaged engine. In the excitement of the moment, the wrong engine was shut down, and because the plane was so badly damaged, it could not be restarted. At this point, we were flying on only two engines, both on the port side of the plane. One of the damaged engines started to windmill and the plane began shaking violently, worse than the most severe weather conditions I had ever encountered.

The pilot decided we had to bail out and gave the order to do so. The three men in the rear – Sgt. Joseph W. Dory, tail gunner; Sgt. Charles A. McBride, ball turret gunner; and I, as the waist gunner, went out the waist door. The others, Lt. Brink, co-pilot; Lt. Roy R. Denure, bombardier; Sgt. Clarence D. Becker, top turret gunner; and Sgt. William Millard, radioman, went out the front. The pilot, Lt. Davidson and the navigator, Lt. Willard J. Blanchard, decided to stay with the ship and try to fly it back to a neutral zone. I believe I was the last enlisted man to leave the plane. I was really scared. When I finally jumped into the unknown, the slipstream tossed me around like a cork in the rapids and I tumbled over and over. Our training was to keep our feet together and free fall as far as we could to avoid detection. You don't realize how rapidly you can fall at twenty thousand feet.

I was wearing a breast pack, a chest-type parachute. When I finally pulled the ripcord, the chute opened and hit me in the jaw. I thought my neck had been broken. Luckily it only caused some neck discomfort. It must have rained heavily in this area prior to our mission, because when I landed in a field, my butt fell into a puddle. While gathering my chute, Lt. Denure landed within twenty feet of me and the two of us quickly gathered our gear and headed for a nearby wooded area. Once reasonably secure, I opened my survival kit to look at the map. It had to be due to shock, but to my eyes the map was completely blank. I know this could not be true. The Air Force does not put blank maps into escape kits.

We were in the wooded area less than a half-hour when two German soldiers in blue uniforms approached with guns drawn and captured us. I believe both were airmen in the German Luftwaffe; one was a non-com and the other a private. They relieved us of our pistols and ordered us to pick up our chutes and marched us to a nearby farmhouse. There, German soldiers had a car with a flat tire and we were told to pump it up. Dumb me; I refused, citing the Geneva Convention. Lt. Denure did the pumping. Luckily, I was not shot.

My first prison camp was the notorious "Sweat Box" at Frankfurt am Main. By this time I had lost all contact with all my fellow crewmembers. I was put into solitary confinement, total darkness for at least two days. The Germans used this method on practically all airmen to break down their resistance. I was taken to an interrogation room where a German officer who spoke "Oxford" English questioned me. I quickly learned that he knew more about my unit than I did.

Following interrogation, about twelve of us, all airmen and non-commissioned officers, were marched to the train station in Frankfurt. Before we reached the station we had to cross streetcar tracks. German citizens who gathered there angrily pleaded with our guards to force us to lie down across the tracks. Thankfully, the guards ignored their pleas. Our group, along with the guards, was put on a train car that reminded me of a remodeled caboose. The seats were wooden benches and I suppose it was what would then be classified as third-class accommodations. I do not remember how long the journey took, but it was early December 1944 when we finally reached the railroad station at Keifheide in northeastern Germany near the Baltic Sea. It was close to the port city of Stettin. Today, the area is Polish territory and Stettin is named Szczecin.

Guards, with police dogs who yapped constantly at our heels, met us. On the two and one-half mile run to the prison camp, a few of the men came too close to the dogs and were bitten. The camp was Stalag Luft IV and the prisoners were predominantly airmen with the rank of sergeant. After processing, I was assigned to a barracks in Compound B. The barracks contained ten rooms and each room was originally designed to hold twelve to fifteen men, but now there were eight triple bunks to accommodate twenty-four men. Since I was the twenty-sixth man assigned to this room, my bed was on the floor.

Stalag Luft IV was a large camp with four compounds holding between 10,000 to 12,000 prisoners. Most were American airmen but about five per cent were British servicemen. I was there from early December 1944 through January 1945. It was extremely cold and very boring. Food was nutritionally inadequate, but Red Cross parcels were good whenever we got them. There was never enough food; twenty-six men in our room shared two parcels. The Germans generally fed us black bread and thin potato soup or oatmeal. Once in awhile there was some horsemeat in the soup. One time they fed us pea soup; almost every pea had a worm enclosed. We ate the soup, worms and all, and joked that the Krauts finally gave us some meat. When you are hungry, anything goes. A German sergeant, who was known as "Big Stoop," was brutal and mistreated everyone.

Near the end of January, the Russian Army was approaching from the east. They were getting close to the camp and we expected that we would soon be liberated. Suddenly, we were told we were being sent to another camp. During the night of February 1, 1945, with snow covering the ground and the weather bitter cold, we were marched back to the railroad station at Keifheide. There, we were tightly packed into boxcars with no room to sit much less lie down, and only a single bucket to handle our body waste. Our trousers were soon wet with urine and dysentery and the stench became unbearable.

Locked in a boxcar without a portal, we had no way of knowing where we were or where we were going. Our destination was Nuremberg, a trip that normally took about six hours by train. Our train was frequently delayed and we spent a good bit of time sitting at various railroad sidings. This nightmare went on for seven days and eight nights during the coldest winter in northeast Germany in years. Adding to our misery, we were strafed several times by our own planes. Long, slow-moving freight trains made ideal targets for our fighter planes and the pilots were unaware of the human cargo they carried.

This journey to hell would be the single worst experience of my entire life. Survival became paramount; we somehow made the food last. With no heat and no room to move, we all suffered terribly from frostbite and other ailments, and fought to retain our sanity in the confinement of the dark boxcars. I prayed for God's help. My faith gave me the strength ad assurance that I could survive this terrible ordeal. It is truly amazing what the body can stand.

We finally arrived at the prison camp at Nuremberg about February 10, 1945. The compound was filthy. At Luft IV, I had slept on the floor. Here, I slept in a bed, but on a straw mattress that was infested with fleas and lice. We came in contact with American soldiers who were captured during the Battle of the Bulge. It was hard to believe, but they appeared to be in worse condition than we were. The Germans had taken all their winter clothing and obviously had fed them starvation rations.

While at Nuremberg, the city suffered a night bombing raid by the RAF. The Germans moved us outside and put us in slit trenches. From this vantage point, we watched as pathfinders lighted the area by dropping white flares and then red flares marked the target. Flak filled the air. This was a sight to behold. It made me think of a steam locomotive on a railroad in the sky and the fireman was spilling red-hot embers from the firebox into the atmosphere. The bombers followed and the sound of exploding bombs was deafening and it all seemed like a gigantic fireworks display. In London, I had been through bombings by German buzz bombs, but it was never anything like this.

The war was coming to an end as American Forces were rapidly closing in from the west and the Russians from the east. It became time for us to move once more. This was around March 1, 1945, and we were back on the road again heading south. Food was now almost nonexistent and we ate whatever we could scrounge from the fields as we passed by. If we were lucky we slept in barns, but mostly we slept out in the open. Old men, who had been pulled from their farms and their jobs to aid in the German war effort, now guarded us. They had no heart for this job and we could have escaped at any time. However, we knew the war could not last very much longer; also, there were SS troops and Gestapo agents out there who would kill you on the spot. We stayed together and concentrated on surviving. My two and one-half years of infantry training conditioned me and helped me survive the prison camps and the marches.

After about a two-week trek, during which we learned that our beloved President Franklin D. Roosevelt had died, we arrived at Stalag VIIB at Moosburg. There, we were quartered in tents about the size of a circus tent. The weather was now warming and we even had enough space to lie down. Late in April, we could hear the thunder of guns in the distance, and then suddenly one night, all the German guards left. We were free to go. Instead, we stayed and waited and were treated to a sight that none of us will ever forget – General George Patton standing in a half-track with his bright helmet and ivory-handled pistols, his jaw jutting forward. He seemed to be saying, "Men, fear no longer, you are back in the arms of the American Armed Forces."

We were taken to Reims, France for delousing, new clothing and debriefing. From there we went to Camp Lucky Strike, where I met my former crew including all of the officers. It was there that I learned that my pilot had tried to fly the plane back to neutral territory and unable to accomplish this, he and the navigator, the other crewmember who had remained aboard, had to bail out. However, the navigator was frozen with fear and would not jump. The pilot practically threw him out of the aircraft, thereby saving his life.

I returned to the United States via a Liberty Ship into the arms of my loving family. The Good Lord really took care of me. I could have easily been with my fallen comrades of the 29th Division in a cemetery in France or blown to pieces over Germany. My life today is built around Vera, my loving wife of sixty-four years, my son, Milton O., Jr., (Buddy) and his dear wife, Jane Klein; my dear daughter, Vera Jean (Pixie) and her dear husband Jim Bittner; and our dear youngest, Cindy and her dear husband, Robert Manas.

The family is most important in our world, and would not be complete without our precious grandchildren, Sandy Price Shefcheck, Scott Milton Price, and Jennifer Bittner DeVille.

In June 1999, my wife Vera and I visited Normandy for the 55th anniversary of D-Day. It was a very emotional trip filled with memories, especially when we visited the American military cemeteries. My 29th Division Company Commander and two of my former squad members are buried in the Coleville Cemetery. Others from "B" Company are buried in other American military cemeteries in Europe or their remains were returned home for burial. I will never forget my "buddies" from B Company with whom I lived and trained for two and one-half years.

Milton O. Price, Sr. was honorably discharged in October 1945, at Fort Meade, Maryland at the rank of Staff Sergeant. He was twenty-five years old. He was awarded the Air Medal; POW Medal; European, African Middle-Eastern Campaign Medal; World War II Victory Medal; American Theatre Medal; and Good Conduct Medal.

Vera & Milton Price – December 1941

100

Maneuvers, North Carolina, 1944
Milton is in front of line holding mess kit.
Half of these soldiers were killed in action.

Milton O. Price, Omaha Beach, 1999

On March 18, 1944, Joseph Spontak was awarded Navigator's Silver Wings and commissioned as a 2nd Lieutenant in the AAF

JOSEPH SPONTAK

*"I began jumping frantically on the nose wheel
doors and they finally opened and I fell out"*

JOHN SPONTAK EMIGRATED from eastern
Austria-Hungary and came to the United States in
1904 when he was sixteen years old seeking work in
the anthracite coal region in eastern Pennsylvania. John
married Barbara Kozar who had emigrated from the
same region in 1906 when she too, was sixteen. They
settled in Pottsville and together raised eight children,
seven sons and a daughter. The King Coal Company
contracted with John Spontak and other independent
miners who supplied their own tools and paid them for
every ton of coal they produced. This brought Joseph
and his brothers into the mines at one time or another to
help their Dad. If you hit a good vein, Joseph recalls,
you could make a lot of money.

The Spontaks enjoyed the fruits of their labor and
the family prospered. They loved the freedom and
opportunities their adopted homeland offered and taught
their children to cherish it and protect it always. When
the tyranny of World War II threatened their freedom,
John and Barbara offered the solemn sacrifice of five of
their sons to fight for the cause of liberty and freedom.

When the United States entered the global war
following Japan's attack on Pearl Harbor, the Spontak
brothers knew what was expected of them. Following his
graduation from Pottsville High School in 1940, Peter
Spontak enlisted in the Army Air Corps, and in 1942
served with the Field Artillery in Iran where he rose to
the rank of Master Sergeant. At age 25, his brother

Stephen enlisted in the Marine Corps and in September 1944, he entered the war in the Pacific Theatre and fought on Iwo Jima as a combat engineer. Pfc. Stephen Spontak has a special claim to fame. As part of the original group of Marines, who scaled the steep slopes of Mount Suribachi on Iwo Jima, he helped raise the first American flag there. The event made famous by Joe Rosenthal's prize-winning photo was simply that a bigger flag replaced the original.

Joseph, age 18 and recently graduated from high school, enlisted in January 1943. He earned his Navigator Wings at Randolph Field and served with the 15th Air Force in Pantanella, Italy. On his twenty-second mission, Enemy fighters attacked and severely damaged Joseph's plane and he had to bail out. He was captured, interrogated and spent ten months as a prisoner of war.

George Spontak was teaching mathematics and science at Downington High School before being inducted into the army on June 25, 1944. The youngest of the Spontak brothers, Charlie, at age18 enlisted in the Army Air Forces and became an Aviation Cadet.

Joseph, the second youngest child, was a straight "A" student all through Pottsville High School and graduated second in a class of 340. At six feet tall and 215 pounds, he was an outstanding athlete. He played both offense and defense on his high school's football team as a lineman, was a heavyweight wrestler, and a star on the school's track team. At the time, the Army Air Forces (AAF) had an ambitious goal to identify and train 42,000 pilots. Scholar-athlete Joseph Spontak proved to be an ideal candidate for their aviation cadet program.

Joseph Spontak took his oath on October 7, 1943 and immediately went to the AAF training center in Miami Beach, FL. The AAF was recruiting men faster than they could support logistically. Because there were not enough uniforms available, Joe had to go through basic training in his civilian clothes. This five-week basic military training included exhaustive physical, psychological, and mental testing to determine one's fitness for the flying program and to ascertain the specialty to which one was best suited. Joseph was selected for flying training.

The AAF had an acute shortage of nearly everything including airfields. AAF Commanding General Henry H. "Hap" Arnold developed a plan to provide Air Cadets primary flight instruction in civilian-operated schools that provided all services and facilities except aircraft. The AAF provided the aircraft. The plan was hugely successful. As many as forty schools scattered across the United States began training operations and at any given time, an estimated six hundred potential pilots, navigators and bombardiers were attending classes in these schools. Joseph attended Mount Union College in Alliance, Ohio, where he took courses in codes, mathematics, maps and charts, aero-physics and altitude equipment training. Trainees who successfully met requirements advanced to the next stage of flight training.

Before bombardier or navigator training, crewmembers had to qualify as an expert gunner. Joe attended aerial gunnery school at Harlingen, Texas. After gunnery school, bombardier and navigator trainees separated. Joseph completed a twenty-week accelerated navigator course at Hondo Air Force Base near San Antonio, Texas. Courses there consisted of celestial and dead reckoning navigation, meteorology, spherical trigonometry, astronomy and the use of a Weems computer plotter. The final exam was to navigate a plane across the country making seven different location stops. He successfully met all requirements. On March 18, 1944, Joseph Spontak received his commission as a 2nd

Lieutenant in the US Air Corps and awarded Navigator's Silver Wings. He immediately began combat-crew flight training on a B-24 Liberator heavy bomber and following almost two years of continuous training, he was now fully prepared for combat.

The crew flew their B-24 from Manchester AFB in New Hampshire to Marrakech, French Morocco via Gander AFB in Newfoundland reaching their destination, Pantanella Air Force Base near Canosa, Italy on June 16, 1944. They were assigned to the 780th Bomb Squadron, 465th Bomb Group and went into action almost immediately, attacking a score of targets in France, Germany, Austria, Hungary, Rumania and the Balkans.

During Operation Overlord - the Allied invasion of Normandy, the U.S. Eighth Air Force and the British RAF came under the direct command of General Dwight D. Eisenhower. Under the code name "Transportation Plan," their tactical objective was to disrupt movement of men and supplies into France, and their primary targets were railroad marshaling yards and repair centers in northern France and Belgium. During and following the invasion of France, they provided supporting firepower to the invading ground troops.

While the Eighth Air Force supported Operation Overlord, the Fifteenth Air Force assumed primary responsibility for the Allied Air Forces strategic objective for the destruction of Germany's capacity to wage war with the focus on reducing Germany's capacity to produce oil. The Rumanian Oil Center at Ploesti was Germany's biggest supplier of fuel and was also one of its most heavily fortified industrial sites. From April to August 1944, the Fifteenth Air Force flew twenty missions over the refinery and rail yards where the oil was loaded onto trains, pounding it into a virtual standstill. Aviation fuel production slumped from

175,000 tons in April to a mere 7,000 in September. However, the cost was high as the Fifteenth lost 223 planes and more than 2,200 men during this period. Joe's squadron flew in several of these raids.

Cal Carson was a WWII fighter pilot with great respect for bomber crews. In an article in the *Pantanella News* in 1997, he wrote about what he believed was the difference between air war and war on land or at sea. He opined that air war is a war of attrition. Each mission is a new engagement, a new battle, a new war. Air combat is usually brief but extremely intense. He indicated that bomber crews under enemy fighter attack go through a hellish experience. Joseph Spontak agrees with this, but he believes the more frightening experience in air combat is seeing heavy flak ahead of you - puffs of dense black smoke, exploding shells and deadly shrapnel, and knowing that you must fly through it. Enemy fighter attacks, although intense, are over so quickly you hardly had time to think, he explained. Though more fearful of flak than enemy fighters, he ultimately suffered the consequences of an attack by German fighter planes. While flying his twenty-second mission, sixteen enemy fighters attacked his group and shot his and seven other bombers down.

Following the reduction of the oil center at Ploesti, the U.S. Strategic Air Forces in Europe next gave the highest priority in South Germany to installations related to jet propelled and pilotless aircraft. This included the Manzell jet-airplane assembly plant in Friedrichshafen, Germany. Although severely damaged in previous raids, by midsummer the Air Forces Command decided to completely destroy the facility to prevent enemy jet-propelled aircraft from becoming operational.

On August 3, 1944, an armada of B24 Liberator Heavy Bombers from 21 Bomb Groups from the 15th Air Force's 47th, 304th, 5th and 55th Wings accompanied by seven Groups of Fighters set out on Mission #56 Friedrichshafen, Germany. There were a number of targets to be destroyed including railroad bridges, chemical works, aircraft and gear wheel factories. The Dornier aircraft factory in Manzell/Friedrichshafen was the target assigned to four Bomb Groups from the 55th Wing that included the 465th Bomb Group.

This is Joseph Spontak's Story:
During the intelligence briefing prior to take-off, the briefing officer emphasized the significance of the target and advised that we could expect intense flak over the target area but pointed out that its accuracy should be diminished due to our fighter escort and lead attack units dispensing chaff. He also alerted us to the possibility of an intercept in the North Adriatic area from enemy fighters based at or near Udine. He estimated that in the target area the scale of enemy effort would be between 125-150 aircraft. He added that on previous raids in this area, enemy aircraft had been very aggressive and enemy aircraft had followed bomber formations 50 to 60 miles from the target area. We all knew this was not going to be a milk run.

Another briefing officer gave the flight plan for the attack. The formations were to continue another 30km after dropping their bombs, then make a right turn, recreate the formation and return to Italy. The weather forecast for the morning of August 3, 1944 was clear sky. The route called for patchy to heavy clouds and moderate over the target. Air-ground visibility was 15 miles or better. We should have no trouble seeing the target.

Thirty-two B-24 Liberators from the 465th Bomb Group took off at 0611 and divided into two attack units. Major Olen C. Cook was formation leader and Captain

Stanley D. Pace led the second unit. Each plane carried 10,500 lbs. of general-purpose bombs. The Group made Wing rendezvous over Spinazzola. An escort of P51s and P38s including the "Tuskegee" airmen joined the formation at 1050 to furnish penetration, target and withdrawal cover. There were four early returns.

The flight to the target was without incident and our bomb run was normal. As we approached the target, the ground forces opened up and the flak became heavy. Several planes were hit and one of our group's planes lost an engine. Our plane was lucky to make it through without taking a hit. After the bomb drop, our group continued to fly easterly beyond the turning point while the rest of the formation turned right to return to Italy as planned. So for a few minutes our group of 28 B24s was flying east while the rest of the formation was flying in the opposite direction heading home. I was surprised to see the degree of separation.

The 465 Group left the target area with the planes in A, B, and D boxes in combat formation but the lead plane in C box had lost an engine causing the planes in C box to trail the group. At first, I thought we fell back because Major Cook ordered our group to decrease speed in order to provide protection to the trailing planes. However, from my vantage point, it became obvious that we had not made the turn at the rally point according to the flight plan and by the time our formation leader realized this error, our group had separated from the main force by at least twenty-five miles. He tried several corrective actions to reunite with the main force; however, due to our damaged planes, these maneuvers only spread our 28 aircraft into an even more detached formation and further increased the degree of separation of from the main body of planes by miles.

The Germans detected that our bomber group had separated from the main body of planes during the return. They dispatched fighters from their base at Kaufbeuren and about 150 miles into our return, near Ehrwald, Austria, the quick fighter planes climbed through the cloud cover and attacked from our rear. Their main target was the tail of the bomber. They came in waves of four with each wave almost V-shaped, firing their machine-guns and 20mm cannons. The slower moving, damaged bombers were like ducks in a shooting gallery. We tried to tighten the formation. Our gunners fought valiantly shooting down several enemy aircraft, later confirmed as eight, but we were no match for the fleet enemy fighters. We called for help from our P-51 escorts. They came quickly and encountered the second wave that was attacking my craft, broke up the third wave, and drove the attacking fighters off; but it was too late to prevent the disaster that resulted. Eight of our bombers, crewed by seventy-nine airmen, were shot down and thirty-one men lost their lives.

We were flying about 24,000 feet when the second wave of enemy fighters attacked our B24. I felt the plane rock with a jolt, turn left and begin to descend. From the navigator's window, I could see our right wing on fire. I looked up into the cockpit and, unexpectedly, all I saw were two oxygen masks burning. Lt. Crane and 2nd Lt. Bob Kurtz, the co-pilot, had already bailed out. Then someone else jumped out the bomb bay. I immediately opened the door to the nose turret; tapped S/Sgt. Lawrence J. Hamilton, the gunner, on his shoulder and motioned downward with my finger. He nodded his head in acknowledgement.

Due to the crowded conditions on the aircraft, the crew did not wear their parachutes during a flight but stored them in the fuselage and put them on right before the jump. American sources later reported that gunner

Hamilton was unable to find his chute in the chaos of the burning aircraft. He passed up an offer from a fellow crewmember to double jump with one parachute. Instead, he went on a frantic search for the reserve chute, which we learned later was not aboard this flight.

I pulled the emergency handle for the nose wheel doors to open but nothing happened. The plane continued to lose altitude and "G" forces were pinning me against the wall of the plane making it difficult to move. I was finally able to free myself and began jumping frantically on the nose wheel doors, and they finally opened and I fell out. The plane was flying at about 19,000 feet when I left it. When I pulled the ripcord on my chest chute, nothing happened, and while plummeting rapidly, I frantically began to peel the chute out. When the pilot chute came out, the main chute opened.

As I descended, I saw several other parachutes in the air, but I could not tell from which plane they were coming. We were over the Alps, and I dropped about nine thousand feet and landed on a mountain peak above the clouds. As I drew close to the mountain, an updraft caught the chute and I landed on a short angle. The dogfight in the sky continued. I crawled behind a large boulder because bullets began to hit all over the rocks.

Since I had landed above the clouds, I was sure that no one on the ground saw me, so as soon as I felt it was safe, I made my way down to the tree line. My plan was to proceed toward Switzerland, which I estimated was about sixty miles away. My "escape" package was of little value. The maps did not show contours. Had I had my navigator maps and a few extra K-rations, I could have stayed hidden on the mountain longer and perhaps escaped. Unbeknown to me, the village people had telescopes and they were scanning the mountainside for any sign of movement.

As I descended into a wooded valley, I saw a woman who also spotted me. Intelligence had briefed us that we might find friendly civilians in this area. I could have run but, because of the major air battle, the area would soon be crawling with enemy troops and it would only be a matter of time before they captured me. On the other hand, if she were friendly, she could assist in my escape. So, I decided to approach her and pretended to be an Italian airman. I did not think my act was very convincing. She pointed to a chalet farther down in the valley and said, "Kamerad Schweizer." I interpreted this to mean that there were comrades in the chalet who could help me get to Switzerland so I politely smiled, thanked her, and walked toward the building.

I was surprised to learn that the chalet was a training facility for Hitler Youth. As I approached, the matron of the house and seven or eight young people gathered and stared at me as if I was some foreign devil. The matron was a very dignified-looking woman who obviously was in charge of the chalet. Around her neck, she wore a two-inch medallion with a swastika in the center. I knew immediately that I was in trouble. She firmly advised that I was a prisoner of the German government, and an elderly man at her side produced a pistol and pointed it at me. With pistol in hand, he escorted me down the mountain and transferred me to a German soldier who took me to the police station in the village of Ehrwald, Austria and put me in jail. That afternoon they brought in another flyer and that evening two more American airmen were brought in. One was badly injured and I learned later that he had died.

The jailer turned us over to German Mountain Troops who took us to Garmisch-Partenkirchen, and several days later transported by train to the Interrogation Center in Oberursel, a suburb of Frankfurt am Main. They placed me in a soundproof cell with only a wooden table to sleep on. Twice a day, they fed me two small pieces of bread and a cup of water, escorted me to the bathroom, and did not allow me to talk to anyone. They kept me in solitary confinement for four or five days. The scariest thing was the continuous bombing nearby. I feared our own planes would kill me. Finally, my turn in the interrogation room had arrived. It was like an executive suite of a large corporation. The German officer was impeccably dressed and spoke perfect English. He offered me a cigarette but I refused. On a table, he had the organization of the 15th Air Force in several binders. He opened a binder and said, "The 465th Bomb Group is composed of four squadrons but Lt. Spontak is not listed. Can you explain?" I responded, "The rules of the Geneva Convention, of which the German nation is a member, requires me only to give my name, rank and serial number." "Yes, yes, of course," he answered. Then he picked up a piece of white cloth about the size of a handkerchief. "Can you tell me what this is?" he asked. I did not have the slightest idea but I repeated my name, rank and serial number. I was in the room for a few minutes and then returned to my cell.

The next day, I was taken to the smaller office of a Luftwaffe officer. He too offered me a cigarette then withdrew saying, "I forgot that you only smoke a pipe." This was true and it became immediately clear that they had convinced someone to talk. He handed me a form and explained that if I would fill it out completely, they would turn it over to the International Red Cross who would advise my family of my situation. The form had a number of questions about my squadron, bomb group, personnel, other officers and more. I filled in my name, rank and serial number and handed it to him. He gave it back and said that I had not completed it. I told him that I did not intend to provide any information other than what I had given him. He called for a guard to return me to my cell in solitary. I protested that the Geneva Convention rules prohibited keeping captives in solitary confinement. He simply waved me off and I was returned to my cell.

During the night, guards came to my cell and escorted me to one of the barracks. I did not want to disturb the sleeping men so I slept on the floor. That day I had food other than bread and water for the first time in a week. I even took a shower. Several days later, I was transported in a special prisoner car to Stalag Luft III located in Silesia, near Sagan (now Zagan in Poland), and placed in the North Compound with RAF prisoners. Following the "Great Escape" the Germans focused more security on this compound. Perhaps, my belligerent attitude marked me as a troublemaker who needed the extra attention provided in this compound.

The "Great Escape" took place from this compound in March 1944. Seventy-six RAF officers escaped but only two made it safely back to England. The Gestapo, under Hitler's orders, executed fifty escapees. The remains of forty-six are buried in a British Military Cemetery in Poznan, Poland. After the escape, security was increased. Periodically, the Gestapo would make us strip naked and stand outside while they tore apart the barracks looking for potential escape material.

Stalag Luft III was composed of five separate compounds. American flying officers were in four of the compounds and RAF officers were in the other. The total number of men imprisoned there was approximately 8,500. Life was quite solitary at first. Because of the lack of food and severe cold weather without heat, many prisoners became irritable and withdrawn. Tempers would flare from time to time, but I do not ever recall a fistfight.

Under the circumstances, I felt fortunate to be in the compound with the imprisoned RAF officers. Many were graduates of Oxford or Cambridge Universities or the Royal Military Academy at Sandhurst. They conducted courses in college algebra, calculus, German, French, Swahili and other diverse subjects. We even had an all-male theater group that performed classical plays with great expertise. They were good enough for Broadway.

Our diet consisted of potatoes, cabbage, German bread mixed with sawdust as a preservative, and barley soup. We received Red Cross parcels once a week. Usually six men shared one parcel. Although minimal, it was helpful. We talked mostly about food, recipes, and the meals we would have when we were free. When your focus is primarily on your next meal, you think of little else. There were seldom conversations about sex and I sensed some men began to lose feelings for their families. Their letters home became cold and uncaring and this likely contributed to a higher than normal divorce rate after they returned home.

We had a very effective counterintelligence group in Luft III, of which I was a member. Since the Nazis would infiltrate their prison camps with German-Americans who had returned to their homeland to fight for the Nazi cause, the British POWs were very suspect whenever the Germans placed an American within their compound. It took some time, but eventually I gained their trust and was determined to be a legitimate US Air Force officer and included in their counterintelligence group.

I was responsible for Block 106 security. One of our functions was to assure that German ferrets were not under our building listening to our conversations, especially following distribution of the *Canary* report. This report was the latest BBC bulletin on the war's progress obtained by means of a clandestine short-wave receiver in the compound. These reports gave us hope, encouragement and helped keep up our morale.

We became concerned about what the Gestapo might do on Hitler's orders, after a group of new prisoners mistakenly passed through the Bergen-Belsen concentration camp where they were eyewitnesses to the destruction of human dignity and life at this death camp. Now knowing what the Nazis were capable of and that the war was going badly for them, we were fearful that one day a vengeful Hitler would order our execution.

To prepare for this eventuality, we developed a comprehensive survival plan. The British had several intelligence agents deliberately captured knowing they would be sent to our camp. They coordinated the plan within the prison and with people outside. In *The Great Escape*, the British dug *Tunnel Harry* from Block 104 to the wooded area on the north side of the camp, which was discovered. Very few prisoners knew about *Tunnel George,* a second tunnel that extended from the camp theater, below the German's armory and into the woods on the eastside of the camp. The authorities never detected this tunnel. Entry was through a theater seat put together like a jigsaw puzzle. I served as a part of the security team during the digging of this tunnel.

The plan subdivided all prisoners into squads and squad leaders were designated. They were privy to only those elements of the plan that they had a need to know. My job was to make copies of area maps obtained from cooperative guards and other sources. I developed a makeshift "ditto machine" made from a large flattened tin can, which contained gelatin from Canadian Red Cross parcels. By tracing the maps on wax paper and using ink, I could make an impression of a map on the gelatin and then transfer the impression from the gelatin to paper. I next color-coated the fields, paths, trees and streams on the reproduced maps. Each squad leader had a survival kit that contained the maps and other items if a breakout occurred.

A group of Polish RAF officers were to serve as commandos and through *Tunnel George*, dig up into the arsenal and seize the weapons. A pre-arranged signal to the RAF and/or USAF was to be sent via a secret, one-time-use transmitter notifying them that the survival plan was in effect. They were expected to drop supplies, weapons and ammunition and, if conditions permitted, paratroopers. The squad leaders were to organize their squads and with the captured weapons shoot their way out of the camp. If we made it out safely, we were to head south toward Czechoslovakia where Czech partisans would meet us.

There was no need to implement the plan because the authorities evacuated the camp when the Soviet armies began approaching from the east. We moved out in the dead of winter, and traveled about eighty kilometers until we reached a German army tank armory that became our quarters for several days. Next, we boarded boxcars and spent three horrendous days locked in these cars without food or water as we traveled west toward Nuremberg.

There, the camp was a bombed-out former Hitler Youth camp near the railroad marshaling yards. American and British bombers bombed Nuremberg constantly. Although we feared for our own safety, we spent most of our time lying on our cots trying to conserve energy due to our weakened condition caused by lack of food.

I met our pilot Larry Crane and co-pilot Bob Kurtz for the first time since we went down and we had a frank discussion about the raid and the German fighter attack. They explained that when the plane was hit, it obviously lost its communication system and the hydraulic system was on fire. It was a critical situation and they believed all crewmembers had received the word to bailout. They opined there was nothing more they could do.

Besides Crane, Kurtz and me, Bombardier 2nd Lt. George N. Britton, S/Sgt. Leonard E. Bracken, S/Sgt. John S. Cooper, S/Sgt. Leeland T. Engelhorn, and S/Sgt. Anthony J. Jezowski made it safely out of the plane. All were captured and became prisoners of war. Gunners, S/Sgt. Charles F. Sellars and S/Sgt. Lawrence J. Hamilton died that day.

When Patton's 3rd Army crossed the Rhine River, we were again forced to evacuate our camp and spent the next six weeks walking south toward Stalag VIIA at Moosburg, which is located northwest of Munich. Although conditions on this march were deplorable, I felt they were better than what we had at Nuremberg.

On the march, we foraged the fields for food stealing whatever we could and when we passed through a village, we would knock on doors and beg for food and often received some. In several larger villages, the German people would set out buckets of fresh water and throw bread into the streets as we passed. Our guards were mostly older men who did not want to be on this march any more than we did and, on several occasions, we even carried their weapons for them. The war was winding down and the defeated German people were now acting kinder toward us but we still had other worries. Early in the march, American fighter planes had attacked the tail end of our column, seriously wounding several POWs. They had to believe we were German soldiers on the march. The allies apparently realized their mistake because after that incident, American reconnaissance planes began to track our movements.

The camp at Moosburg was a sprawling mass of men and chaos with more than 130,000 prisoners strewn all over the fields. Twenty-seven Soviet Generals were imprisoned there along with Americans, British, French,

Australians, Canadians, Sikhs, and others. We were housed in tents and had nothing to do except wait.

On April 29, 1945, we could hear shelling and small-weapons fire taking place in town, and a few hours later a battalion of 3rd Army tanks arrived at the camp. I was greatly relieved to know that this terrible war and my personal ordeal were finally over. I no longer had to fear the threat of being executed.

My weight fell from 215 to 140 pounds. Much of that 75 lb. weight loss occurred in the final three months of captivity. Following liberation, I became seriously ill and transferred to a field hospital in Rouen, France, where I spent several days. Following release from the hospital, I went to Camp Lucky Strike in northern France to await transport by a ship back to the US.

Prior to my discharge from the military, I had enrolled at Lehigh University and eventually earned a Bachelor of Science degree in Engineering Physics. Later, I married Anna Mary Harding from my hometown of Pottsville. We had three children, two girls and a boy. Unfortunately, the little fellow did not make it.

In afterthought, the dining room table in my parent's home that was usually crammed with people for every meal was more than half-empty during the war years. The half-empty table was even more chilling to a mother who lived constantly in a nightmare that some of these chairs might stay empty forever. It was tough on us but pretty tough on my mother and father, particularly during the period of uncertainty after my plane was shot down, until the day they were notified that I was alive and a prisoner of war. They worried constantly about my brothers and me but with the help of God we all returned safely.

In 1995, I visited New Zealand and Australia and was able to catch up with my old POW roommate from Stalag Luft III, Phil Farrow. He was a Flight Lieutenant with the Royal New Zealand Air Force attached to the RAF when he was shot down in 1944. He and I were roommates until we evacuated the camp early in 1945, and we went our separate ways, never to hear of each other again. Elderhostel home-host Denise Green turned to a former RAF airman, who keeps a wealth of such information on his computer, for help in locating Phil, but it was a simple matter of flicking through the telephone directory to find him and his wife Marjorie living nearby. Time and distance simply melted away as Phil and I spent hours reliving old memories of Stalag Luft III and catching up with those fifty years since.

In the Spring of 2000, I returned to Stalag Luft III. I photographed the entrance to the great escape tunnel and acquired a piece of the chimney through which the escapees bored to get under the building in Block 104. I also visited the crash site near Ehrwald where a local historian updated my knowledge about the eight B-24s shot down in the area. He pointed to the spot in a high valley between two peaks where our plane crashed and he gave me pictures of the crash site and a piece of our crashed B-24, which I carried home. He also told me that the remains of our nose gunner, Lawrence Hamilton, were found a few years later about two miles away, but no parachute was evident. Apparently, he had abandoned the plane without a chute.

On August 3, 2001, the citizens of Ehrwald held a commemorative ceremony honoring all the airmen killed or captured on that day in 1944 when a total of sixteen aircraft, eight B24 Liberator Heavy Bombers of the 15th USAAF and eight German fighter planes were shot down over the area. Survivors from both sides with their families along with kinfolk representing others attended the ceremony. Town officials selected the Soldiers' Memorial in the center of Ehrwald as the site for a monument dedicated to the remembrance of that fateful day in 1944. Bronze monuments, describing the event in both German and English and listing the bomber group and squadron and the names and status of the various crewmembers, now permanently mark where each plane crashed. I attended the event and had the opportunity to meet the families of former crewmembers and become acquainted with onetime combatants Otto Bosch who piloted an ME109 and Willie Unger who flew a FW190 during the battle. I went to our B24 crash site. As I walked through the area picking up and holding remnants of the plane, I became overwhelmed by the memories of that fateful day that have haunted me for 57 years. It was a very emotional experience.

Joseph Spontak received his honorable discharge from the Army Air Corps on November 21, 1945 at the rank 1st Lieutenant. He was twenty-one years old. His awards include the Air Medal; POW Medal; WW II Victory Medal; European, African, Middle-Eastern Campaign Medal with Three Battle Stars; American Theatre Medal; and the Good Conduct Medal.

Personal Message

To my daughters Mary Jo and Jane and their husbands Dewey and Michael, and grandchildren Andy, Jack, Lexie and Adam: This is my story as I recollect after sixty-one years. I am very thankful that I survived my ordeal in a terrible World War. By returning, my dear wife Anna Mary and I were blessed to have such a wonderful family as you all are. I love all of you dearly and please remember that America is a great country. Try your best to contribute to its greatness.

Anna Mary & Joseph Spontak, 1990

Former combatants reunited, Ehrwald, Austria, August 2001
Joseph Spontak, Navigator B24; Otto Bosch, Pilot ME 109;
Willie Unger, Pilot FW 190

Memorial to the air battle over Ehrwald, August 3, 1944

Charles Milton Rutkowski, 1945

CHARLES M. RUTKOWSKI

"We had our share of heroes.
While they were performing their heroic deeds,
I was probably digging my foxhole a little deeper.
But I was not alone. We were all scared to death."

C HARLES MILTON RUTKOWSKI came of age in the decade when the world was going mad. On September 1, 1939, Germany's invasion of Poland triggered the war in Europe. On September 16, Charles celebrated his nineteenth birthday. It was during this period that Adolph Hitler was readying his army for a bold march into the Rhineland causing unrest in Europe and concern in our own government. However, Charles and his friends were not too worried about what they considered political quarrels in a faraway land. Public sentiment at the time was that the USA should avoid involvement in another European conflict. Irrespective of the public's feelings, the government introduced a peacetime draft in September 1940, and the government began to conscript men between the ages of twenty-one and thirty-five and Charles began to lose friends to the military. Suddenly, on December 7, 1941, the Japanese attacked the US naval base at Pearl Harbor and plunged the nation into war. The USA declared war on Japan and Nazi Germany.

Charles was drafted into the U.S. Army. He reported to Baltimore's Fifth Regiment Armory for active duty on September 17, 1942, the day following his twenty-second birthday. Assigned to the infantry, he began his infantry training at Fort McClellan, Alabama.

Following basic training, some recruits remained for advanced infantry training while others were assigned to other branches, such as, the artillery, tank corps, medics or other disciplines. Charles was selected for Officer Training School, the first step on the path to becoming a commissioned officer. He was progressing very well. Candidates had very little free time; they trained all day and studied all evening. One evening, Charles made an unwise decision to leave study hall, without authorization, to go to the PX and buy his wife a Christmas gift. Roll call was taken and when he did not respond, he was considered absent without leave and thereby subject to dismissal from OTS. The Army demanded that its officers obey all orders.

The next day Charles was on his way to Camp Forrest , Tennessee, for advanced infantry training, with the 8th Infantry Division, 28th Infantry Regiment. After two months of training, including maneuvers and war games in the Tennessee Mountains, the Division set out for Fort Leonard Wood, Missouri.

After a brief respite, the Division moved to Camp Laguna, Arizona, for desert training in anticipation of duty in the African desert where war was raging. The desert was a miserable place. Fortunately, the Allies were victorious in Africa and the remaining desert training was canceled. The Division returned to Camp Forrest, Tennessee, and began preparations for an overseas assignment. On December 5, 1943, a convoy bearing the 8th Division sailed from New York harbor on the perilous North Atlantic run to the British Isles.

Charles tells his story:
There were several thousand troops aboard and we were really cramped. My bunk was three levels down and for the next ten days, I spent many hours there. We were allowed on deck twice a day for fresh air and exercise, but the decks were so crowded there was not much room to move.

Because we sailed through sub-infested waters, we were not allowed to venture out at night. A lit cigarette could be seen a great distance in the black night of the North Atlantic. The weather was cold and the seas were rough, but the crossing was uneventful except for a severe winter storm near Iceland. Everyone was seasick.

The weather cleared and finally we reached Belfast, Northern Ireland. Our regiment was assigned to a camp at Enniskillen, where we lived in Quonset huts. Each hut held two squads. I was assistant gunner in a machine-gun squad. Sammy Brooks was the gunner; Garrett Kelly, Marion Miller and Lester Tate were the ammo bearers. Our training was as varied as the limited terrain permitted. Emphasis was placed on small unit tactics.

General Dwight D. Eisenhower, Supreme Allied Commander, visited Enniskillen in April to review the Division. He walked among the ranks talking to approximately every tenth soldier asking where we were from and what our jobs were. He was a gentleman. In his remarks he stated that when the time came he was confident that we would be fit and ready to do the job for which we had trained so long.

General George Patton, 3rd Army Commander, also inspected the troops in Northern Ireland. There was no parade or review. He stood on a grandstand built on a flat bed truck and gave a resounding speech to the gathered troops. I will never forget his charge, "When you get the Hun," be bellowed, "show the S.O.B. no mercy. You get him by the balls and you squeeze them until he is dead. If you don't," he warned, "he'll get you by yours and squeeze them until he kills you." His remarks preceded the reputation he would earn as the fiercest general in the U.S. Army. Patton's nickname was "Old Blood and Guts." We learned later it was our blood and his guts.

On July 1, 1944, a convoy of four troop ships and twelve motor-transports steamed out of Belfast Harbor. As we approached Utah Beach, war became a reality. We could see destroyed buildings, sunken landing ships, damaged tanks and equipment strewn everywhere. On July 4, we entered Normandy, where for the first time in our lives we heard Fourth of July fireworks in their original key. Allied planes were scouting the area and anti-aircraft fire was plentiful. Our naval guns were firing on pockets of enemy resistance. German resistance was heavy in most sectors. The German's ability to contain the beachhead for so long was a very impressive achievement.

On July 6, the 28th Regiment moved into an assembly area, and received orders to take over a section of the front line just north of La Haye-du-puits, and relieve the 82nd Airborne Division who had jumped into Normandy on June 6. We were scared then, but not nearly as scared as we were going to be. That night, before going into combat, everyone became your buddy. The conversations were solemn. It is such an overwhelming feeling that it is hard to describe. All of us were filled with fear that tomorrow we may die.

At dawn, trucks transported us close to the front and as we approached the takeoff position on foot, troops of the 82nd Airborne began coming off line. They had been in combat for thirty consecutive days. I saw a machine gunner.

"Hey, buddy," I asked. "Any hints on staying alive?"

"Yeah," he grumbled, "Get rid of every tracer in your box." Every fourth round in a cartridge belt of machine-gun ammunition is a tracer and is intended to show you where you are hitting; but, of course, it also shows the enemy where the fire is coming from.

A Chaplain crawled by. "How are things up there, Father?" I asked.

"God, Son, terrible, terrible!"

"Father, we are relieving the 82nd."

"Thank God for that, Son. Thank God for that," he responded.

Early on July 8, 1944, we got our baptism of fire. The attack jumped off at 0700 and the Germans, anticipating action in this sector, laid down a heavy concentration of mortar shells before we reached the line of departure. They must have known we were green troops. The shelling was a rain of death. Captain Ross, our company commander, was our first casualty and Lt. Hobbs, his executive officer, took command and he was also killed. The first platoon leader took over. Four men were killed and nine more were wounded. We had been in combat only ten minutes. To say we were shaken is an understatement. We panicked. Shells were hitting everywhere, men from our company were being killed or wounded all around us, and our only thought was to get out of the inferno. We ran backwards like scared rabbits. Only some very aggressive leadership pulled us through.

Panic is a soldier's worst enemy and to this moment, the 8th Division had been rated as one of the best trained in the European Theatre. In our first hour, we discovered the difference between an expert infantryman and a combat infantryman.

We regrouped the next day and again went on the attack. Because of fog and mist, we had no air support. We had advanced about two hundred yards before the Germans counterattacked. They laid down a smoke screen and began advancing, when suddenly out of the smoke rumbled a Panther tank. My buddy, Lester Ramsdell, and his squad were positioned behind a hedgerow, and we were to their left. There had been no time to dig foxholes, so when the tank was directly in front of Ramsdell's squad, it opened fire. As it approached, the 88mm shell screamed a song of death and with a blinding flash the hedgerow erupted, throwing Ramsdell into the air. Blood poured from his skull flooding his face as he tried to crawl toward his helmet. He never made it. He lay down to die in a pool of blood. We were paralyzed by fear, unable to move, but slowly the iron monster turned away from us.

When it was safe to move, we hurried toward Ramsdell's squad. Both squads had shared the same Quonset hut for eight months in Northern Ireland and we were as close as brothers. The others were all in shock but alive, but Ramsdell lay motionless on the blood-soaked ground. Lester Miller, an ammo bearer in my squad and a very close friend of Ramsdell, held his head in his lap and tried to talk with him. He became covered with blood. We coaxed him away, "Leave him to the Medics. There's nothing you can do." Fortunately, Lester Ramsdell somehow had survived, and I was able to contact him following the war. He had been unconscious for twenty-one days and spent two years in rehabilitation recovering from his wounds.

The afternoon sun burned off the fog and our fighter-bombers roared over the roads and fields. The superior guns of the German Panzers were of little use now. A number of enemy tanks were destroyed, their counterattack was stopped and the Germans began to pull back. In those first two days, we had fourteen casualties.

On our third day of combat, July 10, 1944, we again went on the attack. God, I was scared. Everyone was scared. The Germans counterattacked again, and continued their tactic of firing smoke bombs and advancing behind the smoke. Everyone on line began firing. My squad was intact. We started firing our machine-gun. Sammy Brooks, gunner, was firing away when suddenly I heard, "Uh." Sammy fell over backwards. He had been killed instantly. I was feeding the cartridge belts so I took over the gun. Lester Tate was now feeding and we kept firing. We couldn't see anyone because of the smoke, but we fired as rapidly as we could and when we ran out of ammunition, I yelled for ammo. Garret Kelly, on my left, came running

He was partially protected by a low hedgerow, and as he ran toward me I saw him flip out. His arms went into the air and the boxes of ammo went flying. His head hit the ground no more than two feet away from me. I pulled the gun down. Sammy Brooks was lying dead behind me and Garret Kelly was lying dead next to me. Neither knew what had hit him and, at the time, I was unable to comprehend what was happening because the action was so intense and chaotic.

We got more ammo, put the gun back in place and continued to fire. The shelling finally stopped, and the German counterattack had been stopped. When the fighting ended, I became filled with emotion because two of my "brothers" had died right next to me. I started to go into shock. The shakes continued until I realized I had survived. Eventually, I learned that each time a buddy gets killed, a piece of you goes with him and the next moments are filled with the inevitable searching question, "Who else got hit?"

Those first three days were miserably rough. We would attack. The enemy would counter-attack. Progress was slow due to the inexperience of our troops in hedgerow fighting, but each day the gains were a little greater. The hedgerows greatly affected the fighting methods used. Rarely could we see the enemy, who was hidden behind the next hedgerow. When we put our machine-guns atop a hedgerow, we were exposed and invited enemy fire, so we replaced our tripods with a spike to which the machine was mounted. The spike was rammed into the hedgerow and allowed us to fire with more stability, and also permitted us to fire the weapons without lifting our heads above the hedgerow.

The hedgerows definitely favored the enemy. The frequent draws dividing the fields provided easy avenues of escape for the Germans. Conversely, they were well aware of the exact location of each draw and could place murderous fire on the Americans almost at will.

Division Command insisted on more rapid advancement. They had expressed satisfaction with the showing of the troops so far, but we were pressured to push harder. On the morning of July 11, we went on attack again. We were immediately met by heavy resistance from machine-gun fire and heavy mortars. Four Sherman tanks rolled to the front. Although the German infantrymen feared the Sherman, they were no match for the more powerful German tanks. As the Sherman tanks rolled forward, a single Panzer Tiger, armed with the unequalled 88mm gun, fired. The gun roared and the lead tank burst into flames. The crew attempted to bail out, but they were cut down by enemy fire. Shells fired from a second Sherman tank slammed against the Tiger, but it continued to turn and fired again, propelling the turret of the tank ten feet into the air and blowing apart the men inside. The enemy cheered as shells struck each tank. All four of our tanks were destroyed. After four days of fighting, those of us still in one piece were becoming increasingly combative; however, watching one German Tiger tank readily destroy four American tanks was a severe blow to our confidence.

The Tiger was damaged and as it backed away, I heard a voice cry, "Comrade, Comrade." A German soldier about eighteen years old jumped over the hedgerow with his hands up. He was scared to death. He spoke some English and said he wanted to surrender. I had the privilege of escorting the prisoner to the rear, and as we walked through the field where the Sherman tanks lay destroyed, we could smell burning flesh and saw parts of bodies scattered over the field. After hearing the enemies' cheers during the battle, I thought to myself, "I will kill this S.O.B. if he makes one wrong remark." He did not. He was too frightened and his war was over.

Despite our losses, the German's main line of resistance began to collapse in several places, and the tempo quickened as the enemy began a major withdrawal.

A captured POW reported that the Germans were in retreat as our artillery fire was too much for them. We had become battle wise and the hedgerows were becoming more familiar. Our battalion went into reserve and the troops got a much-deserved rest. We received new clothing, fed hot meals and read our first mail since entering combat.

On the morning of July 26, 1944, E and F Companies again moved out under the cover of artillery and mortar fire, with tanks and tank destroyers. German resistance was heavy, with extremely accurate mortar and artillery fire. We advanced slowly. One of our tanks was knocked out by enemy fire and two others were stopped by land mines. Then the enemy countered with a tank attack. Our tank destroyers fought them. Later, ten enemy tanks were located hiding behind hedgerows, but because we only had three tank destroyers, we were told to hold up and dig in. We had fifty-five casualties evacuated that day, and we took twenty-four enemy prisoners.

The enemy's strongpoint pulled out during the night, so on the next day, we were able to penetrate the enemy's defensive position with little resistance. Dust and smoke covered the land, and as we moved forward, we saw many dead enemy soldiers, body parts, wrecked vehicles and enemy material.

Resuming the advance on the morning of July 28, we moved rapidly against light resistance. We followed several armored divisions from George Patton's 3rd Army, who had passed through our sector. We were moving south through Avranches. A bridgehead had been won across the river south of Avranches and, with this, the Allies had kicked open the door for a breakout into the French countryside. A seemingly endless convoy of vehicles and men were passing through when we heard the piercing wail of a siren blasting. Rolling past the other vehicles was a Sherman tank, with the flamboyant General Patton standing in the turret. With helmet gleaming in the sunlight and a pair of Colt 45 pistols, one on each hip, he was an inspiration to us all. "Give 'em hell, General," we shouted.

On the fourth day of August, exactly one month after landing on the beach, the Division reassembled just north of Rennes on the Brittany peninsula. Our next mission was to attack and capture the port at Brest. We received another group of replacements. Of the one hundred eighty-seven men originally in our Company, there were only sixty-five of us left. We had lived and trained together for two years. Everyone knew everyone else and now they were gone. Replacements were our salvation. It was a new experience to see strangers among us, who outnumbered our old buddies.

The port city of Brest had been turned into one of the world's most formidable fortresses. There were 50,000 enemy troops garrisoned there with the famed 2nd German Parachute Division as its nucleus. The commanding officer, General Ramcke, had strict orders, "Hold the city and destroy the harbor installations."

The 6th Armored Division prepared to attack the city. Elements of the 8th Division were brought up to help and two other divisions were called to join in the attack. As our Regiment began infiltrating the preliminary objectives from which the attack was to jump off, we found the Germans to be deeply entrenched. Combat patrols were sent to engage and destroy the enemy, and to reinforce these patrols we added machine-gun squads.

On the night of August 10, Sergeant Alexander Schrobat, a good friend whom I had known since our training at Camp Forest, led a patrol to which my squad was assigned. We moved several hundred yards to a farmhouse, where we found a Frenchman lying dead near the house. Close to him was a dead dog. There was an eerie quiet. We moved another fifty yards past the farmhouse when Schrobat hissed, "Halt! Get Down!"

We froze. Several Germans were coming forward and one had a white rag tied around a rifle indicating that they wanted to surrender. We got up and began to assemble the prisoners, but apparently, other German soldiers disapproved of their comrades' decision to surrender. A grenade exploded near the group and suddenly all hell broke loose. Completely outnumbered and out-gunned, we lost Schrobat while fighting our way back to our line. This really bugged me. He was my friend. I pleaded with the Lieutenant to go back, but my pleas fell on deaf ears. They would not jeopardize the mission for one man.

On August 25, 1944 at 1300, the offensive against Brest began. Our Regiment again ran into point blank heavy artillery and mortar fire. Smoke was all over our front and progress was slow. As night approached we had moved about 1,200 yards, but darkness prevented any further advance. Along with other casualties, we had lost our platoon leader. His replacement was a new 2nd Lieutenant who had recently completed officer training at Fort Benning, Georgia.

We were set to attack again the next morning. Our new platoon leader talked to us that night, and since he had no combat experience, he suggested the platoon sergeant take over the platoon for the next day. While talking to us, he took off his helmet, and I was surprised to see that he was completely bald on the top of his head. He was not that much older than I was.

The attack began at 0800 hours. We were hardly out of our holes when the Germans pinned us down by artillery and mortar fire. Casualties were occurring at a morale-shaking pace. As we advanced, I saw two bodies side-by-side, one with his helmet off. I recognized our new platoon leader by his baldhead. He had reported on line at 1800 hours and was dead at 0800 hours the next day.

We spent the following day repulsing a violent counter attack, but, our fighter-bombers blasted them, halting their attack and they retreated. They left their wounded. I heard combat-hardened wounded German soldiers crying for their mothers. A truce allowed each side to evacuate their dead and wounded. We had not yielded one yard, but the day was lost for attacking.

Our tanks moved up to be on line with the rifle companies, and again we went on the attack, but the Germans had set up crossfire of small arms, machine-guns and mortars. Casualties were heavy and our progress stopped. Division Command was insisting that we advance. We needed that port. Since we could not move during the day, we were ordered to attack at night.

Night attacks are one of the most terrifying experiences an infantryman has to endure. E and G Companies had orders to move forward at 0200 hours, seize their objectives, dig in and prepare an all-around defense. We tied white strips of parachute material to our back so we could tell friend from foe, our rifles were loaded and locked and our bayonets were fixed. We were not to fire our weapons under any circumstances before dawn. We were given extra hand grenades, and I removed my canteen from its pouch, filled the pouch with three grenades, and using the chain on the cap, I looped the canteen around my cartridge belt.

We slipped out of our assembly positions like shadows in the night, and shortly after midnight, we began to penetrate the enemy's line. We had advanced about 1,000 yards, when to our left we saw flares and heard gunfire. We were so close we could hear Germans talking and their trucks starting up. When we reached our preliminary objective, we notified Headquarters that we were in position. We had not realized that the enemy had allowed us to pass through their lines. As we began to dig in, flares suddenly exploded overhead, turning night into day. We froze, but it was too late. The Germans had seen us. When the flares died out, we began to dig in frantically. Fear had robbed us of sleep that night.

As dawn broke, we heard firing on our left flank that became stronger as it got closer. Someone shouted, "Tank coming!" Several of the riflemen had rifle grenades and began to position themselves. "Look, it's a Sherman!" was the cry of relief. The relief was short lived as we realized it was a Sherman that had been captured by the enemy, and the tank began firing into G Company on our left. The GIs were flat in their holes to evade the fire. The tank advanced and began crushing the holes burying the men beneath it.

Several riflemen began firing their rifle grenades. The tank came to a hedgerow and its gun came over. The grenades had damaged the mechanism and prevented the tank from raising or lowering its cannon, but it could still traverse. It did, and was aimed directly at our squad and the several riflemen around us. I stared right down the barrel of that tank's gun. I began to dig as hard as I could. As the tank opened fire, the first shell went to my right and caused no damage. The second shell was closer and covered me with dirt. I was flat in my hole. The next shell burst right next to the hole blowing me out of it. I had the sensation of floating through space. When I hit the ground, I could hardly hear due to the ringing in my ears. My mouth and nostrils were filled with dirt, and then I heard someone shout, "They're surrendering."

Well, I had heard that cry before, but it was always directed toward the enemy. I looked around and the machine-gun was blown away. I looked for a weapon. I thought if I am going to round up surrendering Germans, I have to have a weapon. I picked up a rifle when, suddenly, a German paratrooper jumped through the hedgerow. He had a machine pistol in one hand and a hand grenade in the other. "Cease fire," he ordered, "Hands up." All around me, hands were raised. I was still dazed from the tank shell. A soldier knocked the rifle out of my hands. The battle was over. I had been in combat less than two months and I was now a prisoner of war.

They moved us over the hedgerow and into a roadway where the rest of their regiment was lying in ditches along each side of the road. Their stares cut into us as we passed. We had not traveled too far when an artillery shell burst nearby. We guessed that a spotter had seen us and thought we were Germans. Now we feared our own artillery would kill us.

There were about thirty of us in this group. The Germans had us double-time to avoid any incoming artillery fire. I was beginning to feel sorry for myself. I had two teeth broken, my lip was bleeding, dirt was in my mouth and nose and the ringing continued in my ears. As we approached a crossroad, there was a German soldier directing movement. His top lip was gone. I could see his teeth and gums. He gestured as he repeated, "Come, come." I thought to myself, "I am feeling sorry about broken teeth and a bleeding lip and here is someone with no lip at all conducting himself as if nothing were wrong."

After about another mile, we reached their rear line. As we milled around, I wanted to wash the dirt out of my mouth. My canteen was still looped over my belt by the cap chain. I asked the guard, "Water O.K.?" He did not respond and I assumed it was all right and began to unscrew the cap to get my canteen off my belt. Suddenly he fired his weapon and a bullet passed over my head. Another German came running over. "Was ist los?" he demanded. I tried to explain that I wanted water. He turned to the other soldier. "Dummkopf, Soldat wünscht Wasser!" he laughed. It really scared the hell out of me.

Next, we walked to a sand quarry and boarded a large bus that held about sixty people. I looked at the roof of the bus, and if it had one hole, it had a thousand. Once again, I worried that one of our planes would spot this bus and attack it, but that did not happen. They drove us to a French castle in the city of Brest, where we were detained overnight in what I would describe as a dungeon.

The next morning we went before a German officer for interrogation. He warned us that execution was the penalty for failure to cooperate and obey his directives. I had to empty my pockets. The only things I had were my wallet, a handkerchief and cigarettes. Next, he ordered me to empty the wallet. It contained my I.D., some photographs, money, and – filled with the fear of God – an SS medal I had taken from a dead German. I decided to leave the medal in the wallet. One of the packs of cigarettes was a regular 20-pack of Camels and the other was a 10-pack of Chesterfields that came in our C rations. The officer asked which were better; I told him the Chesterfields. He picked up the Camels and said, "I like Camels. Do you mind if I keep?" As if I was going to say, "Yes, I mind." "Help your self." I replied. He took my money and asked if I would exchange it for French francs. I was in no position to say anything but yes. He checked my I.D. and looked at my photos. He never picked up my wallet, believing it was empty. He pushed everything across the table and I put them in my wallet.

Following the interrogation, we were taken to the upper level of the castle where there were rows of steel-framed cots, each with a rolled mattress on top. I had not slept in a bed for two months and was physically drained by the ordeal of the last several days. I fell fast asleep. During the night, I was startled awake by the wail of an air raid siren, and we quickly returned to the dungeon.

The following day, we were marched to the waterfront on the Bay of Brest, where Germans had built a submarine pen. What an impressive sight! The building was huge but the only vessels there now were a landing barge and a tugboat. While we stood lined up, they brought in several truckloads of wounded German soldiers. When they saw us they shouted, "Kill them now and save us the trouble."

Those were the same remarks we would have made if the situation were reversed.

Later that night, we were loaded into the landing craft and at about 0100 hours, we began to move across the bay. We had not gone very far when we heard the roar of airplane engines as American "Black Widow" night fighters flew overhead. There was quite a commotion at the front of our craft, which turned around and returned to the safety of the submarine pen. The next night we embarked again. This time we hugged the shore and reached our destination around 0500 hours. We were now on the Crozon peninsula, a small French fishing village, and were billeted in village houses.

Being a prisoner of war was not a horrible experience for me. The Germans realized their tenuous position and the distinct possibility that eventually they would become our prisoners. As a result, they probably treated us far better than we would have been under different circumstances. To me, the most notable thing about being a POW was the feeling of relief from the stress of battle. I knew I was not going to be killed that day.

We ate three meals a day. In the morning, they gave us a cup of chicory, a substitute for coffee. At midday, we ate either apple soup or sugar beet soup. If a horse was killed by artillery fire, we could expect meat in our soup. For dinner, we were usually given a can of sardines or two small pieces of sausage. Our ration of bread was a third of a loaf every three days. The bread was dry and hard and had sawdust filler. It was at least thirty to forty days old. The date baked was stamped on the end of each loaf.

One of our guards was an old man in his mid-sixty's. One day I asked him if he had been a front-line soldier. "Nein, nein," he replied. The rifle he carried was unusual. "Do you know how to use it?" I asked. "Nein, not loaded," he responded, opening the chamber to show me it was empty. I said, "What good is that? If I run you can't shoot me." "You run," he retorted, "I yell. Somebody else shoot you."

On September 16, 1944, I spent my twenty-fourth birthday as a prisoner of war.

While I was a prisoner, the 8th Division continued moving toward Brest. This seemingly impregnable port city was to provide some of the bitterest fighting the 8th Division was to experience. The troops pounded the enemy's strong points. We could hear their artillery fire. They forced their way into the enemy's outside perimeter; and elements of the enemy's forces withdrew from the action at Brest and repositioned on the Crozon Peninsula.

Crozon represented a strongly held threat to the Port of Brest that would prevent its use after it fell. The brass knew Crozon was going to be a hard nut to crack. For a few days, the fighting was as vicious on Crozon as it had been at Brest. I learned later that we had captured German documents that showed the positions of the German guns and their route of withdrawal, and that was all we needed. Two hours later a tremendous barrage fell silencing every German gun on Crozon.

Our own 28th Infantry Regiment cleared Camaret Point and the village we were in, and liberated us on September 18, 1944. We greeted our troops as the French had greeted us when we liberated town after town. We asked for cigarettes, chocolate and chewing gum. We acted like children. It is hard to describe the elation we experienced. We showered, put on new clothes and ate real food. The entire division enjoyed this period. It was the first respite from the sound of cannon fire since landing on Utah Beach.

Our rest period ended abruptly. On September 26, the Division moved to the German border. Our Regiment set up in Luxembourg, on October 1, facing the formidable Siegfried Line, Germany's first line of defense into their territory. Our forward advance stopped due to supply shortages and stiffening German resistance.

During the night of November 18, we traveled through rain, sleet and snow, and moved into the Huertgen Forest to relieve the badly decimated 28th Infantry Division. This began two and a half months of the hardest fighting that our Regiment was to experience. The Huertgen Forest has been described as a chamber of horrors combining the worst elements of warfare, weather and terrain. I thought it was the worst place in the world.

The Germans greeted us with a torrent of mortar and artillery blasts and over 5,000 rounds fell into our area during these first two days. Casualties began to pile up immediately. Jeeps and other vehicles were unable to carry supplies to the front-line companies because the narrow roads had become frozen rivers of mud covered with snow. Horses and carts were brought in, but they failed because the horses shied away from the frightening noise of the artillery and mortar fire. The front had to be supplied.

I was assigned to Regimental Reserve because of the lingering effects from the concussion received prior to my capture. All available ambulatory personnel were now organized into parties to carry food, ammunition, water and other supplies to the front-line companies and bring out their wounded, some on litters. Although we always moved under the cover of darkness, carrying parties were continually under attack and suffered heavy casualties from the incessant artillery and mortar fire, and small arms fire.

The five-month battle for the Huertgen Forest ended on February 9, 1945. Battle casualties mounted to 24,000 dead, wounded or missing. Trench foot or other non-battle casualties disabled an additional 9,000 men.

While the battle for the Huertgen raged, Hitler initiated a counteroffensive in the Ardennes, known as the Battle of the Bulge on December 16, 1944. The attack achieved complete surprise and two German armies broke through thin American defenses, recapturing towns and villages. The enemy's main thrust was stopped at Bastogne and the great counteroffensive was repulsed. Now out of their defensive positions, the German armies were vulnerable for destruction.

After the Battle of the Bulge, the war was completely on our side. Although the battles were fierce and German resistance stiff, our advance was swift. It was during this period that the Divisions initiated a new detail called Combat MPs. I headed up one of the Combat MP squads for our Regiment. A squad consisted of six men, all combat veterans and most had suffered a debilitating wound. Our job was to coordinate the movement of the many prisoners from the front line to Regimental enclosures.

Along the entire west bank of the Roer River, infantry and armored divisions were poised to assault the water barrier west of the Rhine. Our offensive continued. We commenced crossing the flooded river close to Duren on February 23, 1945 following the heaviest artillery barrage ever fired by the Eighth Division artillery. We were the second battalion to get men across but not without loss. All the boats were swamped or overturned by the twelve mph currents that resulted from the destruction of control valves at the Schwammenauel Dam, or enemy artillery fire, but sixty men from the 2nd Battalion made it across and established a foothold.

We were in the Ruhr Pocket when I made a trip to the front line to secure more prisoners. I ran into Staff Sgt. Marion Miller, who was from Tennessee and always had a smile on his face. He had been my gunner in Normandy. We warmly greeted each other, as Army buddies tend to do. He invited me to stick around for a while as he had to take mail to his group, and when he returned we were to swap war stories.

While he was gone, I began to interrogate my prisoners. Suddenly, another GI burst into the room and excitedly asked, "Did you hear that Miller was killed by a sniper?" I rushed to the scene and found him lying in a pool of blood. Several GIs were crouched inside a nearby building fearful of the sniper. Dragging him by his ankles, I pulled him inside. The bullet hit in the back of the head and exited through the front. Another good man lost his life so close to the end of the war. I was sickened and outraged. When I returned to my prisoners I really felt like doing them harm to avenge Miller's death but I maintained my composure. I later learned that his squad had killed the suspected sniper.

One of the men in my squad reported that he had learned of a Nazi concentration camp near the town of Wobbelin. When we arrived, the camp was swarming with reporters from *Life, Look* and other newsmagazines. Because we were MPs, no one questioned our presence. Some of the prisoners were so emaciated that they just lay on the ground and took no notice of what was going on. Others were stronger and we found a prisoner who spoke English. He stated that most of the dead had starved and/or beaten to death. In one building, I saw several hundred bodies stacked like cords of wood.

The local citizens were required to attend the funeral services and witness the burials. Nearly all who went through the concentration camp were profoundly affected. Some civilians admitted that they had realized that terrible things were going on in the camp, but they had been powerless to do anything. Others claimed that they knew nothing of the atrocities. The camp was like a chamber of horrors. It was like stepping back into the Dark Ages.

The 8th Division fought in the battles of Duren, Bonn, Cologne, Dortmund, and Paderborn, and I continued to round up prisoners captured by our front line assault troops. After the Allies crossed the Rhine in March 1945, the thin crust of German defenses crumbled. From the Rhine to the Elbe, American armies hounded a beaten and disorganized enemy in one of the swiftest most stunning pursuits in military history. GIs were advancing almost at will.

Everyday, Germans surrendered in droves. The roads were jammed with columns of prisoners. On foot, bicycles and horseback, in motor vehicles and horse-drawn carts, the defeated German armies were moving southwest away from the Russians. All available personnel were now engaged in directing the men of the disintegrating German army into regimental prisoner of war enclosures. Over two hundred thousand prisoners overwhelmed these already crowded facilities. Here, were the men who had given us so much hell since July 1944, now calling it quits. It was over for them, but we could not cheer. The road to victory had been too long and difficult to celebrate. We just sat down and breathed a sigh of relief, thankful that we were alive.

Units of the 28th Infantry Regiment crossed the Elbe River on May 2, 1945, and light initial resistance was subdued. The thousand-year-old city of Schwerin fell that day and here we made contact with advance elements of the Russian armies of the north. It was a joyous occasion and the celebration lasted all day. The next day however, the Russians emplaced barriers and strung barbed wire. These were the earliest elements of the iron curtain.

On May 7, 1945, General Eisenhower sent this message to the combined Chiefs of Staff: "The mission of this Allied Force was fulfilled at 0241, local time, May 7, 1945." The war was really over and Hitler was dead. The Germans had surrendered unconditionally, but even then we didn't feel like celebrating. It was anticlimactic!

From Schwerin we traveled by truck back through Germany, Belgium and France. We boarded the Liberty Ship *Ebersol* and left the port of Le Havre on June 28, 1945. Eight days later, we disembarked at Newport News, Virginia and were transported to Fort George Meade, where I had been originally inducted. I was home safe in the arms of my darling wife, Virginia. I had spent the past year with people who were trying to kill me and now I was with those who loved me. I never wanted to leave again! My leave was for only thirty days and I feared going back. The war with Japan raged.

On the morning of August 6, 1945, the American B-29 *Enola Gay* dropped an atomic bomb on the Japanese City of Hiroshima and three days later another B-29 *Bock's Car* released another bomb over Nagasaki. Both caused enormous casualties and physical destruction. These two events have preyed upon the American conscience ever since. I truly believe that if President Truman had not ordered the dropping of the bomb, you probably would not be reading these memoirs.

Following my thirty-day leave, I was aboard a train destined for Fort Leonard Wood, Missouri, but before we departed, whistles began to blow, people were shouting and dancing and embracing. Japan had surrendered. The war was finally over. I went from Fort Leonard Wood to Fort Francis E. Warren, Wyoming for processing out of the Army. I caught a troop train to Chicago and then on to Baltimore. I was home. It was over.

In ending my story, "Captain Good Fortune" has stayed with me over the years. On September 16, 2005, I celebrated my eighty-fifth birthday. My darling Virginia is still at my side. My four wonderful children have given me seven grandchildren and one great-grandchild. As the years silently drifted by, I lost contact with my brothers-in-arms.

Reflecting on my experiences of the war, I believe my story is not very different from the stories of thousands and thousands of other infantrymen, and of other men and women who served their country during WWII. I was certainly not a hero. I was not even brave. I did my duty the best I could. I believe I was a typical Joe. We had our share of heroes. While they were performing their heroic deeds, I was probably digging my foxhole a little deeper, but I was not alone. We were all scared to death.

146

Charles Milton Rutkowski received his honorable discharge on October 23, 1945 at Fort Francis E. Warren, Wyoming at the rank of Private First-Class. He was twenty-four years old. His awards include the Combat Infantryman Badge; Bronze Star Medal; POW Medal; WWII Victory Medal; European, African, Middle-Eastern Campaign Medal with Four Battle Stars; American Campaign Medal; and the Good Conduct Medal.

Virginia and Charles, 1945

MY SQUAD
God Love Them All

This photo was taken outside of our Quonset hut
Enniskillen, Northern Ireland, autumn, 1943

From left to right, Standing – *Marion Miller, killed two weeks*
before the war ended, and Lou Parson, who survived.
Kneeling – *Lester Tate who suffered a hand-wound;*
Lester Ramsdell who was seriously wounded in Normandy;
Charles Rutkowski, who survived;
Garrett Kelly, and Sammy Brooks, both killed in Normandy.

Anthony Gullace

ANTHONY J. GULLACE

"Get in the plane, Tony.
You won't have to use that parachute today."

D URING THE SECOND WORLD WAR, the task of the combined Allied Air Forces was to destroy Germany's military and industrial systems and undermine the morale of the German people to fatally weaken their capacity for armed resistance. Round-the-clock bombing prevented the enemy from getting any rest, as the RAF raided at night and the U.S. Bomber Command attacked during the day. To meet the growing demand of the rapidly expanding Army Air Forces, the American aircraft industry began turning out record numbers of aircraft beginning in 1942. In turn, the AAF needed thousands of pilots, navigators, bombardiers and tens of thousands of crewmembers to fly these aircraft. The AAF offered inducements such as extra pay, quick promotions, the right to wear wings but above all the attraction was the allure of flying.

There is glamour to flying but in reality, flying combat missions as a member of a heavy bomber team during World War II was a hazardous calling. A mission was a long, drawn-out ordeal. Airmen spent five to ten miserable hours jammed into a cramped duty station and flying at high altitudes introduced them to the rigors of extreme cold. Discomfort accompanied grinding tedium. Underlying the physical torment was the human emotion - the fear of dying. I only flew five combat missions. On June 25, 1943, while on my fifth combat mission, enemy aircraft attacked our plane and shot it down. I bailed out, was captured, and spent the rest of the war as a prisoner of war suffering indignities, deprivations, declining health and accumulating a lifetime of memories.

My story begins in June 1940, when I graduated from Washington High School in Rochester, New York. Jobs were scarce and I had demonstrated some artistic talent while in school so I moved to New Albany, Indiana to live with my Aunt Agatha and Uncle Joseph Pulitano and he began teaching me clothing design. I had found a job to support myself, met the woman I would one day marry and I felt things were going reasonably well until December 7, 1941, when Japan attacked Pearl Harbor and plunged our nation into war. Three months after Japan's attack, at age 20 years, I enlisted in the Army Air Forces and selected airplane mechanic as my military occupation specialty. Four weeks of basic training at Jefferson Barracks, Missouri included physical conditioning, aptitude testing, and close-order drills under the direction of a tough drill sergeant. We were taught discipline and to react immediately to commands. Pulling KP (Kitchen Police) taught me that this experience was not going to be all fun and games. One lesson learned that I thought I would retain throughout my military career was never volunteer for anything.

Following basic training, I transferred to Chanute Field at Rantoul, Illinois and successfully completed five months of comprehensive airplane mechanic schooling. The air force required its specialist to be accomplished in more than one specialty, so I volunteered for glider pilot training. The appeal of flying had seduced me and I anxiously waited, but there were many qualified volunteers and the long waiting list grew longer. After several weeks, I had to select another specialty. I had the greatest respect for the men on the ground who kept the planes in the air, but the allure of flying caused me to apply for aerial gunnery school.

There was no waiting list here. I went immediately to Las Vegas, Nevada for five weeks of intensive aerial gunnery training using a variety of firearms that ranged from B.B. guns to .50-inch caliber machine-guns. The final test was air-to-air machine-gun firing at a towed target. Different colored bullets identified our hits. This test was crucial if you wanted to join a bomber team. Failure meant you returned to your original specialty or some other non-flying discipline. I qualified as a marksman and upon graduation received my gunner's wings and a promotion to the rank Staff Sergeant. I was proud of my progress when assigned to Gowen Field Air Base at Boise, Idaho to begin training as a member of a 10-man bomber team on a B-17 Flying Fortress. During the schooling, I specialized in flight engineering and the companion job of upper turret gunner. Seemingly, I learned my lessons well because they kept me at Gowen for several months as an instructor.

Captain Mason, our flight instructor, was to become operations officer for one of the squadrons of a new bomb group and encouraged me to request assignment, so I volunteered to join the cadre for this new group. The 379th Bomb Group was formed in November 1942 and was composed of four bomb squadrons - the 524th, 525th, 526th, and 527th. There were six Flying Fortresses to a squadron and each plane had a crew of 10 highly-trained men. I was assigned to the 524th Squadron and Captain Mason became the squadron's operations officer. Paul Hartman was our pilot. The other crew crewmembers were co-pilot, Charles Howe; navigator, James Gore; bombardier; John Francis; flight engineer and top ball turret gunner, Anthony Gullace; waist gunner, Robert Greeley; radio operator, James Blick; waist gunner, Harold Schrader; tail gunner, George Hill; and lower ball turret gunner Clyde "Slug" Schlagovski.

The group/squad training was a four phase training with one month allotted for each phase. We began at Boise, Idaho where individual crewmembers demonstrated their specific responsibility and versatility while flying a B-17. Each crewmember was a specialist but was also trained to perform at least one other job. The second phase was at Wendover, Utah where we practiced formation flying in a "combat box" a defensive formation that resembled a slanted flying wedge. We referred to Wendover as "no man's land" because the nearest civilization was Salt Lake City, about 100 miles away. In January 1943, the third phase of our training was at Sioux City, Iowa where we practiced simulated bombing raids. For the fourth phase, each squad was assigned to a different satellite base. The 524th squadron was sent to Watertown, South Dakota but the winter weather was so severe, we would periodically fly to El Paso, Texas to complete training requirements. Upon completion of the team-building training, we were ordered overseas for combat duty.

We received a 10-day furlough but after only a week at home, we reported immediately to Kearney, Nebraska to begin processing for an overseas assignment. The Group received new Boeing B-17Fs and the crews made their initial checkout flights. The pilots had to demonstrate their proficiency for instrument flying. While in flight, the windows were covered and the pilots had to return to base and land the plane using instruments only. Lt. Hartman completed this part of the checkout very nicely.

Our flight plan took us from Kearney, Nebraska to Bangor, Maine following a quick stop in Detroit, Michigan for refueling. This was in March 1943 and the weather was bitter cold. The runway was iced and we must have skidded half way down the runway before coming to a stop. We refueled quickly and continued on to Bangor. As we neared Rochester, I asked the pilot if he would fly over my hometown. Not only did he fly over the city, he flew low over the street where my family lived. He waved his wings as I made a loud noise by changing the prop pitch. This startled a group of youngsters playing in the street and they looked up and waved. Later, I learned that one of those children was my kid brother, who clearly remembered this event.

After several days in Bangor, the group proceeded to Goose Bay, Newfoundland. This was our take off point for the nonstop crossing of the North Atlantic to Prestwick, Scotland. Due to bad weather, we had to lie over at Goose Bay for several days. This gave us time to perform a required 50-hour inspection. I directed the crew's efforts that included changing the oil and spark plugs. When we finally took off, we were heavily loaded with fuel, carrying two additional tanks in our bomb bay as well as some other equipment. The take off was scary and after a couple of bounces, we all breathed a sigh of relief when we were finally airborne. The first and last minutes of a bomber's mission were frequently the most dangerous times of all.

Our orders were to fly at varying low altitudes and slow airspeeds to conserve fuel. After several hours, the navigator needed celestial navigation readings. The ascent through the clouds seemed never ending and we finally broke through above 15,000 feet. The navigator did his job and we quickly descended. The weather turned fierce and the forward edges of our wings became covered with ice. Activating the deicer boots broke up the ice but we had to be patient not to reactivate them too hastily. Next, a carburetor began icing and the engine was backfired, always a dangerous procedure when you are airborne. Moments later a supercharger turbine wheel began to act up which too was caught and fixed in time. The flight was hectic and our anxiety intensified when our radio operator reported that a plane from another squadron went down in the mid-Atlantic. I am certain that all aboard were lost.

We arrived at Prestwick, Scotland with about 50 gallons of fuel remaining, which equates to about 20 minutes of flying time. That was close! Soon after, we began practicing formation flying. Our orders were to stay in close formation and no aborting unless necessary. On the very first flight our plane developed serious problems. One engine stopped and the propeller could not be feathered, causing much drag. Suddenly, a second engine's oil pressure dropped. The pilot, co-pilot and I, as flight engineer, determined that this was an emergency and we had to break formation and return to base. As soon as the plane touched down on the runway, the remaining three engines quit. During his examination of the engines, the maintenance officer removed the oil filters and found that they were clogged with fine metal filings. I advised the maintenance officer that we had changed the oil during a 50-hour inspection in Newfoundland. We suspected the planes were sabotaged learning that the plane that went down in the Atlantic also had its oil changed during a 50-hour inspection in Newfoundland.

The 379th Bomb Group next moved to its permanent home, a new base at Kimbolton, Huntingdonshire in the south of England. During this period, American fliers were swarming into England and the AAF was having logistical problems of staggering dimensions. It took a while for our base to become functional with supplies and food. At the beginning, our meals were prepared mostly from canned C-rations, powdered eggs and beans. Breakfast was so bad that many of us became sick to our stomachs particularly at higher altitudes. At 25,000 feet, temperatures inside a plane would drop to minus 40-50 degrees so special clothing was needed to protect against frostbite and allow the crew to function inside the aircraft. The aircrew usually wore long johns, regulation GI trousers and shirt and a two-piece electrically heated flight suit that plugged into receptacles on the plane, along with special caps, boots and gloves. For crewmembers, a strategic bombing mission was an arduous, monotonous, physically discomforting ordeal. More than anything else, it was hard, complicated work.

Combat began, on May 29, 1943. On my first bombing mission, a force of 191 bombers raided the U-boat pens at Saint Nazaire on France's Brittany Peninsula. During the early morning briefing, the operations officer described the weather outlook and the target and flight path plan was shown on a huge map, along with the kind of flak and fighter opposition expected. To a rookie, this did not seem too bad. All we had to do was to fly across the channel and the peninsula to Saint Nazaire, take the proper approach to the target, drop our bombs, and turn around and head for home.

Colonel Maurice Preston, the group CO, announced that since this was the group's first combat mission, he would lead the attack. He chose the 524th as the lead squadron, and our plane as the lead ship. I believe he drew names out of a hat, but I am not sure. I was thrilled but both the pilot and tail gunner were rather unhappy because they were bumped and had to stay home. The Colonel and his operations officer, who flew co-pilot, replaced them. Our co-pilot took the tail gunner position.

We had an escort of British and US fighters but they broke off as we approached the French coast. They had reached the outer limits of their operating range due to the limited amount of fuel they could carry. As we approached the target area, enemy fighters rose to intercept but we successfully kept them at bay. Nearer the target, the enemy fighters veered away to give a clear field of fire to the German's ground defenses and the anti-aircraft batteries went to work. We faced a gauntlet of enemy flak that detonated at predetermined altitudes and it was so heavy that it looked as if we were flying through a black cloud. We took several hits but nothing serious. The Colonel's evasive flying avoided any more hits. Others, however, were not so lucky. Our group lost three planes on that first mission and 30 of our comrades were killed or captured that day. On the return trip, we were all edgy, weary and eager to return to base.

After every mission, a debriefing session was held. All uninjured returning aircrew participate. We were solemn, glancing about to see who had made it back. The colonel assessed our performance and results and then directed a remark toward me. He asked if I was in the room and I stood and identified myself. The Colonel announced, "On the return flight, my engineer decided to leave his turret to have a smoke." (The point made was not to leave any section of the plane unprotected.) So, I got a little chewing out from the colonel and lots of ribbing from the others. In my own defense, we were not far from the English coast and I believed out of harm's way. Besides, this was my first combat mission and we were all a little jittery on the return, so I felt it was time for a breather. However, I never did that again.

My second mission was on June 11, 1943 and the target was Wilhelmshaven, the submarine-building center on the North Sea about 40 miles from the Dutch border. For this mission our squadron flew with a composite group composed of squadrons from various bomb groups. This arrangement turned out to be a disaster. The lead plane's crew was flying their 23rd mission and it quickly became apparent that their priority was to get in and out as quickly as they could. After all, if they survived this and two more missions, they became eligible for relief from combat duty. Their actions disrupted the formation and caused the group to separate. We were no longer flying in a compact, defensive formation. Each squadron was now on its own and more vulnerable to attack. Our plane was flying wing to our squadron lead ship when it was hit by flak and went down. The next lead plane also went down. The next thing we knew, we were flying alone. Enemy fighters swarmed to attack from all directions.

We fought well under the circumstances and even scored a few hits but our plane was riddled with holes. Despite the breakup of our formation, the raid was not a complete disaster. We dropped some bombs on target, shot down several enemy fighters and survived. I hoped to get credit for a downed ME-109, but since we were separated from the others, there was no confirmation from another plane. Skillful flying by our pilot saved our lives that day.

The return flight path carried us over the German border and out to the North Sea. When we were over water, Lt. Hartman asked if I would exchange places with the co-pilot who wanted an opportunity to operate the machine-gun in the top turret. Squadrons in a group formation fly close at the beginning of a raid and usually loosen up when the planes approach the English Channel. I had settled into the co-pilot's seat and noticed that the pilot was drenched with perspiration following our ordeal, when a single ME109 made one last desperate pass at us. We heard the burst of the top turret machine-gun firing as the co-pilot wailed away. The English coastline came into view and we still had quite a distance to our base when the pilot turned the controls over to me. At Boise, flight engineers had been encouraged to gain experience flying in the event both the pilot and co-pilot became incapacitated; therefore, I had had some previous stick time. After crossing the English coast, the pilot took back the controls when suddenly we saw a barrage of cable-suspended balloons directly in our path. He quickly made a sharp 180-degree turn to avoid the cables and fortunately, we got out okay.

We began our approach to the airbase and began the pre-landing checkout procedure only to discover that our hydraulic system was inoperable. The radio operator notified base of our situation and the runway was cleared. Landing a damaged plane is a life or death challenge. Ambulances and fire trucks were at the ready. We disregarded the usual pattern approach and flew straight in. When the wheels touched, as flight engineer I pulled the emergency brake handles located overhead between the pilot and co-pilot. This was a one-time pull and the hydraulic pressure dropped indicating that we had no brakes at all. The pilot immediately turned off all except the number one engine. Simultaneously, I unlocked the tail wheel and with full power and full rudder, Lt. Hartman made a beautiful ground loop at the end of the runway and onto the grass. This skilled maneuver prevented injury to the crew. When the ball turret gunner climbed out, his face was bright red. I thought he had been wounded but as it turned out he was covered with hydraulic fluid. The plane had holes everywhere including one huge hole in the tail surface. The control cables located at the lead edge of the wings were so frayed I would never know why they did not break. The plane, damaged beyond repair, became a "hanger queen" to be stripped for salvageable parts. The 379th Bomb Group lost six more planes, sixty more men that day and a number of badly damaged planes returned with wounded aboard. Another squad's top turret gunner/flight engineer, Staff Sergeant Cliff Erickson, actually flew his plane back to base and landed safely with some verbal directions from the pilot who had been shot in the face. The copilot was unconscious. For this heroic feat S/Sgt. Erickson was awarded the

Distinguished Flying Cross. In another plane, a top turret gunner had his head blown off.

As soon as we acquired a new plane, we were scheduled for our third mission on June 13, 1943. The target was the U-boat installations located at the North German port of Bremen. What I recall mostly about this raid was that I suffered frozen fingertips and hands when I foolishly removed my gloves to free a jam on one of the machine-guns. I spent a few days in the hospital for treatment. Following my release, I returned to flight status. We had to abort our next mission when the 10-man lifeboat broke loose from storage and wrapped itself around the tail of our aircraft. The metal cylinder that inflated the raft destroyed one of the horizontal stabilizers in the tail. Our crew owes our lives once again to two cool-headed pilots who brought the aircraft back to base. Every combat aircrew member flew in the face of constant danger not only from enemy aircraft or ground defenses but also from mechanical failure or accidents and, sometimes, just plain error.

When U.S. Air Forces began operations in Europe, they were confident that their aircraft armed with heavy-caliber guns and flying in close formation would be more than a match for the German fighters. This confidence was proving to be ill founded as all bomb groups began to experience unsustainable losses. Because of the lack of long-range fighter escorts, most of our targets were in occupied France and Germany's western border towns. The target for our fourth mission on June 22, 1943 was a synthetic rubber manufacturing plant located near the Dutch-German border.

June 25, 1943 was my fifth and final mission. The target was Hamburg, Germany's second largest city with a population in excess of one million and a half and its largest and most important port. Its shipyards produced 45 per cent of the total output of German submarines and it contained 3000 industrial establishments. Hamburg was of utmost industrial importance to Germany and as such, it was, after Berlin, the most heavily defended city in Germany. The British, flying at night, had made many attacks against Hamburg in varying degrees of intensity, but damage had not been significant. Despite the lack of fighter escorts it was time for the "Yanks to give it a go" with their precision bombing on pinpoint targets. When Hamburg was announced as the target during our briefing, we heard some "whoopee's," "whistles," and "hurrahs." After only four missions the 375th Bomb Group was now in the big leagues, up there with the big boys.

As the planes began to taxi into position for take off, I stood outside our plane fumbling with my parachute. After the previous day's mission, I sent my parachute to the rigging shop to be repacked, and was issued a new one. When I put the harness on that morning, it was too large and not properly adjusted. The fort's engines were running and it was getting close for our turn to taxi out for take off, and I was still outside the plane feverishly trying my best, but unsuccessfully, to adjust the harness. The cockpit window slid open and my pilot, Paul Hartman, shouted what would become never-to-be-forgotten words, *"Get in the plane, Tony. You won't need that parachute today."*

It was cold and rainy at take off time. Where clouds did not cover the sky, condensation trails did and we flew on instruments most of the time. The German ground defenses around Hamburg were growing in effectiveness. They could hurl 22-pound explosive shells six miles high from their 88mm batteries. Before we reached the target area, we were hit by burst of flak and our number-four engine was damaged. The plane immediately began to lose power and we were unable to stay with the formation. We dragged behind to where we were alone. Luftwaffe fighters that came at us firing .30-inch caliber machine-guns and 20-mm canons. I could see the cannon bursts and estimated that they must have been set for 600 yards. With my computer-operated gun sight I could pick up the fighter and track him from a thousand yards out. The battle was fierce. Our pilot took evasive action and made the plane go up and down and side to side. This made it very difficult for the gunners to aim and fire, but it was appropriate action to take. Waist gunners had to be especially careful not to shoot and hit our plane's wings. They used .50-inch caliber machine-guns on a swivel mount. The top turret had interrupters that would cut off the gun firing so as not to hit wingtips or horizontal tail fin. At one point, a fighter was coming at us from one o'clock. I managed to bracket it in my adjustable cross hairs and opened fire at about 700 yards. As he got closer, he began to go down fast with some smoke trailing. I believe I hit him. As the battle raged, we could see huge clouds ahead and hoped to make it into them for cover. During a battle, there is not much communication among the crew except to call out the location of incoming enemy fighters. I did hear the pilot ask the navigator for compass headings to England and France. We made it to the cloud cover and for several minutes, we felt safe, protected by the clouds. However, our luck ran out. The clouds opened up and there waiting for us were several enemy fighters. Before we could make it to the next cloudbank, we again were hit hard and the number-four engine was now on fire. Soon, the entire wing was burning. The pilot ordered us to bail out but I did not hear the order. I was still firing when Lt. Hartman pulled on my leg and shouted, "Get out!" I was not wearing my parachute because of the improper fit and also, it got in my way. I quickly put it on and started for the bomb bay doors but they were closed. I could see the radio operator, Jim Blick, at the other end waiting for me to pull the emergency cable to release the bomb bay doors. I yanked and pulled hard but the doors would not open. I shouted for Jim to go out through the fuselage door then I turned to go out the front hatch. I glanced at the instrument panel. We were at about 10,000 feet with an air speed of about 300mph. Just as I stepped down through the flight-deck door to the lower section, the floor under my turret exploded. Oxygen bottles stored there were hit. Particles of the decking struck my back. I saw the navigator coming up from the nose. He motioned me to jump. I squared my feet, said a little prayer and out I went. I let my body tumble and I could see the earth come around a couple of times before I pulled the ripcord to open the chute. It opened with a bang and as the harness straps went past my head some silk material fluttered in my face. Thinking it was my parachute, I looked up and saw a hole at the top of the chute and I thought I had had it, but as it turned out the silk was the scarf I was wearing and there was nothing wrong with the chute. The poor adjustment on the chute injured my back. I looked around and down and saw a fighter coming right at me. My first thought was he is going to spill my chute by flying so close but instead he just gestured OK by waving his wings. Looking down I could see people dressed in white and I thought they were farmers. I landed hard in a field of grain that was several feet tall, quickly took off my chute and lay low. Suddenly I heard a voice and looked up into the barrel of a machine-gun held by a white-uniformed soldier. He shouted, "Rouse," and motioned with his gun for me to get up and raise my arms. I did and said, "Nix Pistol."

The soldiers herded the survivors and took us to a small jail-like building. Waist gunner, Bob Greeley's legs were seriously wounded and he was in pain. I gave him a shot of morphine from my escape kit that the Germans later confiscated. Using his belt, we tied a tourniquet around his upper leg to control the bleeding. A tail gunner from another aircrew was wounded in the hands and bleeding badly. We administered first aid and although undoubtedly needed, the Germans did not provide any medical help. Afterwards, I found that my back and pelvic area were black and blue, and covered with dried blood specs.

Later, the Germans brought in two boxes that contained the remains of two of our aircrew, S/Sgt. Jim Blick and Sgt. Harold Schroder. Our guards forced us to parade through the village carrying the caskets. Emotional villagers lined the street and gestured wildly as they screamed profanities. Some came forth to spit on us while others hurled stones at us. We were the "Terrorfliegers" or "Luft Gangsters" and their rage was frightening. I believed we were about to be lynched or murdered in cold blood, but the soldiers returned us to our cells and the situation quieted down.

From this point, we traveled by truck to an interrogation camp near Frankfurt and I was confined to a small 5 x 10 foot cell without lights or a window. Several times a day, I was interrogated and asked the same questions repeatedly. If we refused to answer their questions, our life was threatened. This treatment lasted about a week.

Eventually we were marched to a railroad siding where we were loaded onto boxcars. En route while stopped at the marshaling yards in Cologne, the air raid sirens sounded. The guards kept us locked in the boxcars and they took off. Fearing that our own planes would hit us, we began screaming and cursing. Finally, a German officer had the doors opened and guards escorted us to a shelter. In the shelter, an SS officer began to push some of us around and he grabbed me by my shirt under my chin and shook the hell out of me. I did not show any signs of retaliating so he finally let me go. There was a lot of damage to the main yards and rail tracks were all torn up but our train was still there, engine and all. We returned to the boxcars and it took a lot of maneuvering to get us out of the marshaling yards.

After a day or two, we finally arrived at our destination, Stalag VIIA, Moosburg, Germany. Here, they issued prisoner of war identification numbers and tags, and photographed us. My number was 112657; I still have this tag and the photos taken. I believe I was about the 250th American enlisted airman taken prisoner by Germany. During the course of the war, the Germans captured or killed a total of 90,000 USAAF airmen.

We never received Red Cross packages at Stalag VIIA but other groups did. Once, we thought a wagon loaded with Red Cross parcels was coming into camp but it went right past our compound to the French compound. Our camp leader did some negotiating with the French and we got one package for seven men. This was not very much.

Americans were not allowed in the other compounds. One night, Sgt. Pacicotti and I who both spoke Italian and an army corporal who spoke fluent German convinced several other GIs to let us trade their government-issued wrist watches for food. The Corporal bribed the guards with a few cigarettes to let us go to another compound. We first went to the Indian barracks where we entered after explaining we were Americans and interested in trading. Inside, we all sat on the floor and our hosts served tea with butter in it. We drank it since we did not want to insult the Indians, and then began to negotiate watches for food. They really wanted these radiant dial watches when they saw how they glowed in the dark. From there we went to the Italian barracks. When Italy capitulated in 1943, many Italian soldiers who had refused to fight for or had fought against the Germans were brought to this Stalag. While we were negotiating, the lights flashed off and then on. This was the sign for lights out. In the dark, I understood an Italian say, "Grab their food." Before they could, I told my buddies to grab their stuff and get out. We got near the gate to get back into our compound and saw that the guard had changed. Our Corporal went up to talk with him while the two of us hid behind the barracks. After he gave the guard a couple of cigarettes, the gate opened a crack and the corporal pushed in. The two of us rushed past the guard and put some cigarettes in his hands. This turned out to be a good night's work. We exchanged food for watches and one watch owner even got a replacement watch back. We now had some food and still had some watches for future trading.

Once or twice a day we fell out for roll call, a count of the prisoners standing in columns of five men deep. The guards had this nasty habit of walking the dogs in close and letting them leap at us and occasionally bite us in the legs. I would always try to fall out early to get in the middle of the group. At times after the count, or any time of the day, some guards would turn one or two of the dogs loose. We were particularly wary of this whenever the dog trainer entered the compound with a dog. To avoid being bitten, we would run for the barracks and try to make it to the upper bunks or rafter post. One time a dog got this GI by the arm and he made a sudden turn and came out of his jacket, which wound up in the dog's mouth. Most GIs were not easily frightened but those viscous animals with their deadly eyes put fear into us. They stared at you as if they could see right through you. Prison life at Stalag 7A was a miserable experience.

On October 14, 1943, the Germans moved all Air Force non-commissioned officers from Stalag 7A to Stalag 17B located at Krems, Austria. After receiving some bread, we marched to waiting railroad boxcars.

While en route, we had an opportunity to attempt escape. The guard had fallen asleep sitting on the floor near a slightly opened door. The train was moving rather slowly up a grade. My buddy and I talked about it but decided to wait until the next camp hoping to be better prepared. We did not know where we were; we had no food and could not speak German. In hindsight, I think perhaps we made a mistake not attempting to escape, especially after the torment I experienced at Stalag 17B.

We arrived there at night; it was a scary looking place. As we walked between two rows of barbed wire fencing toward a group of storage buildings, the air filled with the odor of gas. I recalled the stories I had heard about the Nazis using gas chambers to murder civilians in their extermination camps. We had to disrobe and enter this large white empty room with showerheads in the ceiling. I really thought this was the end of my life when suddenly water came pouring down. It was a shower room after all. The odor was coming from the delousing building. After delousing, we went to our barracks area.

Each barracks was divided into two sections and I was assigned to Section B in Barracks 37, which was located next to the warning wire that ran along the perimeter fence. The Germans assigned 130 to 140 men to a section and each section had an appointed leader. The men within a section were organized into seven smaller groups and a leader was appointed for each group. I was in charge of a group of 20-25 men.

Every day several men would go to the kitchen outside of the compound to get their barracks' daily rations. Usually this was one or two wooden tub containers. Two men carried each tub with a long pole going through two holes at the top. The tubs were filled with soup made from dehydrated vegetables. In the early months at Stalag 17B we could almost always find meat in our soup, of course, the meat was maggots. The barracks' "ration king" would dish out one can (about 12 oz) to each man. We would line up in our subgroups, rotating the groups every day to be first in line. Sometimes there were leftovers and the first group would get back in line. We took our soup to a dark place to eat it so as not to see what was in it.

We also received three loaves of dark bread per group daily. Some of the bread was wrapped in foil with a seal dated 1937. It looked like rye bread and sawdust was an ingredient used as a preservative. The coarseness of this bread made our mouth sore and raw. As group leader, I was responsible for cutting each loaf into seven or eight pieces using my German dog tag to measure. In addition to the bread and soup, we usually got two or three potatoes per man. Sometimes we would end up short and when that occurred, I would share mine. Occasionally, they gave us ersatz coffee. This was our daily ration of German food.

Red Cross parcels kept us alive but the parcels, like packages from home, did not come very often. After several months, we began receiving Red Cross parcels in quantities sufficient to distribute one parcel per man. A package contained one can of powdered milk, 2oz of powdered coffee, a small can of margarine, one "D" ration bar, three packages of 10 cigarettes each, two small bars of soap and maybe one or two other items.

We made fuel from shaved bed boards and some timber removed from the outdoor latrine. Someone designed a blower built from tin cans in our Red Cross packages. The blower worked like a forge. It was about one and a half feet long and six to eight inches in diameter, with a blower wheel, also made from tin cans. This device could heat water rapidly with very little fuel.

We had a good trading system. All items traded were valued based on a pack of ten cigarettes. For example, a can of coffee may be worth two packs of cigarettes. The market would fluctuate based on supply and demand, usually supply since there was always a demand.

In the summer of 1944, I was in a combine with Slug, my ball turret gunner, but it did not last too long. Card games were the most popular form of recreation and there was always a game to join. We held bridge tournaments and other card games but poker was the game for the gamblers. The stakes were food. One GI received playing cards and chips from home so he became the houseman and set up a poker table and supplied candlelight made from margarine when the games were played at night. He got a cut of each pot. Slug was a gambler but I valued my food too much to risk losing it so we had to break up our combine. Still, when he won, he shared some of his winnings with me and if he lost, he could count on me to share my food with him.

For months, I was very sick. Due to the lack of proper nourishment, I began to suffer from vitamin deficiency and malnutrition. My blood was thin and pink. When I got a scratch, it would take a long time to heal. Then I contacted scabies. Scabies infestation is very contagious and spreads like wild fire. My body was infested from the waist down. At the infirmary, the medics would paint my body with a tar-like substance each day and for three or four days I wore a pair of long johns and then I would finally take a shower. It got to the point that my skin became black. The scabies kept reoccurring so they sent me to the camp hospital referred to as the "Lazarette." My pain was almost unbearable as I dragged my legs through two or more feet of snow for nearly an hour. Two of us went that day. The other airmen was paralyzed on one side of his body and he had to be carried on a stretcher. The paralysis resulted from beatings received from civilians and Hitler Youths at the time of his capture. At the Lazarette, they put me into a small empty cement room that had a single cement bench and told to remove my clothes. The room did not have any heat and it was so cold I passed out. When I came too, I found myself in bed in a larger room with six other GIs and a few Italian and British prisoners. Our doctor was an imprisoned captain in the French army.

I remained in the hospital for about five months. The medics treated my skin with a purple liquid called gentian violet and then silver nitrate. My legs were bandaged and I could not sleep. The slightest touch of my legs against the mattress would start an unbelievable fiery itch. They had to restrain my arms by tying them to the bed to prevent me from scratching. The pain was almost unbearable. My right leg discolored so badly that the doctor thought he might have to amputate. Thankfully, it began to improve. During this time, I also received treatment for pleurisy. Then the German Command issued orders that all patients hospitalized for more than three months had to go back to camp regardless of their condition. I returned to my compound even though I had not fully recovered.

During the summer of 1944, we started to dig a tunnel from under barracks 37 that extended about 50 feet beyond the double barbed wire fence and into the woods. Following completion, all of the escape plans were in place. As the first GI came up out of the tunnel, German guards stepped out of the woods. They were aware of this attempt and that was the end of our tunnel digging. The Germans forced those still in the tunnel to return to the barracks back through the tunnel. We had to tear it down, but we worked so inefficiently, the Germans eventually had Russian prisoners fill it up.

We had heard rumors of prison camps up north that were in the path of the Russian advance being evacuated and the men forced to march for months, so we were uncertain as to what was in store for us when we evacuated Stalag 17B on April 8, 1945. We marched westerly along the Danube River from one end of Austria to the other and eventually reached the German Bavarian border. Before I left, I used my spare shirt to make a backpack and filled it with some cigarettes, foodstuff, soap bars and whatever else I could carry. Soap was the best item for trading for food with Austrian women. As we marched passed farmhouses on the road, we did a lot of begging for food. Sometimes if we wandered too far from the road, a guard would shoot in our direction. I do not think they were trying to hit anyone. In one small village, I saw a sign that looked like "Bakery." My buddy and I stepped in and the shelves were full of bread. We asked and received a loaf each. By this time, the store filled with of GIs, who quickly emptied the shelves. A guard came in shouting but he quieted when given a loaf of bread. At times, our guards did not have any more food than we had. They were older men and we called them "Gross Pappa," our version of "Grandpa" in German. The younger soldiers were at the Russian front. One day we passed a camp that appeared to be a concentration or slave labor camp. We could see the inmates behind the wire but we were unable to identify their nationality. As we passed, SS soldiers came out and their glares made us thankful that we were not imprisoned there. Another day we encountered a group of civilians going in the opposite direction. They appeared to be Jews and our guards told us they were Hungarian. They looked gaunt and were really in bad shape. I will never forget the time we saw a German soldier picking up dead bodies along the roadside and stacking them in a horse drawn wagon. The wagon was full and some looked as though they may still be alive sitting up in the wagon. It was a gruesome sight.

We marched mostly along the banks of the Danube River crossing from one side to the other a few times to avoid villages that had been bombed. One night, while bivouacked in a field next to an airfield we came under air attack. We could hear the roar of airplane engines overhead mixed with the sound of sirens wailing as the dark sky suddenly lit with flares fired high into the sky. There was a large swale located between the airfield and us, which we ran into for protection. The bombers dropped their bombs and as suddenly as it started, it was over. The next morning, we saw that the airfield was a dummy with props made to look like aircraft and that raid was for naught. Although we were close to the action, I do not think that any POWs were injured as a result of that raid. That morning we marched double time through the village to avoid the wrath of the villagers. Near the end of April, I became very ill. We bivouacked in an open field and there was a cold rain coming down. I was burning up with a fever. The next morning, my buddy Spud Paciotti heated water over a small fire and cooked a potato and gave it to me. I told him that he should go on without me because I was too sick and would stay behind and take my chances with the civilians. Spud insisted that I go on. He practically carried me about 20 miles that day. That night, we stayed in an area where some of us slept in fields and others made it to barns belonging to a group of farmers. I slept in a barn loft with plenty of straw. That evening, we ate hot soup prepared by some GIs and local farmers' families. During the night, my fever broke and the march continued. In the morning, we learned that President Roosevelt had died. We thought that this was just more propaganda but it turned out to be true.

By the end of April, we could see and hear gunfire on the other side of the river. We approached a small town and saw a white flag flying from a church steeple.

Our spirits lifted when we heard the sound of a tank coming up the road through the woods. The hatch opened and a tall captain was standing in the turret. As he got out and began walking amongst us, GIs gathered all around him. He patted one POW on the head and said reassuringly to all, "You are going to be all right now." The moment was so emotional; I could see tears on many of the POW's faces. We really had made it. The next day several jeeps of GIs led by a colonel came into our encampment and officially liberated us. We took the guns from our German guards, and they now became our prisoners and marched off to a temporary encampment. The GIs in the jeeps had C rations and fresh eggs and began to hand them out. This caused a grab fest with POWs struggling for the food and many an egg was broken. Although now free, we remained cautious. A sniper had killed a soldier after the town had surrendered. I went from house to house in the area pleading for food. The Austrians were so happy to see the American army rather than the Russians; they gave us whatever food they had.

We were so anxious to get home, we decided to march another 12 miles rather than wait for trucks to transport us to a bombed-out factory that was to be our night's shelter and pick up point in the morning. Along the way, the army fed us hot C-rations. The next day, we rode to a nearby airfield where C-47's were waiting to fly us to a camp in France. There, we were deloused, showered, given a change of clothing, more food and then shipped to camp Lucky Strike at LeHavre, France to wait for a ship to take us home. At Camp Lucky Strike, we had some good meals and all the milkshakes or eggnog that we wanted. We now rarely finished a meal when we would have to run to the latrine tent where there often was a line. After months of starvation, food now passed right through us.

After four-days, we boarded a liberty ship and on June 10, 1945, we passed the Statue of Liberty and upon entering New York Harbor, we heard the sound of car horns honking and saw people waving. As we disembarked, Red Cross women met us and offered us coffee and doughnuts, and a very warm "Welcome Home!" We next went to Fort Dix, New Jersey where, following a cursory physical examination, we received a 60-day leave, partial pay, and orders to report to Atlantic City by August 15, 1945 for either reassignment or discharge. While home, I received a telegram notifying me to report to the Rochester Hotel in Rochester, New York. There, agents from the Military Intelligence Service interrogated me regarding the treatment I had received while a POW at Stalag 17B. I think they were collecting information in preparation for the war crime trials that were to follow.

On August 4, 1945, Katie Giarrizzo and I married in New Albany, Indiana. We celebrated VJ day while on our honeymoon and on August 15, 1945, I reported to the Redistribution Center at Atlantic City, New Jersey. I had accumulated sufficient 'points' to be discharged immediately but somehow my military records could not be located and my discharge from the military had to be deferred. In the interim, the Air Force offered me the opportunity to select a base for assignment until my records were found. I chose Bear Field, which was close to my wife's family in New Albany, Indiana. By mid-October, the Air Force still had not located my records; so, after first being forewarned that false information would subject me to fines up to $10,000 and imprisonment, I agreed to sign a statement under oath attesting to my military service. I received my Honorable Discharge on October 22, 1945.

The post war years have been very stressful. I continued to experience health-related problems including chronic back pains and periodically my skin disorders would flair up. The pain, discomfort, loss of work and mental fatigue became so stressful that I would go into depression. I had nightmares of wartime incidences, became unusually impatient and easily agitated. I was no longer the person I once was. All this had an adverse impact on my marriage and personal relations with others. For years, the war was something that I could not talk about. When I tried, I would get very emotional and begin to cry and would lose my voice. Even today, it is difficult. I continue to receive care from the Veteran's Administration for my service-related health problems.

Fifty-eight years following my discharge, I received the Purple Heart and the Air Medal along with several other decorations. General Scott Gray made the presentation at Andrews Air Force Base, Maryland on August 19, 2003. I was the only one honored that day. My family and four Ex-POW comrades were present for this ceremony.

Staff Sergeant Anthony J. Gullace was Honorably Discharged on October 22, 1945. He is the recipient of the Purple Heart, Air Medal, POW Medal, WWII Victory Medal, Presidential Distinguished Unit Citation, European-African-Middle Eastern Campaign Medal with a battle star, American Theatre Medal and a Good Conduct Medal.

Personal Note

Every combat airman flew in the face of constant danger knowing all too well that he might not come back from his next mission. During WWII, more than 90,000 American airmen were lost or taken prisoner in Germany. The day I was captured, I felt blessed to have survived the fighter attack and destruction of our plane. The day I was liberated, I thanked the Lord for getting me through all of the ordeals and illnesses I had suffered in prison camp and on the march. Through God's grace and all of the prayers said for me by my mother, family and fiancée Katie, I was brought home safely. Katie and I were married in August of 1945. We had two children, Sharon and Bob and five wonderful grandchildren. Unfortunately, we lost our daughter in 1992, at the age of 41 to breast cancer. We are certain, even though she is not here to read this memoir; she knows all that I went through. My wife Katie has stood by my side for 60 sometimes difficult but wonderful years and I hope we will stay healthy to continue to enjoy our golden years.

Katie and Tony Gullace

*General Scott Gray awarding Tony the Purple Heart
and Air Medal, August 2003*

Tony Gullace at the National Prisoner of War Museum,
Andersonville, Georgia

Daniel D. Dudek in Brussels, Belgium, May 1945
Shortly after being liberated from POW
Dan was twenty years old

DANIEL D. DUDEK

*"Then we collided; he cut us in two and sheared
our tail section off from the waist windows back.
His right wing broke off."*

D ANIEL D. DUDEK grew up in Baltimore's
Canton area. His home was across the street
from the Enoch Pratt Branch Library located at
Elwood Avenue and O'Donnell Street. He attended St.
Casmir's Parochial School and Baltimore's prestigious
public high school, the Polytechnic Institute, informally
known as Poly. He graduated in June 1942, and went to
work for the Bethlehem Steel Company at Sparrows
Point, Maryland.

Dan was eighteen years old when he was drafted
into the U.S. Army on February 1, 1943, and took basic
infantry training at Fort McClellan, Alabama. The Army
Air Forces (AAF) was looking for men and women with
the qualifications necessary for the more than five
hundred skills that contributed to the success of a routine
bombing mission. The principal source for pilots,
navigators, bombardiers, and technical, administrative
and service officers was the Aviation Cadet Recruiting
Program. Dan dreamed of becoming a pilot, so at the
first opportunity, he volunteered and was selected for the
program.

Personnel assigned to the AAF for aviation cadet
training were given a five-week basic military course
which included exhaustive physical, psychological and
mental tests to determine their fitness for the flying
program and to determine the specialty for which they

181

were best suited. Dan took his AAF basic training at Keesler Air Force Base in Mississippi. Beginning in 1943, everyone entering the Aviation Cadet Program was assigned to one of forty college training detachments throughout the country for a period of one to five months depending on their advancement based on their scores on tests at both the basic military course and the college training detachment. During 1943, approximately six hundred potential pilots, navigators or bombardiers were attending each school at any given time. Dan attended Springfield College in Massachusetts for pre-flight training.

Following successful completion of this training, he was sent to the AAF Classification and Pre-Flight Center at Nashville, Tennessee. Final classification resulted from test scores achieved during academic training, and physio-motor tests that evaluated coordination and a comprehensive physical examination, both given at this center. When he failed the physio-motor testing, Dan was so disappointed, he petitioned a review board but his appeal was denied. Candidates, who were unable to meet all requirements to become a pilot, navigator or bombardier, were offered an opportunity to become an aerial gunner.

During gunnery school at Laredo, Texas, Dan became proficient in weapons; ballistics; turret operation and maintenance; gun repairs; air, sea and land recognition; shooting from a moving base and from a turret; and firing from the air at ground objects, towed targets and other aircraft with a gun camera. Skeet shooting with shotguns was designed to improve reaction and quickness. Following completion of gunnery school, he began training as an aircrew member on a B-24 Liberator at Boise, Idaho.

The AAF replacement unit training program provided replacements for overseas aircrews that had been lost in combat or rotated home for reassignment. On August 11, 1944, Dan sailed aboard the *SS Argentina* in a convoy that took twelve days to cross the Atlantic. Following arrival in Northern Ireland, he was assigned to the 8th Air Force, 489th Bomb Group and 844th Squadron. On his ninth mission, October 19, 1944, Dan's plane had a mid-air collision with another squadron bomber over Mainz, Germany. He bailed out, was captured and became a prisoner of war

Dan tells his story:
I was the tail gunner on Lt. John Aiken's crew, and on September 16, 1944, we were assigned to the 489th Bomb Group, which was made up of the 844th, 845th, and 846th Squadrons. We were assigned to the 844th and our stay with the group was a short one.

We went into action almost immediately. My first combat mission, on September 21, 1944 was a bombing run over Koblenz, which is about eighty miles inside the German border. The next day we hit Kassel and three days later, we were again over Koblenz and our target was the marshaling yards located there.

October 1944 was a dull and gray month with twenty-three days of cold, rain and mud, but it did not keep us on the ground. On October 2, 1944, we hit the railway siding, shipment sheds, and industrial buildings in the city of Hamm. It was our Bomb Group's third mission to this target within a week. The next day, we flew lead on a run to Speyerdorf, which was a messy mission and our results were considered poor. Two days later, we hit the oil refinery in Rhine, about twenty miles inside the German border. Rain and fog "souped" us in for about ten days and on October 14, 1944, we bombed the marshaling yards at Cologne, Germany's third largest city, and its third heaviest defended with 286 anti-aircraft guns. The flak was heavy but inaccurate and there were no casualties as we hit their railroad lines, rolling stock, and warehouse buildings. We returned the next day, October 15, 1944. This time the flak was accurate and intense. When we were right over the target, the Krauts opened up with everything they had and every ship came back to base with holes in it.

On my ninth mission, October 19, 1944, our original target had been the buzz bomb plant at Mainz, but we had to go after the secondary target, the marshaling yards. We were flying *Bombers Moon*, and I was in my normal station in the tail turret. After we had assembled with our squadron and while we were crossing the English Channel, my electrically heated suit failed, and I began to get cold and numb, so I called Lt. Aiken and informed him of my problem. Sgt. Bruce Anderson, the left waist gunner, volunteered to switch places with me, as he was familiar with the tail turret. We not only traded places, we also swapped parachutes because you could not wear a back-type chute in the tail turret, just the harness. The chest chute was placed outside the turret on the floor. When I got to the waist-gunner station, I put a flak suit on over my chute and then plugged in the casualty bag and put it over me to get some heat.

We were in the slot position on this mission, and everything went fine until we reached the initial point, opened the bomb bay doors and began the bomb run. The flak was heavy and all around us. As I looked out of the left waist window, I saw *Pregnant Peggy* on our left side flown by Lt. Lee Lithander slide right over on top of us. They were so close as they passed over us; I could almost touch the bombs in their bomb bay. All of a sudden there was a loud THUMP, and I remember saying "Oh, my God, he dropped his bombs on us!" Apparently, Lithander had hit some prop wash, fluttered up and came down right on top of us. After the planes separated, Lithander lost control of *Pregnant Peggy* and the two planes collided. He cut us in two and sheared our tail section off, from the waist windows back. *Pregnant Peggy*'s right wing broke off and she spun in. Our plane also went into a spin and I was pinned against the fuselage roof, on the right side of the plane.

My first thought after clearing the plane was to reach out in front and pull the ripcord. As I did, I realized that I had the flak suit on. Normally, you would pull the red tab and the suit would separate at the shoulder and waist snaps, and fall off; but as I was tumbling through the air, only the waist snaps came loose and I could not pry the shoulder snaps apart to release the suit. In spite of my struggles I could not get it off, so I reached under it and pulled the ripcord. When the chute opened, it must have flipped the flak suit up, breaking several teeth and knocking me out for a while. When I came to, the flak suit was up against my oxygen mask, and I could hardly breathe. I felt as if I was being choked to death, so I pulled the oxygen mask off and, when I let it go I could see it falling below me. It was then, with great relief, I knew that my chute had opened. Finally, I was able to loosen the shoulder snaps and release the flak suit. I was just about to let go of it when I remembered that it weighed twenty-seven pounds and that it would help pull me down faster, so I put it between my legs and held on to it until my right foot began to get numb from the cold. I had lost the flying boot on that foot getting out of the plane. Then I saw two other parachutes, so I let the flak suit drop.

Now I could see two small towns and German soldiers with their dogs. Although I had landed in a soft farm field out in the country, I sprained my foot. Despite my injury, I had time to hide the parachute in a ditch before I limped into a nearby orchard to hide. German soldiers quickly surrounded the orchard and sent in their dogs, so I came out with my hands up. While the soldiers searched me, a farmer punched me in the face for messing up his field. Then a truck arrived carrying another crewmember, Clarence Harding, the right waist gunner. The Germans drove us into a town of Speyerdorf where we picked up the co-pilot of the other B-24 involved in the collision, Lt. Lloyd Krumrey. He had come down in town and had broken his right ankle when he hit the edge of a building. We were driven to a Luftwaffe base where a German medic treated the Lieutenant's broken ankle and wrapped my sprained foot so that I could walk.

We were returned to Speyerdorf, where we spent that night in a lice-infested cell in the local jail, and ate a piece of moldy bread as our only meal for the entire day. The next morning we traveled by streetcar to the train station and along the way local German civilians shouted hateful obscenities and spat at us. We rode all day until midnight and, when we got off the train, Harding and I had to carry the Lieutenant because he couldn't walk. We carried him several miles before we arrived at the Dulag Luft Interrogation Center near Frankfurt am Main, where each of us was put into solitary confinement for several days. I was so tired, all I wanted was sleep, but I was taken before a German officer who spoke perfect English. He asked where we left from, what our targets were, and how many missions I had flown. I only gave my name, rank and serial number as required by the Geneva Convention.

Later, I learned that there were only two survivors from each crew, Sgt. Clarence J. Harding and myself from *Bomber's Moon,* and Lt. Lloyd W. Krumrey and Staff Sgt. Richard F. Phillippy, from *Pregnant Peggy.*

Our pilot, Lt. John M. Aiken, Jr.; Lt. Charles A. Rath, co-pilot; Lt. Loyola F. Doherty, navigator; Lt. Lewis C. Francis, bombardier; S/Sgt. Glen L. Smith, tail turret gunner; S/Sgt. Virgil Everhardt, radio operator;

and Sgt. Bruce D. Anderson, waist gunner were all casualties. As fate would have it, I owe my life to Sgt. Anderson who offered to take my position as tail gunner. Lt. Lee B. Lithander, Lt. Robert J. Hurley, S/Sgt. Robert R. Butler, Jr., Sgt. Henry L. Stock, Sgt. Geza Torek, S/Sgt. Eugene I. Kader and Sgt. John H. Crompton all lost their lives when the *Pregnant Peggy* crashed.

Paul Menzenki's plane was flying on the left wing of the two planes that collided and he filed a report that was later published in the *History of the 489th Bomb Group.* "On the way to the target, two airplanes on our right wing were flying a real loose formation. When we got into flak they tightened up, but it must have been a little rough, because the planes were moving up and down, as if the air was bumpy. One plane came down on top of the other and (they) came apart again with little visible damage. At least I could not see any. Almost as soon as the planes separated, two parachuted men jumped out of the top plane (*Pregnant Peggy*). They pulled their chutes much too soon. They must have been terrified. One missed the tail by a narrow margin, and the other got hung up on the tail surface. He let himself out of the chute and went down. The question in my mind will always be – did he know what he was doing, or was he so terrified that he lost all reason? Or did he think the plane would not function with him hanging there?"

From the interrogation center, we were sent to a nearby Red Cross station, where we were de-loused, had a shower, and were issued new army clothes, boots, overcoat, blanket, and a toothbrush. We had a good meal. From this point, we were herded like cattle into boxcars, with only some straw on the floor, for a two-week journey to northeast Germany to a POW camp named Stalag Luft IV, near the Kiefheide railhead.

When I arrived at the camp gates, I was thrilled to be greeted by a boyhood friend, Walter Czawlytko, who had been a prisoner since June 29, 1944. Walter and I renewed our friendship and have remained friends ever since.

I was in this camp from November until the end of January 1945. When the Russians started to advance from the east, we moved out and were forced to march from camp to camp toward the western front, a journey that stretched hundreds of miles and lasted nearly three months during one of the coldest winters on record. The very sick were placed on horse-drawn wagons. German troops and their dogs guarded us constantly. Finally, on May 2, 1945, paratroopers from the British 2nd Army liberated us near the Rhine River.

We were turned over to American forces and sent to Le Havre, where we were gradually fed rich foods such as eggnog to build up our body weight. For the past six months, I had been fed poorly and had survived the forced marched by eating mostly turnips scrounged from the fields. When I finally ate my first full meal, I became very ill. Eventually, my health improved and I returned home on June 8, 1945, on the Liberty Ship *Brazil*. Following a thirty-day furlough, I was re-assigned to several AAF installations and ended my service with the Army Air Corps at Bolling Air Force Base near Washington, D. C.

November 6 was my Dad's birthday. In 1944, instead of receiving the usual happy birthday greeting from me, he received a telegram informing him and my Mom that I was "missing in action." The day that should have been filled with joy became a very, very sad day and the family became frantic with worry.

As families usually do when faced with tragedy, they found strength in their faith and support from loved ones and friends. Neighbors gathered in silent prayer and many went to church to light votive candles for special intentions and asked God, in his mercy, to spare my life and protect me.

On the very day my family received the telegram, fifteen-year-old Dolores Wisniewski was visiting her grandmother, Catherine, who told her that she was going to St. Casimir's Church to pray for a boy who was missing in action. Young Dolores asked her grandmother for the boy's name and then she went to church, lit a votive candle and prayed that Danny Dudek would return safely to his family. Little did she know then that she was praying for the man who would later become her husband and the father of her children. I met Dolores for the first time in 1947 and we were married the following year. I learned of this story at my 50th Wedding Anniversary celebration. Prayers are indeed very powerful.

On December 6, 1944, my parent's unfaltering faith in God was fortified when the American Red Cross notified them that I was alive and a prisoner of the German government. My brothers, Martin, Leo and I all went into the service within a ten-month period. Their anxiety, fears and loneliness were matched by millions of other parents around the world. War is as difficult for those at home as it is for those who fought the bloody battles. My parents were deeply religious people and their faith gave them the strength to carry them through their terrible ordeal. Their prayers were answered when all three sons returned home safely. My youngest brother was called to the priesthood and is now Father Bernard Dudek, a Franciscan priest.

189

Personal Note

I will always remember the date of October 19, 1944, the day I became a POW, all the hardships I endured, especially the infamous forced march, and all the atrocities that I suffered during my time as a captive. Life goes on. In my later years, I am a very happy man who has been blessed with a loving wife for fifty-six years. Dolores and I are very proud of our three wonderful children and their spouses, four grandchildren and two step-grandchildren. Dan, Jr. and his wife, Jeannette; Fred and his wife Marlys, and their precious children David and Kelly and Alan and Audrey; daughter, Darlene and her husband, Paul Kolech and their precious children, Barry and Shari. This story is for them, my family whom I love so very much and I thank the dear Lord every day for all my blessings.

Daniel D. Dudek was honorably discharged on November 10, 1945 at the rank of Staff Sergeant. He was awarded the Purple Heart; Air Medal; POW Medal; European, African, Middle-Eastern Campaign Medal; World War II Victory Medal; American Theatre Medal; and Good Conduct Medal.

Daniel D. Dudek was called for his final mission on May 26, 2005 at age 81 and was given a military interment at St. Stanislaus Cemetery in Baltimore. He soared where eagles never dared.

Crew Members (opposite):
Top row, left to right – Lt. L. Doherty, navigator; Lt. Francis, bombardier; Lt. L. Rath, co-pilot; Lt. Aiken, pilot; S/Sgt. Daniel Dudek, tail gunner
Bottom row, left to right – S/Sgt. B. Anderson, left waist gunner; S/Sgt. Edwards, ball turret gunner (he was taken off our crew); S/Sgt. C. Harding, right waist gunner; S/Sgt. Smith, engineer; S/Sgt. V. Everhardt, radio operator

Dan and Dolores Dudek, October, 1998

Ken Barnes

RALPH KENNETH BARNES

"I did not want to become a prisoner of war.
I was prepared to die in those woods."

THE GERMAN counteroffensive in the Ardennes Forest area in mid-December 1944 is considered the biggest battle on the European western front during World War II. Because of the bulge it put into allied lines, the counteroffensive became popularly known as the "Battle of the Bulge." Between December 16, 1944 and January 25, 1945 more than 100,000 German soldiers were killed, wounded or captured and American forces suffered 81,000 casualties including 19,000 killed and more than 23,000 captured.

Following the breakthrough in Normandy, the Allied Forces swept across France and by October were poised along the western frontier of Germany. In some ways, the break-neck advance through France was just as disorderly as the German's retreat. The rapid progress and resulting extended front pressed the limits of logistical support. Supply problems became so acute that a continued large-scale forward movement became impossible. Yet, there were American commanders who were determined to maintain the initiative and continue the drive into Germany. Plans were prepared for the 1st Army located north of the Ardennes to advance to Cologne through the Huertgen Forest while Patton's 3rd Army, positioned south of the Ardennes, would strike at the Saar Basin.

However, the Germans were not about to call it quits at the time. The allied supply problems afforded them a breathing spell. Hitler now had a continuous front line in the west amply backed by their main line of defense, the West Wall and other natural obstructions. Despite the ceaseless war in the air, German industries were maintaining production in many areas including artillery, airplanes and tanks. The German's defense had changed radically in character and spirit. Units all along the front were standing to fight. Introduction of the new jet-propelled plane gave additional cause for optimism for stability in the air.

However, Adolph Hitler knew he could maintain this line of defense for only so long. He also knew that in order to succeed, he had to reverse the tide of battle and regain the initiative lost since the landings at Normandy. Hitler developed a daring, reckless and yet brilliant plan to launch a major counteroffensive through the Ardennes Forest area of Belgium and Luxembourg.

The attack would strike with the force of those magnificent blitzkriegs that had won him most of Europe during 1939 and 1940. His plan was to catch the over-confident Americans and British by surprise, send their armies reeling in retreat, recapture the port of Antwerp and cutoff the British army and annihilate it or push it into the sea as they had done at Dunkirk in 1940.

Elaborate deception plans were made, as the element of surprise was the key to success. So, while the American and British were preoccupied with attacks in other areas, the Germans amassed a force of 12 Panzer divisions, 16 new Volksgrenadier (people's infantry) divisions and 12 artillery corps in the Ardennes. Our intelligence somehow managed to remain completely ignorant of the German preparations.

The Ardennes region is rugged, difficult terrain with high plateaus intersected by many deep valleys. The limited road network made supply for the defenders difficult, and even more difficult for advancing attackers. At the time, the Ardennes region was considered a "quiet area" where newly arrived divisions were indoctrinated to combat and battle-weary veterans would be sent for rest and recuperation. Its 85-mile front was thinly held. The 99th Division, an inexperienced outfit that had been on line less than a month, defended the region on the north. South of them in the Losheim Gap, a seven-mile pass on the northern end of the Schnee Eifel, was the 14th Calvary Group, a battalion-size mechanized reconnaissance unit.

On the Schnee Eifel (Snow Mountain) ridge was the newly arrived 106th Division. At their southern flank was the 28th Infantry Division, which had suffered more than 6,100 casualties in the Huertgen Forest. Next, was a battalion of the green 9th Armored Division and the 4th Infantry Division, which also suffered 6,000 casualties in the battle of the Huertgen Forest.

The 106th Division had two regiments, the 422nd and 423rd, perched on the Schnee Eifel while the third regiment, the 424th was positioned at the base of the ridge south of the Alf River. From the day they had replaced the 2nd Division on December 12, 1944, the 106th Division's commanders were dissatisfied with the defensive positions they were ordered to occupy. Efforts to obtain authority to make desired adjustments went without success. Roads running westward were at both ends of the ridge and they converged at the village of Schonberg. Attacking forces could envelope the Schnee Eifel and link up at Schonberg, cutting off the forces on the ridge. That is exactly what happened. Four days following the arrival of the 106th, the Germans launched their attack at 0530 on December 16, 1944 and before their preparatory artillery shelling had quieted, two Volksgrenadier regiments had surged through the

195

Losheim Gap and by mid morning were three miles behind the 422nd Regiment's northern flank.

On the southern end of the ridge, a Volksgrenadier regiment streamed up the valley of the Alf River, overrunning the 423rd's anti-tank company and began buffeting the 424th Infantry that had already begun to withdraw. The German advance closed around the southern end of the Schnee Eifel and by nightfall of the first day of battle, the two regiments of the 106th Division on the ridge were in great peril. At 0830 on December 18, 1944, enemy infantry forces linked with a German tank column and the 422nd and the 423rd Regiments were surrounded and cutoff.

Ken Barnes was there. Newly arrived at the front, this was his baptism under fire. Now, more than sixty years following those fateful days, his memory is still sharp enough to recall many events of the four days of fighting that preceded his capture and the months following.

Ken Barnes's Story:

I grew up in the city of Baltimore and graduated from Baltimore's Polytechnic Institute with a specialty in mechanical engineering. I had selected German as my required foreign language never realizing then how useful knowledge of the language would be in the near future. My older brother Ted had enlisted in the Marine Corps shortly before my Dad died suddenly in July 1942. That left me as sole support for my widowed mother and younger brother Calvin. Following two six-month deferments, I was twenty years old when I was inducted into the United States Army on March 31, 1944 and sent to Camp Blanding, Florida to begin 17-weeks of strenuous, rigorous training to become a combat infantryman specializing in heavy weapons such as the 60 and 81mm mortars and the bazooka. Following completion of the training, I transferred, to the 106th Infantry Division at Camp Atterbury, Indiana. The 106th was activated in 1943, and after undergoing standard infantry training, it was ready for combat in early 1944. However, units already overseas were badly in need of individual replacements and the 106th and other newly formed divisions were cannibalized for replacements. By the time I arrived, most of the enlisted men there had little more than basic infantry training. Our training during our six-week stay at Atterbury focused on honing our infantryman skills and developing the teamwork needed in combat but time was of the essence.

In mid-October 1944, the 106th Division deployed en masse to Europe on two ships. The former luxury liner *Queen Elizabeth* and the four-stack ocean liner *Aquitania* departed New York harbor and a week later reached Greenock, Scotland. We spent the following six weeks near the town of Bancroft, England where we again honed our marksmanship skills and received tactical training in combat situations. Our morale was high. We were ready and anxious to join the fight. The war was going well for the allied forces and we wanted to be a part of it.

We arrived at the French port of LeHavre in the first week of December and set up bivouac in Rouen. After several miserable days in the rain, we were loaded onto the versatile deuce-and-a-half (two and a half ton) trucks for a two-day, 270-mile motor trek through Amiens, France and Brussels, Belgium to the front. We arrived at Saint Vith on December 10, 1944 and, under the cover of heavy fog that blanketed the area, began immediately relieving the 2nd Infantry Division from their posts along the Schnee Eifel, one regiment at a time; man for man, and gun for gun. By December 12, 1944, the 106th Division assumed full responsibility for the sector.

The division's area of responsibility extended from the north at the Losheim Gap, southward through the Schnee Eifel ridge to the southern nose of the ridge.

From December 11 to 15, 1944, the weather was cold and damp and temperatures hovered around freezing. Snow, sleet and rain fell intermittently maintaining 6 to 12 inches of snow over the area. The enemy's concealment was good; pillboxes provided excellent command posts and allowed German soldiers to avoid some of the discomfits of the cold and snow. Each night, one or more enemy patrols would infiltrate through regiment lines resulting in some minor firefights. I recall the eeriness of the first night as I was assigned guard duty from midnight to 0400. Footsteps on the crested snow reverberated throughout the woods and I was sure that an enemy patrol was in the area. Several times I gave the challenge to "identify yourself" only to be greeted by the sounds of silence. I was never so happy to be relieved and able to crawl into my sleeping bag inside the two-man pup tent I shared with another GI.

Supplies were generally adequate with the exception of winter combat gear. Ammunition was closely controlled, particularly mortar and heavy weapons ammo. Only half of the daily-allotted supply was authorized for use; the other half remained under regimental controls loaded on unit vehicles and kept near regimental supply points. Communications were provided through existing wire lines to all the units and Division and regimental command posts. Radios had been issued to all units in England but since radio silence had been imposed, there was no opportunity to test or calibrate properly. Patrolling was active on both sides.

On the nights of December 14 and 15, 1944, patrols reported unusual wheeled and track vehicle movements.

VIII Corps intelligence commented that the sounds were probably German Divisions making a change.

The First Day

On 16 December 1944 at 0530, an outpost guard called to report unusual flashes of blue light throughout the region. Moments later the shells came bursting in. The German counteroffensive through the Ardennes began with heavy artillery fire interspersed with mortar fire and rocket launchers whose projectiles made a screeching noise the GIs nicknamed them "screaming meemies." While the artillery attack was taking place, two Volksgrenadier regiments surged through the gap on the 422nd's northern flank and easily overran the 14th Calvary Group. By mid-morning they were three miles behind the 422nd's northern flank. On the southern end of the Schnee Eifel, a Volksgrenadier regiment stormed up the valley of the Alf River overrunning the 423rd's anti-tank company. During this early battle, the 423rd used up much of its available heavy weapons ammunition. The Germans formed a fishhook around the southern flank threatening the exposed regiments from the south as well as the north.

When the attack began, my battalion, the 2nd Battalion, 423rd Infantry, was in Division reserve near Saint Vith. The suddenness of the German attack delayed critical decisions until the upper echelons could get a better understanding of the strength and direction of the attack. It was not until the afternoon of the 16th, that the 2nd Battalion was dispatched to Schonberg with orders to set up defenses around the village and block the roads and hold this important road center. This was the doorway out for the men on the Schnee Eifel. Yet, no sooner had we dug in and prepared our defense, when we were ordered to move again and support the 589th Field Artillery Battalion, which was under attack on the left flank of the 422nd Regiment.

199

We moved out in blackout conditions through sleet and snow, got lost and did not reach our objective until 0100 the next day. There was little to do but dig in again.

By nightfall of the first day, the 422nd and 423rd Regiments were in great peril. Artillery fire destroyed the telephone wire lines and the Germans were jamming our radio signals. Communications between units and command posts ranged between difficult and impossible. The VIII Corps commander sent word that ammunition, food and medical supplies would be dropped and advised that the 7th Armored Division was racing from Holland to provide relief. However, he emphasized that if the two regiments could not secure their flanks, they should vacate the ridge and pull back toward Saint Vith. In army tradition, that decision usually rested with the Division's Commanding Officer.

The Second Day

At dawn, the next morning of December 17, 1944, while protecting the displacement of the 589th Field Artillery Battalion we became heavily engaged with the German forces. Ammunition was running low and I was part of a squad of men ordered to locate the regimental ammo supply but we could not locate it. Some units of the 589th were able to get through the German's defenses and made their way back to Saint Vith. However, the larger part of the battalion was unable to break through the German resistance to the west, so our two battalions fell back into the Schnee Eifel. The 423rd Regiment now had all its battalions together and notified the Division Command Post that "We will hold the perimeter. Drop ammunition, food and medical supplies."

Meanwhile the 7th Armored Division, who was rushing to our assistance, was caught in a massive traffic jam caused by so many retreating units. The Division's tanks literally pushed trucks and other vehicles off the road in their desperate attempt to reach the two trapped regiments. Despite Herculean efforts, they would not arrive in time. Later that afternoon, enemy pressure slackened. At this point, our regiment had suffered about 250 casualties. We were critically low of mortar and artillery ammunition. Rations per man were cut in half. None of us had slept in two days but our spirits were bolstered when word was received that an airdrop would be accomplished the next day. The 423rd Infantry would hold.

The Third Day

Early on December 18, we received communication that a Panzer Regimental Combat Team was advancing on Schonberg and it posed a threat to Saint Vith. The 422nd and 423rd Regiments were ordered to proceed to positions south of Schonberg, dig in and engage the approaching enemy and delay his advance until reinforcements could be brought in. The promised air drop of ammo and supplies had not been received and we were critically low on ammo and medical supplies, but orders were orders so we had to make do with what we had, which wasn't very much. Both regiments moved out in unison and we had not progressed very far when we were hit by a barrage of mortar fire and our advance ground to a halt. Another radio message brought orders for us to make our way through Schonberg then back to the Saint Vith area. This was easier said than done. At this point, the 423rd could only muster about half of its rifle strength and our mortar ammo was nonexistent. We changed direction and were able to advance to about 800 yards from the village where a hail of heavy small arms and mortar fire stopped us again. Casualties began to mount. In all units, small arms ammunition was nearly exhausted. As the shelling continued, we burrowed deeper into our holes and prayed that the promised relief would soon arrive. Our situation was desperate.

The Last Day

Fear robbed us of sleep again that night and as December 19 dawned, we were cold, hungry and completely exhausted. This was our fourth consecutive day in combat without sleep. A low fog blanketed the area as we emerged from our foxholes like ghosts from their crypts, and with little remaining ammunition, we began another advance toward Schonberg. We knew we had to move or be doomed to die in our foxholes. I can remember that final day as if it were yesterday. We were trudging through the woods when we reached a firewall opening. As we began to queue up, Mark Andersen, a buddy from Minnesota was no more than twenty feet in front of me when a shell that struck a tree, exploded and hit him dead on. Some fragments of shrapnel struck me and I fell to the ground dazed but not seriously wounded.

We were again ordered to make our way across the firewall and as soon as we began, the Germans laid down a direct line of fire and several more men were hit. We jumped back into the woods. There was no way to get across the firewall and live. It was nearing dusk and, strange as it seems, the enemy's tracer bullets that sped by mesmerized me but I was shaken from my stupor when a bullet tore through the front of my field jacket only inches from a grenade carried in my left upper pocket. The bullet singed my skin near the armpit and I fell to the ground again. By some miracle, I had survived two near-death incidents and as I lay on the ground, I thought to myself, "By what miracle am I still alive?"

Since we could not make it past the firewall, we fell back into the woods. The Germans now directed artillery fire at us and we suffered more casualties. As the shelling and casualties continued to increase, both regimental commanders acknowledged that our situation was hopeless and it became apparent that further resistance was nothing more than a useless sacrifice of lives. Therefore, to save their men from almost certain slaughter, they ordered the troops to surrender. We heard our Commanding Officer, Colonel Charles Cavender announce over a speaker, "Men of the 423rd we are surrounded. Throw down your weapons and come forward with your hands raised over your heads." We thought this was a German trick and at first, we refused. As bad as our situation was, it was inconceivable that we were surrendering. Many of the officers and enlisted men, expressed bitter disappointed for this decision. We truly believed that relief would soon come and we were willing to continue fighting in any way until help arrived. I did not want to become a prisoner of war. I was prepared to die in those woods.

Then a German soldier carrying a machine pistol and an American GI carrying a white flag came into our area and we knew the order was valid. We broke down our weapons and threw them away. Then we moved into the firewall clearing and German soldiers came forward and removed any ammunition, grenades or other weapons we may have been carrying. They next went through our personal items and watches, rings, wallets, money, cigarettes and other things of value quickly disappeared. Some men lost their gloves and a few were forced to exchange boots with German soldiers. It all occurred rather quickly and we began our march eastward into Germany.

Author's Note: A report issued on January 18, 1945 indicated that the 106th Infantry Division had suffered 8,663 casualties including 416 killed in action, 1,256 wounded and 7,001 missing, presumed prisoners of war.

We marched in the dark toward Prum where we were placed in a fenced cattle yard. That was to be our home for the night of December 19. The moon glistened on the crusted snow and we could see that a number of GIs had preceded us. Mitch Boulden and I met during induction at Fort George Meade, Maryland. We became friends immediately and were at each other's side constantly during our entire military experience. Now, as prisoners of war we gave comfort to each other. We selected a place where we could lie and huddle together to help ward off the freezing temperature. I was wearing layers of clothes – my long johns, woolen fatigues, field jacket, knit cap and I had retained my gloves. As I looked around, I saw that a number of men wearing their GI overcoats and how I now regretted that I had abandoned mine because it was too cumbersome. It would have been a great ground cover or blanket now. Before the attack effort, we discarded our cumbersome backpacks losing access to extra rations, several extra pair of socks and other sundry items. In retrospect, had we had them at the time of capture, the German soldiers would have confiscated these items along with everything else they took from us the day. Because the past several days we were emotionally and physically drained and so exhausted, we quickly fell fast asleep on our snow mattress.

Shortly after daylight on the 20th, we were again on the march. Our ranks seemed to have swelled a hundred fold as I looked back and saw nothing but columns of GIs trudging along. Some curious German citizens stood by the road and watched as we passed by. A few pelted us with snowballs. We marched all day, approximately 40 kilometers (25 miles) until we reached the marshaling yards at Gerolstein. Boxcars were stretched along the track as far as the eye could see, awaiting our arrival. Before being loaded onto the boxcars, the Germans fed us soup and a slice of dark bread. Men who did not have a canteen cup used their steel helmets as a soup bowl.

The World War I vintage boxcars dubbed "40 & 8s," held eight horses or forty men but at least sixty-eight men were crammed into our car. The floor was covered with filthy straw and no sanitary facilities were provided, not even a bucket. The men jostled with each other to find a spot where at least they could sit down. I found a spot below a 5"x 20" slide opening and after we began moving, I was able to look out and read the location signs as we slowed and pass through towns en route and kept the group somewhat informed of our whereabouts. My friend Boulden was at my side during this ordeal.

In the opposite corner of the car, a hole carved in the boxcar's floorboard became our latrine for the remainder of the trip. Getting from one end of the car to the other was no easy task, as the men grumbled as we stepped over and sometimes on them. We left Gerolstein on December 21 and passed through Bonn and Koblenz before we reached Limburg, another major rail center, on Christmas Eve. That night became one of the nights of terror I associate with this saga. British fighter-bombers bombed and strafed the marshaling yards not knowing that many of the targeted boxcars held defenseless American prisoners of war.

Locked inside the boxcars, we could hear the sounds of machine-gun fire and exploding bombs that reverberated throughout our boxcar. Suddenly, the door to our car slid open and the men began to scramble out looking for shelter. Boulden and I decided to remain on the train, believing it was safer inside the car. Our car was not hit, but we could see that several of the cars had suffered casualties. Following the raid, bodies were scattered on the siding next to the now nearly empty cars. Word spread that enlisted men and officers were killed during that raid. We could never verify an actual count but the event did amplify how defenseless and vulnerable we actually were.

The German guards collected the prisoners and reloaded them into the boxcars. I have since learned that there was a POW camp outside Limburg and, I understand that some of the men tried to gain entry into this camp and remain there. They figured that anything else was better than being crammed into these boxcars with no food or water and subject to the "friendly fire" of Allied aircraft. We finally got underway on December 27 and passed through the cities of Frankfurt, Erfurt and Leipzig before arriving at Stalag IVB – Muhlberg the evening of December 29. We had traveled eight days and nights without food or water.

We were unloaded from the boxcars and ushered into a heated building. Most of the men were in poor physical condition due to lack of nourishment and being locked in such cramped quarters for so long. As we entered the warm building, some of the men began to lose consciousness. After we were all inside and the men who had passed out revived, our processing began.

We had to strip and moved to a room where some guards showered us with what seemed to be a steam hose. After being cold for so long, the warm moist heat rejuvenated our aching bones. After we dried off, we lined up to receive a tetanus shot administered in the chest just above the heart. We then dressed in the same soiled clothing we had been wearing at the time of capture, assigned a POW number and a POW dog tag. All our clothing was stamped with indelible ink with the form of an equilateral triangle so that we would be easily identified in the event of an escape. Finally, we were given a metal cup filled with hot soup and a slice of black bread. On New Years Eve, we received one Red Cross parcel for each two men.

At this time, I experienced what life was like in a regular Stalag. I recall standing roll call morning and evening. Some days, the guards rushed us out so hastily that we did not have time to put on our boots and had to stand on the cold icy ground in our stocking feet.

Breakfast was a slice of dark bread and ersatz coffee. Its taste was bitter but at least it was hot. The one hot meal we received daily was served at noontime and was usually tasteless potato soup and a slice of dark, sour pumpernickel bread. Our diet was about 200 calories per day and we all began to lose weight rapidly.

On the home front, my mother Lela M. Barnes received a telegram on January 11, 1945 stating, "The Secretary of War desires to express his deep regret that your son Private First Class Ralph K. Barnes has been reported missing in action since 21 December 1944 in Germany." This was followed by another letter dated 13 January 1945 explaining what "missing in action" meant. Mom immediately notified the rest of our family and my sweetheart Catherine Cooney. The family was all horrified. My oldest brother launched a series of letters to the War Department trying to find out more about my status. No information was available until my Mom received a telegram dated April 11, 1945 that I was now a prisoner of war of the German government. There was a collective sigh of relief that I was alive and the Allied Forces seemed destined for victory. There was nothing more anyone could do but hope and pray.

On January 10, Mitch Boulden and I, and thirty-three others were selected to work in a Gbr. Mueller Deckenfabrick (Mueller Bros. Blanket Factory) in the town of Lobau, located about 50 miles east of Muhlberg near the Polish border. Because of my high-school German, I served as interpreter for the group. We were housed in a large metal building with double-decked bunks and a latrine at one end. The facilities were definitely better here than at the Stalag and the quality and quantity of food improved. We occasionally got oatmeal for breakfast, and soup and bread for our noontime meal. Boulden and I worked the night shift and our job was to feed bolts of wool into a roller device that fuzzed the wool. There were a number of other prisoners and forced laborers working at this factory including Russian, Mongolian, Polish and others including a considerable number of women. Life became routine but tolerable.

On March 13, our guards ordered us to collect our few belongings and prepare to march. We did not know why but surmised that the Russian Army was advancing from the East. We walked about 20km and boarded a train that took us through Dresden. The city was destroyed by allied air raids between February 13 and 15, 1945, in what was to become one of the most controversial episodes of the Second World War. Despite the total loss, the Germans had the rail system operable within a week and the rail yards were bombed again on March 2nd by 406 B-17 bombers from the U.S. Eighth Air Force. I will never forget the destruction I witnessed as our train passed through.

The city still smoldered a month following the devastating raid and decaying bodies were still strewn among the extensive rubble and bomb craters were being used as mass graves. There were not enough able-bodied survivors to bury all the dead and American POWs who were encamped in Dresden, some were from the 106th Division, were given this grizzly task. It took more than three months to bury or cremate the estimated 25-35,000 dead.

Hohnstein is a small town on the Elbe River about ten miles southeast of Dresden. The prison camp there, Stalag IVA, was a work camp. We arrived on the14th of March. This was a typical prisoner of war camp with barbed-wire fences, watchtowers, guards and dogs but it was on a much smaller scale holding only about 200 prisoners. It was located on top a small mountain. The next day, we went immediately to work repairing bombed rail lines. To reach the damaged tracks, we had to descend 332 steps down the mountain and cross the Elbe River on a barge. Following completion of our day's work, we again crossed the Elbe on the barge and climbed up those same 332 steps to reach the road back to camp. There they fed us a bowl of thin potato soup and a slice of German dark sour bread. The work was arduous and climbing up the side of that mountain everyday without proper nourishment began to take its toll. Starvation is insidious. Some of the men became so malnourished that they became seriously ill and several died. I personally helped bury three of them.

As we struggled to survive, we began to hear the roar and rumble of artillery in the east and we knew the Russians were advancing in our direction. About May 7, the Germans broke camp and announced that they were going to march us toward the American lines. We marched southeast for several days on winding roads that were loaded with German troops and civilians carrying their worldly possessions. Our group reached the town of Prossen and the next day we awoke to find our guards had left. For the first time in five months, we were no longer under the control of German guards. At first, we were unsure as to what we should do. Small groups of men began to drift away in different directions. Mitch Boulden, George Sampson and I decided to take off on our own and try to find the American lines.

My German speaking skills began to pay dividends. Civilians informed us that American forces were in Czechoslovakia so we began walking southward. We walked about thirty miles when we approached several homes, identified ourselves and asked for something to eat. We did this in each town we came to. They did not have much but usually gave us something. Some families let us sleep in their barns at night.

On May 8, 1945, Germany surrendered. The war in Europe was officially over but there were still pockets of resistance and we had to remain cautious. Russian troops began arriving in tanks and other armored vehicles. There were a number of women troops among them. From my viewpoint, the Russians treated us with courtesy. They questioned us to make sure we were truly American POWs and then let us go on our way.

We were unsure as to what our next steps should be when we learned that Patton's 3rd Army had advanced to Pilsen which we were told was about fifty miles south of where we were. Mitch, George and I decided that was our destination. As we made our way, we continued to stop at houses along the way looking for food and a place to sleep that night. At one farmhouse, a German woman invited us into her home. I believe her family surname was Werny. She was very gracious and told me that I reminded her of her own son and tearfully related that all five of her sons were killed in the war. Her only surviving child was her 17-year-old daughter who lived at home with her. She was fearful that Russian soldiers would rape her daughter, and she begged us to stay at her home and protect her daughter. Although we were anxious to get moving, we stayed at this home for four days. While we were there, no Russian soldier approached the house.

To show her gratitude and appreciation for our protection, the mother gave me her Mother's Cross (the Cross of Honor of the German Mother) awarded to German mothers who had five or more children. She said that since I was one of five children myself, the medal would have special significance. Her medal was a silver cross with the inscription *Der Deutschen Mutter* encircling a black enamel Nazi swastika emblem on a white enamel field. The reverse was plain save for the date 16 Dezember 1938 followed by a facsimile of

Adolph Hitler's signature. Whenever a member of the Hitler Youth met a mother displaying her award worn on a blue ribbon around her neck, he was to snap to attention and give a brisk salute of "Heil Hitler." When Mrs. Werny gave me the medal, she expressed her profound hatred for Adolph Hitler and his regime.

It was time to move on. We somehow learned that a German Hospital Train was to depart the town of Karbitz, Czechoslovakia and head westward toward Teplitz. Maps that we had acquired showed that this would get us closer to Pilsen. We confiscated several bikes and had an adventurous bike ride through the Czech countryside before reaching the hospital train. When we boarded the train, I spoke with some Germans in my elementary German and they forewarned: "You are destined to have war with the Russians. You might as well stay here and finish it now."

After arriving at Teplitz, we changed to an American train and on May 18, 1945, we arrived at Karlsbad. We were met by several American soldiers, provided breakfast and boarded a bus that afternoon for the army base at Pilsen. We arrived the next morning and were taken to a Recovered Allied Military Personnel Center set up for Allied former POWs. At the Center we were registered, deloused, received a cursory medical exam and fed C & K rations.

After a few days, we were transported to the airport where we boarded C-47s and flown to Rhimes, France and then on to Camp Lucky Strike near LeHavre, France. This was the last processing center we would go to before boarding a ship for the good old USA. We had a soothing hot shower, and issued new fatigues and other clothing, mess gear and blankets. We spent more than two weeks at Lucky Strike waiting our turn to board a ship for transport home. Finally, on June 12, we were alerted to stand by, turn in any French Francs we held and prepare for shipment. We were trucked to LeHavre and boarded the *Admiral Mayo* and on June 14, 1945, we finally were on our way home.

While we were at Camp Lucky Strike, my Mom received another telegram from the War Department dated 29 May 1945 advising that I had been returned to Military control. It arrived before my radiotelegraph message that read, "Dear Mom Am safe well will see you soon love and best wishes to all." (signed) Pfc. Ralph K. Barnes.

We disembarked at Boston on June 21, 1945 and I arrived home two days later. In the month following my repatriation, I had regained 45 pounds and now weighed about 160 pounds. Following a 90-day furlough, I went to Miami, Florida for recuperation and then ordered to report to Fort Knox, Kentucky at the end of September. While on the 90-day leave, the war in the Pacific ended on August 8th. My wife-to-be Catherine and I joyously celebrated this historic event with throngs of delirious people in downtown Baltimore.

On 19 December 1945, I received my honorable discharge with the rank of Corporal from the U.S. Army, exactly one year from the date of my capture. I returned to work at F.X. Hooper Company and my beloved Catherine M. Cooney agreed to be my wife. We were married at St. Bernard's Church Rectory on January 26, 1947. I progressed in my job and Catherine and I were blessed with four "baby boomer" children – Clay, William, Joan and Linda.

Unfortunately, my nightmares did not end following my return home. At times, I would kick and scream in my sleep and thankfully, Catherine was there to comfort and calm me. I sought treatment at the VA for a variety of ailments but they virtually ignored me. It was not until the year 2000 when I finally received my disability awards from the VA that I began to be treated with respect and dignity.

Catherine passed away in January 2002. Recently, I married Beverly Beckstrom Gallen who lived four doors up the street from me when we were teenagers. Bev and I now live in Cockeysville, Maryland enjoying our golden years, our home, our families and friends and especially our five grandchildren – Benjamin, Zachary, Natalie, Gina and Ashley.

In closing, I would like to pay homage to G. Mitchell Boulden. Mitch and I were inducted together at Fort George G. Meade in Maryland and we became constant buddies from the time we met. We went through basic infantry training together at Camp Blanding, Florida, assigned to the 106th Infantry Division at Camp Atterbury, crossed the Atlantic to Scotland and England, entered France and trucked to the Ardennes. We were always in the same Regiment, Battalion, Company, Platoon and Squad. We were together as we battled the Germans from 16 December to our capture on the 19th. Together we suffered through the trials and tribulations of being a prisoner of war giving comfort and encouragement to each other only as good friends can do. Mitch Boulden was six years my senior and was the father of a young son when inducted. He had also been a fireman for several years. Since I was a "wet behind the ears" kid of twenty-one, I looked to Mitch for guidance and advice on many things.

Through it all, I never knew he kept a small diary and pencil in his boot. Following his death in the '90s, his wife Ruth mentioned the diary and she had it safely secured in a safe deposit box. She graciously allowed me to reproduce a copy. It contains relevant and realistic information from the time we were inducted, assigned to the 106th Division, the days prior to our capture, our POW experience, including the train route from

Gerolstein to Muhlberg, then until the time of our repatriation.

Following our return home and the 90-day furlough we both received, we went different ways and eventually lost touch with each other except for holiday cards and infrequent telephone calls. I want to use this opportunity to tell Ruth Boulden and her children that I cannot imagine how I could have ever survived the ordeal of captivity without Mitch Boulden's strength and courage and I am forever grateful that I was his friend.

I would also like to recognize George C. Sampson. When inducted, George was thirty years old and the father of two children. It demonstrates how deep the need for manpower was at that time. George, who is now 90-years old, was able to keep up with the younger men during the rigorous training and other exercises and he maintained his sense of humor and sense of duty throughout the ordeals on the front, in the blanket factory, our trek to freedom and Camp Lucky Strike. I am privileged, thankful and indebted to him for being a wartime buddy and a longtime friend.

Beverly and Ken Barnes, 2005

Gilbert Eugene Stover, 1943

GILBERT E. STOVER, JR.

*"Semi-conscious, I could think of nothing else other
than to stay alive and kept repeating to myself,
"Pull your ripcord, pull your ripcord."*

EVEN IN HIS MID-SEVENTIES, Gilbert Stover
has retained the rugged athletic look he must
have had in 1940 when he was a halfback on the
Arcadia football team that defeated the Southern
Greyhounds 65-0 to win the Baltimore City
Championship. I am certain he played football with the
same tenacity he displayed during our interview and that
carried him through the crucible of the Second World
War. He's a tough guy, the kind you want to have on
your side during a fight. He also has a soft spot.
Memories of his experiences bring out emotions that are
sacredly reserved for those who suffered through the
ordeal of war.

Gilbert was nineteen years old when he was drafted
and selected for the Air Forces. His basic training began
at Training Center #9 in Miami Beach, Florida.
Consistent with his competitive nature and athletic
prowess, he had hoped to be a fighter pilot, and had he
not washed out on the "bends test" part of his physical
exam, he would have been a good fighter pilot. All
airmen who could not meet the stringent requirements of
pre-flight training were trained as aircraft armourer-
gunners including a twenty-week course in operation
and maintenance of aircraft armaments. Gil Stover was
given this training at Buckley and Lowry Fields in
Denver, Colorado, and Tyndall Field, Florida.

Graduating September 14, 1943, he was proud to receive his Aerial-Gunner Wings and the Army Air Forces Marksmanship Badge (Expert) with four silver bars for rifle, machine-gun, pistol, and aerial gunner along with sergeant stripes.

Flight crew training took place in Lincoln, Nebraska, aboard a B-24 Liberator, *Sinful Cynthia,* named in tribute to the pilot's new bride. In preparation for their overseas assignment, they flew from Lincoln to Miami, Florida, to Trinidad, South America, then across the Atlantic to Dakar, on the West Coast of Africa, and then north to Tunisia where they received additional combat flight crew training. In March 1944, they reached their destination, Cerignola, Italy.

The 15th Air Force was newly constituted and began operations in the Mediterranean Theatre on November 2, 1943. It was composed of five bombardment wings and the 306th Fighter Wing. The 484th Bomb Group, one of three bomb groups assigned to the 49th Bomb Wing was made up of four bomb squadrons – 824, 825, 826 and 827. Sgt. Stover was assigned to the 827th Bomb Squadron. Colonel William B. Keene and Deputy CO Lt. Colonel Chester E. Busch led the 484th Bomb Group. Their planes were recognized by a "red bow tie" combat insignia carried on the tail assembly. From February 1944 to May 1945, the 484th flew 208 missions from the Torretta Air Base in Italy.

The absence of a fixed, limited tour of combat missions contributed significantly to aircrew anxiety and emotional breakdowns; however, in March 1943, the 8th Air Force operating in the European Theatre of Operations (ETO) directed that bomber crews should be limited to a tour of twenty-five combat missions. The Distinguished Flying Cross was awarded to all 8th Air Force crewmembers who completed their tour of duty; however, policies regarding combat missions differed widely from one theatre to another. For example, in the Mediterranean Theatre, where the 15th Air Force operated, crews had to fly between fifty and sixty missions. Sergeant Stover had flown thirty-one missions, including bomber runs over the coast of France in preparation for D-Day. On his thirty-second mission his plane was shot down and he was seriously wounded.

Gilbert Stover tells his story:

On June 13, 1944, we were one of thirty-seven B-24 bombers heavily loaded with maximum tonnage of bombs that set course for the rail center and marshaling yards at Munich, Germany. Our secondary target was the marshaling yards at Innsbruck, Austria.

As we approached Munich, approximately fifty Messerschmitt 109 and Focke-Wulfe 190 fighters attacked our formation, and as the nose gunner, I had a ringside seat of the action. Our massive firepower in a tight formation proved to be insufficient protection against attacking fighters. The first enemy force swept over the top of the Bomber formation and commenced an air-to-air bombing attack while the second enemy wave subjected the bombers to heavy rocket fire. After expending their bombs and rockets, the enemy fighters continued to relentlessly attack the bomber formation in a desperate effort to break up the formation and destroy the bomber groups.

I watched the enemy fighters come in on the front of the formation. Seven rows of seven German fighters each flashed between the bombers, with guns blazing, narrowly avoided collisions with our planes. At the same time, we were subjected to heavy flak from the anti-aircraft guns on the ground and often both our planes and the German fighters were hit, and some were going down.

Despite the fighter attacks and subsequent intense and heavy enemy anti-aircraft fire, the bomber formation maintained its integrity and continued on over the primary target, but a dense smoke screen had blanketed the rail center and marshaling yards. Near perfect visibility is essential for high altitude precision bombing. Finding conditions unsuitable for a successful attack, and even though enemy air and ground opposition had seriously crippled several ships, we set course to the alternate target, the marshaling yards at Innsbruck, Austria. With wounded men remaining tenaciously at their stations, the severely crippled aircraft were held skillfully within the protective formation. The Bomber Groups passed through another heavy barrage of intense and accurate anti-aircraft fire, and despite the severity of the opposition, the run to Innsbruck was successful with all the bombs concentrated in the immediate target area.

Second Lieutenant Edward Eibs piloted our plane. We had taken several hits and as we neared the target, we discovered that the bomb bay door hydraulic system was damaged and the doors would not open. Making a gutsy call, he ordered the rack to be released and dropped our bombs on the doors, opening them down beneath the plane.

Shortly after we left the target, another plane piloted by Major Halderman was hit and it began to lose altitude. German fighters began to swarm around it. ME 109's and FW-190's attacked any aircraft out of the protection of the formation. Our pilot radioed that he was dropping down to assist, but the Major ordered that we stay in formation. He said that he and the tail gunner were the only two people aboard still alive and he had ordered the tail gunner to bail out. He added that he had taken a shell through his hips and was unable to move. I watched in horror as the tail gunner bailed out and moments later, the plane with Major Halderman and the dead crewmen aboard, exploded in the air. I later met the tail gunner, Bill Hogan in prison camp.

Suddenly, one of our engines was hit by flak and the prop had to be feathered. The plane began to lose altitude fast, taking us out of the formation. Damaged bombers outside the formation are easy meat. Seven or eight fighters swarmed all over us and we took another hit. In spite of that, we shot down several more fighters, for a total of seven kills that day. Six to eight American bombers were lost on this raid. As the battle continued, we took another hit and Lt. Eibs ordered, "Ready to bail out," but on the intercom in the front of the plane all that we heard was "Bail out." Lt. Prodgers, the navigator who was positioned directly in back of the nose gun, went out the nose wheel opening. Either flak from the ground or fire from a German fighter hit the nose turret as I attempted to exit, and I was hit in the face by metal fragments.

Half dazed and without oxygen, I hooked my parachute on one side only and struggled to bail out by dropping through the nose wheel opening the same as Lt. Prodgers had done. In a B-24, the nose gunner had to vacate the turret in order to clip on his parachute. Semiconscious, I could think of nothing else other than to stay alive and kept repeating to myself, "Pull your ripcord. Pull your ripcord." In my anxiety, I pulled it too quickly and my parachute caught on the opened bomb bay doors, swinging me up into the ball turret guns and knocking me out. I finally fell free, but my parachute had lost a four or five foot section ripped out of its middle. As I descended, the air rushing past caused me to momentarily regain consciousness and I remember passing other parachutes, both American and German, as if they were standing still.

Upon hitting the ground, I was again knocked unconscious and remained in that state for eighteen days from 13 June, to 1 July, 1944. When I finally awoke, both of my eyes were bandaged closed and I really thought I was blind. I learned I was in an all-German hospital. When the bandages were removed, I was relieved that I could see and a German nurse was attending me. She said that the doctors had operated on me and removed flak from my right eye, and my jaw had been broken. When I arrived at the hospital, they removed my uniform and dressed me in a hospital gown. While I was unconscious, the attendants believed I was a German fighter pilot, but when they learned that I was an American 'terrorflieger' they put a guard at my door and I was no longer treated quite so well. I remained at this hospital for two or three weeks before being transferred to a POW hospital and prison at Obermassfeld, Germany, where captured American and New Zealand doctors took care of wounded prisoners.

When my wounds were reasonably healed, I was sent to an interrogation center in Frankfurt where I was interrogated for about three weeks. The Nazis were both nasty and nice. They wanted information about my pilot, crewmember positions, missions I had flown, the number of bombers that flew in each mission, and other details. We were fed only bread and water; pushed around roughly, some of which I deserved, and enticed with the offer of spending a night with a woman. During the interrogation, I began to feel better when I realized that they had identified my original crew and not the crew I had been flying with when I was captured. This told me that neither Lt. Prodgers nor I had given them information they were seeking. Following interrogation, I was transferred to the prison camp at Nuremberg, where conditions were deplorable but we made the best of the situation. Food was poor and there was never enough of it, but Red Cross parcels were a lifesaver.

The Americans were closing in so we were moved again to another camp, Stalag VII B at Moosburg. I was one of the lucky ones who were placed on a train for the transfer. The Germans put the letters "POW" on the top of the train, but we were still strafed by our own planes. In the confusion of this attack, three of us grabbed a rifle and took off into the nearby woods, but very quickly SS Troops closed in and recaptured us. We surrendered without resistance and they took us directly to the Moosburg prison camp. As time passed, we could see the flash and hear the thunder of artillery in the west and knew the war would soon end. One day all the guards left. We stayed and waited for the American forces to arrive. I was liberated on April, 29, 1945, and felt a great sense of relief. The war was finally over, we had won and I had survived. Losing had been unthinkable.

After returning home on the Liberty Ship *Sea Robin,* I spent another year in the Newton D. Baker hospital at Martinsburg, West Virginia, where plastic surgery and reconstruction of my face hid the physical scars of my wounds. The emotional scars are still with me today.

Gilbert E. Stover, Sr., after a year of medical care, was honorably discharged from the Army Air Forces on April 17, 1946, at the rank of Staff Sergeant. He was twenty-three years old. He was awarded the Air Medal with two Oak Leaf Clusters; Purple Heart Medal; World War II Victory Medal; POW Medal; European, African, Middle-Eastern Campaign Medal with Five Battle Stars; Distinguished Unit Citation* and the Good Conduct Medal.

*The 484th Bomb Group received a Distinguished Unit Citation for gallant action on the 13 June 1944 mission.

Flak Damage - Gil Stover, the gunner was not injured.

Top row:
Holder, Giamette, Hazelton, McKinney, Stover & Hatch
Bottom row: Ingham, Eibs, Prodgers & Taylor

Janet & Gil Stover, Puerto Rico 1969

Walter D. Czawlytko, prior to going overseas, 1943

WALTER D. CZAWLYTKO

War, Sweet War,
What sort of mistress are you
That you can be pursued
By all those beautiful boys?
- Polish Military Folklore

T HE YEAR 1943 was a memorable year for many young Americans but particularly for Walter Czawlytko. War raged throughout the world, his brothers Frank and Bernie were in the US Navy somewhere in the Pacific and another brother, Danny, was serving with the 100th Infantry Division. Walter's concentration was at home. Young and handsome, this strapping six-footer met and fell in love with the very pretty Mary "Marie" Trzcinski, the girl of his dreams whom he vowed silently to someday make his wife. He had found a good job with the Glenn L. Martin Company, and his hopes and aspirations were just beginning to unfold. However, young Walter knew that his plans for the future would have to be temporarily set aside because he soon would be called upon to serve his country. In August, less than two months past his eighteenth birthday, he was inducted into the U.S. Army. Assigned to the Army Air Forces, he trained as an "aerial gunner" on a B-24 Liberator, a heavy bomber.

If 1943 was memorable, 1944 was unforgettable. Nineteen days following his nineteenth birthday, on his second bombing mission, his plane was hit by enemy flak and damaged severely. It went into a tailspin. The entire crew successfully bailed out and German military personnel quickly captured them all, but not before an enraged German woman wounded Walter. He spent nearly the entire next year of his young life suffering the indignity and hardships as a prisoner of war, and survived one of the cruelest episodes ever perpetrated against American prisoners of war, the forced march across Germany.

Walter Czawlytko is a first generation American and proud of his Polish heritage. For more than 120 years, his father's homeland was partitioned, and its territory divided among its three major neighboring countries, Russia, Austria and Prussia. Between 1792 and 1918, the Polish nation vanished from the maps of Europe and Poland was little more than a name.

Walter's father, John, was born about 1883 in the Russian-partitioned sector where brutality and the humiliation of censorship, police surveillance, arrest, imprisonment or exile overbore public life. Generations of young Poles were conscripted into the ranks of the partitioning powers. John Czawlytko served as a foot soldier in the Russian Army in 1903, and demonstrated virtues admired in the individual Polish soldier. Stamina, fortitude under adversity, the ability to improvise, and devotion to cause are traits that won the admiration of comrades in armies wherever Poles served. It was these same traits that obviously passed from John Czawlytko to his children, and gave young Walter the spiritual strength and physical fortitude necessary to face and overcome the terrible ordeal he was about to face.

At age 24, John decided to leave a homeland that offered him little but poverty and oppression, and forge a new life in the United States. Sponsored by his cousin Ignatius Augustnowicz, he came to America and arrived at Baltimore's Locust Point terminal in the year 1907. At six feet six inches tall, he was a giant of a man, but a diminutive Henrietta Ciesla, less than five feet tall, melted his heart. Somehow, they knew immediately that the world was as big as they could make it. They were married at St. Casimir's church and had ten children together. Walter was next to the youngest. Born 10 June 1925, he grew up in Baltimore's Canton area and attended St. Casimir's Parochial School. His faith in God and devotion to the Blessed Mother, instilled in him by his parents, was fortified at school. Faith and devotion continue to be important to him, even today.

Following graduation from St. Casimir's, Walter attended nearby Patterson Park High School. He found employment with the Glenn L. Martin Company, a giant aircraft plant in Baltimore County. Assigned to "base operations," he began to learn the rudimentary tasks of an airport control operator, a position that was likely responsible for his being assigned to the Army Air Force following his induction. His training began at the Air Forces Training Center at Miami Beach, Florida. More than five hundred separate skills were required to ensure the success of a routine bombing mission. Training men to perform these skills in the little time available during wartime was crucial to the successful outcome of the war.

All enlisted men in an aircrew were aerial gunners irrespective of their other specialty. Some trained specifically to be gunners. At the end of the basic training period, Walter transferred to gunnery school at Tyndall Air Force Base in Panama City, Florida. At the conclusion of specialist-gunner training, he went to Westover Air Force Base in Massachusetts for combat crew training on a B-24 Liberator. Crew training on a heavy bomber was a ninety-day program tailored for specific theatres of war. Following completion of training, the crew flew a Liberator from Mitchell Army Air Force Base in New York to Ayr, Scotland, stopping to refuel in Labrador.

This is Walter's story:

We arrived in Scotland on June 6, 1944, D-Day. There was so much excitement in the air. Everyone gathered around radios listening to news of the invasion of fortress Europe. Soon, we were assigned to another B-24 that our pilot named *Abel Mabel* after his wife. Our crew spent five days flying over the Atlantic "shaking the bugs out" of this new plane and gaining valuable in-flight combat training experience. I was the left-wing waist gunner. We flew south to our new base at Horsham St. Faith, in southern England where we were assigned to the 8th Air Force, 96th Combat Wing, 458 Bomb Group, and 755 Bomb Squad.

After supporting the invasion of France, the Air Forces' heavy bombers reverted to their strategic objective to destroy Germany's war-production capabilities. On the morning of June 28, the 96th combat wing departed at 0400 hours for industrial sights west of Berlin. This was my first combat mission. The flight was long and tedious and the crew was nervous and fidgety. The quarters were so close that I stood back-to-back with the right waist gunner. Our electrically heated flying suits restricted our movement. The noise of the B-24's four engines was so loud the crew could not hear each other talk. Like a tourist on his first flight, I was mesmerized as the beauty of the French and then German countryside unfurled. My thoughts kept drifting back and forth between loved ones at home, and what I was about to face. The closer we drew to the target area, the more anxious we all became.

Then suddenly we were under attack by enemy fighter planes. I watched them come. They appeared as specks in the distant sky but grew rapidly as they approached. They flashed between the bombers, guns blazing. We fought back. My gloved hands squeezed the triggers as I blasted away at the fighters with my .50-

inch caliber machine-gun, but I was so scared, I am sure I did not hit anything. The bombers tightened their formation to thwart off more air attacks. This tactic now made us easier targets for the ground flak gunners. The sky lit up like a 4th of July celebration as armor-piercing shells exploded all around us. I watched helplessly as we flew into the firestorm. As quickly as it started, it was over. Once we regained our composure, the crew checked for damages and found nothing major.

We lumbered on toward the target. Dark, puffy veils of smoke again hung in the sky. It was worse than before. I could not believe how anything could fly through it and survive, but we did. I saw several planes hit and drop out of formation, smoke and fire billowing. Frozen with fear, I prayed harder than I had ever prayed before. Somehow, we made it through the flak, dropped our bombs and regrouped for the return run home. On the way back, German fighters were waiting for us. ME109s and FW190s attacked once again. We made it safely through with relatively little damage. I was thankful. We were now combat veterans, young men who had experienced combat, learned the true meaning of fear, witnessed death and destruction, and returned to talk about it. We never wanted to go back.

The Allied Forces were making a concerted attempt to destroy the German aircraft industry, flying night and day, so the next day, June 29 1944, we were called upon again. Up at 0300 hours, our crew collected at our table in the mess hall, too sleepy to have any kind of conversation. A few jokes helped cut the veil of seriousness that gripped us. Recalling yesterday's experience, none of us were anxious to face that hellfire again. After breakfast, we gathered in the briefing room, and learned that the strategic targets for this mission were in the Leipzig area and included a synthetic oil plant, a bearing works, and eleven aircraft assembly and components plants.

Off we went. The sky filled with planes. A total of 1,150 bombers and 779 fighters formed a stream that stretched 200 miles across Germany. They carried a total of 1,775 tons of bombs. Our group's specific target was a Junker's aircraft factory located in the city of Aschersleben immediately west of Berlin. Forty-seven bombers carrying 147 tons of bombs were in this group.

Our B-24 Liberator was piloted by 1st Lt. Robert Hannaman. Lt. William Perkinson was the co-pilot; Lt. Irwin Eiring, the navigator; and Lt. William Kelley, the bombardier. S/Sgt. Earl Smith was the radio operator. S/Sgt. Roberto Salazar manned the top turret; Sgt. John Haggerty was in the bottom turret. Sgt. Bruce Bean was the tail gunner. Sgt. Lewis Cockerill was the right wing waist gunner and I was the left wing gunner.

As we approached the initial point, the sky again filled with ugly puffs of black smoke that hung in the sky like a veil of death. We were flying about 27,000 feet when suddenly the plane rocked violently. I looked out and could not believe my eyes. The number three engine was completely gone. The wing remained intact but the engine was gone. Almost immediately, we went into a tailspin and plummeted rapidly from 27,000 to about 4,000 feet. Our pilot somehow pulled the plane out of its deadly descent and we began to regain altitude. Lt. Hannaman's actions under unbelievable conditions obviously saved all our lives, but the plane was now on fire and could not be saved. The pilot shouted we had only thirty seconds to "bail out" and ordered us out. I was close to the escape hatch near the bomb bay doors. I hesitated for a moment. The other waist gunner, Louis Cockerill, told me later that I made the sign of the cross before rolling out of the hatch. We all wore the smaller chutes, chest packs that blossomed to about sixteen feet in diameter after they opened. I am not sure if I was the first out or not, but as I descended I counted nine other parachutes that had blossomed. I knew then that we all had escaped from the plane safely.

Like most other airmen who had to bail out of a damaged craft, this was my first parachute jump. I am unable to recall what I felt as I descended, but it had to be relief that I was alive and fearful of what was to come. As I drifted downward, I saw a group of citizens tracking me. Although I tried my best to avoid it, I still landed in a tree. An angry group of German men and women, armed with knives of various types and sizes, approached. They cut the parachute's shrouds, freeing me from the tree. The silk parachute quickly disappeared. Although I could not understand what they were saying, I was able to comprehend "package, package!" They wanted my survival pack, and the money and other items in it. I gave it to them without a struggle. One woman, seething with anger and hatred in her eyes, lunged at me and thrust her butcher knife into my shoulder. The pain was excruciating. Fearing for my life, I waited for the next blow to fall. Fortunately, German soldiers had arrived and ordered the citizens back. They saved me from more retribution from the crazed woman and others in the group.

All ten members of our crew were captured within minutes after hitting the ground. Once rounded up, soldiers put us into a truck and conveyed us to the crash site where our plane was still burning. We were so lucky to be alive. I closed my eyes, and thanked God for His mercy in saving my life and asked for the strength to endure what was to come.

They transported us to the Luftwaffe interrogation center at Frankfurt am Main. I had received only basic medical attention for my stab wound and my shoulder ached painfully. Following about four days of solitary confinement, I was led to an interrogation room where I was questioned extensively by a German officer who spoke better English than I. He wanted to know the number of my bomb group, how many planes were in the mission, the name of my commanding officer, and other information. We were so new to our group that I honestly did not know the name of our commanding officer.

The German officer stated sarcastically that the name Czawlytko was Russian and, with that, a guard struck me in the face with the butt of his rifle knocking out several of my bottom teeth. The officer reprimanded the soldier and expressed his apologies to me explaining that Russians had committed so many atrocities against the German people that it was difficult to control the emotions of his men. Then his eyes narrowed as he pointed out that since my father had served in the Russian Army, I must be a Russian spy. He asked if I understood the penalty for being a spy. My shoulder and mouth throbbed with pain. Filled with anger and disgust and feeling miserable from my wounds, I really did not care what they did to me and I told them so. They were bluffing. They knew all along that I was an American citizen. I was amazed how much information they had. They knew more about my squadron than I did.

With all their bullying, at times they could show acts of compassion. I wore two wristwatches: my personal watch, a Hamilton, and a government issued military watch. During the search, they removed my military watch but allowed me to keep the Hamilton. The officer asked, "What's that?" I explained that the watch was a going away gift from my brother and it was very meaningful to me. The officer stated that German people respect strong family ties. He allowed me to keep the watch.

Following the interrogation process, they took me to a tent, and gave me a postcard to complete and send home. Unable to read German, I asked a prisoner next to me if he knew how to fill out the card. He had already completed his and handed it to me so I could use it as a guide. His name was Walter Wernerski and, to my surprise, his address was 722 Linwood Avenue, which was only three blocks from my home in Baltimore. We became close friends during our internment. Later, we were separated on the forced march and, although I tried to contact him a number of times, we never saw each other again.

For departure to the prison camp, every two men were leg-chained. The radio operator on our plane, Earl Smith and I were chained together. We marched back to the railroad station where we were forcibly packed like sardines into unventilated boxcars. I estimate there were as many as seventy men crammed into a boxcar designed to hold forty. All we could do was sit chained to the man next to us. With no way to relieve ourselves but in our pants, the stench quickly became nauseating. As the train rolled across Germany, conditions rapidly deteriorated from deplorable to unbearable. Once or twice during the journey, the Germans opened the doors, and threw bread into the car and passed a bucket of water along with a ladle. After four desperate days, we finally arrived at the rail spur at Kiefheide near the town of Grosstychow (now Poland). The station was about two and one-half miles from Stalag Luft IV, a prison camp built specifically to house allied enlisted airmen.

As we exited from the cars, our legs were unsteady after being cramped in the boxcar for so long and our eyes tried to adjust to the light. The chains were removed. German guards with snarling dogs prodded us along with their bayonets, and we forced us to run the two and one-half miles from the railroad station to the prison camp. If one did not keep up or stumbled and fell, he was either bitten by dogs or jabbed with a guard's bayonet or both.

Arrival at the camp was a relief. I was too exhausted to feel fear or anything else, but I had survived yet another ordeal. I truly believed that, with God's help, I was going to survive this nightmare, and settled in for what was to become a very slow-moving, boring and depressing experience.

There were twenty-four men confined to a room about 12 feet by x 12 feet. We had double bunk beds, mattresses that were made of wood chips and covered by burlap and one thin blanket. The room had two windows boarded on the outside. There was a small coal stove, but we received coal occasionally, and when winter set in, it was very cold. We doubled up with each other to try to keep warm.

Randomly, German guards would appear two or three times a day, sometimes in the middle of the night for a head count. As soon as it got dark, guards came and locked everyone up. There was no escape. They provided buckets inside the rooms for prisoners who had to relieve themselves during the night. We were all constantly suffering from dysentery. The room reeked.

I would often go to the main gate when the Germans soldiers brought in new prisoners to see if there was someone, I might know. One fall day I noticed a soldier whose face was covered with blood and I recognized him immediately. It was Danny Dudek, a friend from home. He was assigned to Barrack No. 6 and I was in Barrack No. 7. Seeing someone from home was a godsend. He was consoled to find someone he knew and I was elated to see an old friend. We spent many a day reminiscing about old times and sharing plans for the future after the war was over. We have remained friends for the past fifty-plus years.

During my internment, the only recreation available was to walk around several barracks staying within the warning wire. One day, while taking our daily exercise, we saw a German soldier accidentally electrocuted on a telephone pole. The prisoners began to cheer, which enraged the guards in the towers who turned their machine-guns on us and started to fire. We all scrambled for safety. Luckily, no one was hit. There was another incident when a German plane crashed outside the compound and the prisoners began cheering. In order to get us back into the barracks, the German soldiers again turned their machine-guns on us and fired but no one was wounded.

I will never forget a young prisoner named Williams who came into camp with stab wounds all over his body, one hundred and forty nicks to be exact. We counted them. As he ran the gauntlet from the train station to the camp, a German soldier kept jabbing him with his bayonet.

Another airman in our barracks named Schroeder was from Madison, Wisconsin and one of our German guards was a personal friend of his. The guard was also from Madison. He was a butcher in civilian life and had returned to Germany for a visit when the war began. The Nazis conscripted him into the German army and he became a prison camp guard. We never had any problems with him. Most of the guards treated us fairly except for a few. Fortunately, I never had an encounter with the infamous "Big Stoop," but everyone in the compound was familiar with his reputation.

As a prisoner, we had none of life's simple amenities such as a toothbrush, toilet tissue or a bath. I believe I had only one shower during my entire ten months internment. We were all infested with lice. We had a water pump in the compound and one prisoner would pump the water while the other washed but since we did not have soap, the eggs of the lice went unchecked and multiplied. The men would create games, and have competitions for cigarettes picking lice off themselves and collecting them in a container.

Food, or the lack of it, was unquestionably our main concern in camp. We were fed only once a day and our daily ration consisted of one cup of potatoes, two slices of bread made with a sawdust filler, and a cup of ersatz coffee made, I believe, from barley or some other grain. Every so often, they dumped a truckload of kohlrabi or carrots into the compound. At times, we ate them raw and other times cooked them in the few cans we had. My weight began a steady decline following my capture. Red Cross packages helped, but we received them so seldom. When we did, we had to share them with six, eight or sometimes twelve men.

Religion played an important role in my life as a POW. I prayed constantly. Once, a Polish priest visited the camp and spoke to us. Since I could speak Polish, I served as his interpreter. I will not forget his words of assurance and maintaining faith. I still use a rosary that he gave to me.

Much has been written about the forced march across Germany during sub-zero weather. I cannot speak for others. I can only report what happened to me. I faced a number of ordeals as a prisoner, but by far the cruelest, most debilitating experience I could ever imagine was when the German government forced us to walk hundreds of miles in freezing weather with inadequate clothing and almost no food. We lived like animals in the fields with little or no shelter, grubbing for nourishment, no sanitation, and ridden with lice and other parasites. It is a tribute to man's human spirit and his will to live that so many of us survived.

The ordeal started when the Russian offensive began to advance across Poland. The Germans decided to evacuate the prisoners from Luft IV and other prison camps in eastern Germany and Poland. They moved us out in groups of about two hundred. The sick and infirm were put into boxcars and most others walked. On February 4, 1945, I was among one of the first groups to evacuate Stalag Luft IV.

The first night we slept in an open field covered with ice and freezing water. We did not have proper clothing and only a single thin blanket to endure the sub-zero weather. We would huddle together to fend off the bitter cold. We had almost no food except what we could scrounge from the fields. We continued to march for the next sixty days, about twenty kilometers each day. At times, we slept in local barns, to the dismay of the farmers. The German soldiers told the farmers to remove their animals so we could bed down, but some farmers protested the evacuation of their animals, so we had to lie beside them. Others were fearful that we would contaminate the hay because we were so filthy and covered with lice. We suffered from chronic dysentery and had only hay or leaves to wipe ourselves. We smelled worse than the animals.

As our journey continued, prisoners too weak to go on would fall by the roadside. The guards would jab them with their bayonets to get them moving. Some were suffering from pneumonia, others had ugly open sores, our legs were raw and chafed, blisters on our feet and a variety of other ailments. We all tried to help each other but we were so weak ourselves. Men would simply drop out. After a time, even some of the German guards began to desert.

There were rumors that the British were advancing toward us. This gave us hope and the strength to carry on. I was fearful that one day Germans would simply murder us all. By the first week in April, I was ready to give up. Weakened by starvation, dysentery and other miseries, I became convinced that unless something happened immediately, I was not going to make it. So, I lay down in a ditch by the side of the road and no one did anything to help or hinder me. I watched as the group of hollow remnants of human beings moved on. Once they were out of sight, I crawled into the forest and found new strength in my fight for freedom. Shortly after, I teamed up with three or four other prisoners who were unknown to me. We could see the rockets firing in the west and we knew the British were getting closer. The first day we stole a pig from a farm and cooked it over one of the many fires started by the rocket fire. As a layer of the meat cooked, we ravenously pulled strips off with our fingers and stuffed it into our mouths, half-cooked, half-raw. The next day, we came across several Polish laborers. Since I spoke Polish fluently, I was able to communicate with them and traded my prized Hamilton wristwatch for a loaf of bread and two eggs. This was the very watch my brother John had given me as a going-away gift and which the Germans had allowed me to keep at the time of my interrogation – the watch I treasured through my entire internment.

Our group continued to struggle westward toward the British troops who were advancing east. When they found us in the forest, half-starved, half-crazed, they verified that we were American prisoners, and notified the American authorities who immediately sent a plane for us. We flew to a hospital in LeHavre, France, where I removed my filthy clothing, was deloused and issued a new uniform. My old clothing, or what was left of it, was burned. My weight had dropped from 180 pounds to 98 pounds. I was suffering from malnutrition, fatigue, dysentery, frostbitten hands and feet, and showing signs of edema, an early symptom of starvation. How many more days would I have survived?

After a recuperation period at the LeHavre hospital on a diet of ice cream, milkshakes and other rich foods, I managed to gain a few pounds, pounds that fell off as soon as I came home. I sailed home on a hospital ship in May 1945. I was only 19 years old, but I felt like I had lived a lifetime.

Many of us who made that march remain puzzled by the madness of attempting to evacuate nearly twenty-five thousand men and march them across country in freezing weather without any of the basic logistics necessary to support such a move. Perhaps the Nazis considered American and British flyers as elite sons, as the Luftwaffe considered their airmen. Knowing their cause was lost; they intended to use us as "bargaining chips" to achieve more agreeable surrender terms. If my theory is correct, the plan was doomed to fail because the German infrastructure and transportation system completely collapsed. Consequently, prisoners of war fell to the absolute bottom of any list prioritizing humane services. We suffered the consequences.

When my parents stopped receiving mail from me following my capture on June 29 1944, they became concerned about my welfare. My sister Clara began checking regularly with the local Red Cross for news of my fate, and my brother would go to the Baltimore News Post newspaper offices to seek news of any kind about my unit. Almost two months passed before they received notice that I was missing in action and had been missing since June 29. No one could believe it. Had I not just arrived in England a week before? My mother had five sons serving our country, but at the mention of my name, she would burst into tears. I believe my family suffered more than I did. Not knowing if a loved one is dead or alive can be an emotionally draining experience. Their faith, as mine, helped them survive. They were somewhat relieved to learn in late October or early

November that I was alive and a prisoner of war. My mother and Marie, my beloved future bride, began sending packages of foodstuff and sundry items to me every week, but I received only one during my entire internment and that was a box of crushed cookies – nothing but crumbs. Of course, we devoured every single crumb.

I could never express in words the elation I felt upon returning to American soil. We arrived in Boston and were on our way by train to Camp Meade, Maryland, and had to change trains in Baltimore providing a five-hour layover. Although cautioned not to leave the train station, I was close enough to home to make it there and back. When I arrived unannounced at my parents' home, Marie was also there. What a joyous time. We hugged and kissed each other, cried together and gave thanks to God. I hardly recognized my mother; she had lost so much weight from worry. She had suffered so much during my ordeal and that of my four brothers. Now, her tears were tears of joy. A river of emotion swelled and flowed from us all that day. A neighbor drove me back to the station and Marie stayed with me until I boarded the train to Camp Meade. Shortly after, I received a sixty-day furlough. Unfortunately, I became ill and spent most of it at the Fort Howard Hospital in Baltimore.

Following my discharge from the Army Air Forces, I spent the following three years in and out of Fort Howard hospital suffering from vitaminosis, colitis, neurosis, nervous anxiety reaction, frostbite and other ailments. It took years before the VA doctors successfully treated the parasites that had invaded my system.

I returned to the Glenn L. Martin plant to get my old job back, but that did not happen. They had me cleaning gas tanks and in my condition, I did not last long. I tried working for General Motors, but I no longer had the physical stamina to perform the heavy lifting required. I was very weak. I was fortunate to get a job with the Veterans Administration and worked there for 15 years. I really liked working for the VA, but when they began reducing their workforce, I decided to search for another job with more security for my growing family. At age 35, the maximum eligible age for a police officer, I joined the Baltimore City Police Department. At age 47, following several heart attacks, I performed light duty assignments.

As I reflect back, my spiritual strength enabled me to survive when I was so physically broken. I prayed constantly and the image of my beloved Marie sustained me and kept me going. I thought about her all the time. I promised the Blessed Mother that if I survived, I would be indebted to her for the rest of my life. Well, she answered my prayers and granted my wish. I survived a horrible ordeal and returned home to marry Marie Trzcinska. However, my war-related illnesses robbed me of my youth. My loving wife suffered unimaginably because of my flashbacks and all of my recurring disabilities, but together we survived and, today, we have a happy life and a beautiful family.

We recently celebrated our 58th Wedding Anniversary. We have four sons and one daughter. They are married and all are just wonderful to my wife and me. We have nine granddaughters and five grandsons. I will be forever grateful to the Blessed Mother and will continue to thank her for the rest of my life.

Walter D. Czawlytko received his honorable discharge on 5 November 1945, at the rank of Staff Sergeant. He was twenty years old. His awards include the Purple Heart; Air medal; WW II Victory Medal; American Theatre Medal; European, African, Middle-Eastern Campaign Medal with three battle stars; and the good conduct medal. He is a lifetime member of the American Ex-Prisoners of War, the Veterans of Foreign Wars and the Blind Veterans Association.

Walter (2nd from bottom left) & Crew

Walter and Marie Czawlytko

245

Richard Mulcahy
Fort McClellan, Alabama

RICHARD V. MULCAHY

*"We were outnumbered and completely surrounded.
As I saw it, we had two choices surrender or be killed."*

HE WAS A RESTLESS KID who wanted to be part of the war but his dad would not sign until he was age eighteen, so his brother Louis forged his father's signature. In July 1942, when he enlisted in the US Army, Dick Mulcahy was seventeen years old. Following completion of basic and advanced infantry training at Fort McClellan, Alabama, he went to Fort Leonard Wood, Missouri, where he was assigned to the 8th Infantry Division's 28th Infantry Regiment. War in North Africa was being fought furiously between British and American allied forces and German and Italian troops. The 8th Division moved to Camp Laguna, Arizona for desert training in expectation of joining the fight in North Africa. The men quickly learned that the desert was a terrible place to train and fight and were relieved when the allies were victorious in Africa and their desert training was discontinued.

In mid-November, a convoy of ships sailed from New York harbor carrying the 8th Division's men and equipment across the perilous north Atlantic arriving at Belfast, Northern Ireland on November 28, 1943. They spent the next seven months at Camp Lough Coole near Enniskillen in Northern Ireland training intensely in preparation for combat with the German troops in Europe. Dick was ready to go but suffered an emergency appendectomy in early June 1944 and spent D-Day in surgery, and the remainder of the month in the hospital.

Following their successful but costly landing on the Normandy coast on June 6, the American 1st Army concentrated its attention on securing a link between the Omaha and Utah beachheads, cutting off the enemy troops defending the Contentin Peninsula and capturing the port at Cherbourg. The German forces, under orders to "fight to the last round" battled violently. But American firepower from land and sea, air superiority and material were overwhelming. Follow-up divisions were pouring into Normandy. When Cherbourg fell on June 29, 1944, the Americans turned their attention to organizing the breakout operation.

The strategy was simple; find a weak spot in the enemy's line, punch a hole in it and then send mobile forces to exploit it. This required identifying a system of parallel roads sufficient to support the movement and supply of several divisions of mechanized troops. The city of St. Lo with its major highway junction was the key to continued movement but it was very heavily defended and it was going to be a tough nut to crack. The plan was to capture the town of Coutances, about ten miles to the southeast of St. Lo and attack it from the rear. From the north, two roads that led south to Coutances passed through Carentan and La Haye-du-puits. Americans controlled Carentan, but La Haye-du-puits had to be taken.

The attack south toward La Haye-du-puits led directly through some of the worst hedgerow country in Normandy. On July 3, 1944, crack troops of the 82nd Airborne began to move easily initially, and then they ran into fierce opposition that cost them 1,200 casualties in three days. The newly committed 8th Division, which arrived at Utah Beach on July 4, was rushed to the front. Regarded as one of the best-trained outfits in the US Army, the men of the 8th had to learn the hard way how to make their way through the hedgerows. Dick Mulcahy was a corporal in I Company, 3rd Battalion, 28th Infantry Regiment, and fought in the battle for La Haye-du-puits.

Following is Dick's story:
I was still hospitalized when the 8th Infantry Division set out from Belfast Harbor to Utah Beach on July 1, 1944, and I was distressed about being left behind. I knew combat was going to be rough and after having trained with these guys for two years, I didn't want to run the risk of dying with strangers. I pleaded with the doctors to release me so I could rejoin my company. The doctor checked me over and agreed that I had recovered sufficiently to return to active duty. I caught the first transport I could across the Channel and hitched a ride to my regiment's command post, then learned that I Company was not only at the front, they were set to jump off on attack the next morning. A jeep carried me to the front. It felt so great to be back with my buddies and they were all glad to see me. We were confident of our abilities, yet it was still a little tough sleeping that night because we were so pumped up.

The attack began at 0700 and almost everything went wrong from the start. We encountered heavy rains and murderous fire. The superior 82nd Airborne had gained only a few miles in five days of heavy fighting at a high cost of life. We were green troops and we advanced cautiously at a crawl. We knew the Germans were dug in somewhere behind the hedgerows but we could not see them. In this maze, we separated from the other squads and lost contact with them. We kept moving when suddenly we came under attack and dove for cover, firing back in the direction of the enemy fire. Shrapnel from a grenade struck our squad leader, Sergeant Duncan, knocking him out of action. I was the next highest rank so I took command. I ordered one of the men to find his way back with Sgt. Duncan so he could get medical attention, and the rest of us continued to crawl forward until we came to a split in the road. I had no idea where I was or where I was going, but our orders were to keep moving forward and infiltrate the enemy's lines. I chose the left fork in the road. As it turned out, this proved to be a frightful mistake. Unseen, German soldiers watched as we passed and then closed in behind us. "Sich ergeben," (hands up) they ordered. I looked around and saw that we were outnumbered and surrounded. At this point, we had two choices – surrender or be killed. It was a helluva situation to be in so early in combat, yet we made the right choice. We laid down our rifles.

We were double-timed back several miles to a barn where an officer questioned us about the 8th Division. He wanted to know when we arrived in France, what our troop strength was, what our orders were, and many more related questions. They were very anxious and impatient. Citing the Geneva Convention, I gave only my name, rank, and serial number. The German officer became furious with my response and struck me in the jaw with his fist. I reeled and wanted to strike him back so badly, but I kept my composure and just stood there. He had too many soldiers with weapons around him.

We then walked, traveled by truck, and rode in a boxcar until we arrived at Stalag IVB in Muhlberg, located in southeastern Germany, about forty miles from Dresden. There were separate compounds for American, English and Russian prisoners and there were about five hundred men in the American compound.

Prison life was boring. Roll call and headcount was at 0500 hours. The rest of the day we talked to other prisoners, walked around, and played ball, hopscotch, or any other kind of game we could think of. Sometimes the Germans would take us to their headquarters for questioning, but none of us, as far as I knew, gave them more than name, rank and serial number. Living conditions were deplorable. There were no shower facilities. Each of us had a thin blanket and slept on a lice-infested, straw mattress.

At times, we played a game for the cigarettes we received in Red Cross parcels. Ten men each anted up one cigarette. The leader blew a whistle to start and the players had five minutes to pick lice off themselves and put them in their can. The whistle blew to end the game, and the man with the most lice in his can won the game and the cigarettes.

Our diet was insufficient. All we ever had for breakfast was a thick liquid that was supposed to taste like coffee, but it was awful. For lunch, we usually had what they called cabbage soup, but in fact it was just a few cabbage leaves in water. Supper normally consisted of a single slice of bread, nothing else. We received Red Cross packages about once a month. During my ordeal, my weight dropped from 160 pounds to 87 pounds.

Summer passed to fall and fall to winter. The winter was very cold. At times, the snow was three feet deep. I was put in charge of the wood detail and every day I led ten men into the forest to gather wood for our stove. I developed pneumonia from trudging through the snow and working up a sweat in freezing weather while wearing inadequate clothing. German medical treatment was deficient in all respects. We were all lucky to survive.

One side of our compound housed British POWs. They were strict disciplinarians and ceremonial. Once, after they caught one of their own stealing food from fellow inmates' Red Cross parcels, we were all ordered outside. We watched as they brought out the accused man, bound from the waist up, and marched him to the latrine, where they tied a rope around his ankles. Then, they continuously dunked him head first into the slime of urine and feces until he was covered and his clothing saturated, and then they left him lying wet on the ground still tied. The temperature was below freezing and we heard later that he had died. None of us who witnessed this ate anything the rest of the day. War and deprivation brings out the worst in men.

Although raised as a Catholic, I was not very religious throughout my adolescent years, but while incarcerated, religion became an increasingly important part of my life. I had no where else to turn, so every day I prayed to God to give me the strength to survive and each day that I did, my faith grew stronger. The day we were liberated, I fell to my knees and thanked God for sparing my life, and I have continued to do so every day.

As the Russians drew closer to our Stalag, the guards told us that they were going to march us toward the Elbe River and turn us over to the Americans. We marched for thirty days. Every day we were given a single loaf of bread to be shared by a number of men, how many I can't remember, but we each got a slice about 1/8" thick. That was our daily ration! Wherever and whenever we could find them, we dug turnips, potatoes, rutabagas or anything else edible from the farm fields. We slept on the ground or in barns when they were available. We were filthy, lice infested, sick with dysentery, chafed raw, wet and cold.

Bob Simon, from the 82nd Airborne, and I had become friends and he and I decided we had had enough and left the column to try to find something more to eat. After walking aimlessly for two days, we came upon a house on a hill that had signs posted all around it declaring its neutrality, and stating that the house was under the protection of the Geneva Convention. Bob and I asked each other, "What the hell do we have to lose?" We knocked on the door and, to our surprise, found an

American named Al Werner, who had returned to Germany shortly before war broke out to conduct business for his firm. Unlike some others, he was not conscripted into the German military, but he was also not allowed to leave Germany. Therefore, he stayed in his little house for five years protected only by a few homemade signs.

At first he was taken aback by our appearance, but we explained that we were escaped POWs and begged for his help. It was evident that we were in desperate straits so he offered to hide us in the basement of his house until the Russian troops arrived. As it turned out, it was a good move for both him and us. About seven or eight days later, Russian soldiers banged on the door. When they learned that Werner was hiding American prisoners of war, they broke out some vodka and we had a great time drinking repetitive toasts to Stalin, Truman and Churchill. The next day, they transported us to the American lines on the Elbe River, where we walked across a bridge to safety. When I reached the other side, I fell to my knees and gave thanks.

At Camp Lucky Strike, we removed our lice-infested clothing, were sprayed with DDT, issued new clothes, and transported to Hildesheim, Germany. From there, we flew to Antwerp, Belgium, where we boarded a liberty ship that sailed to Newport News, Virginia. We then traveled by train to Fort Meade and finally home.

On The Home Front

On the home front, Dick learned later how difficult life was for his family following his capture and imprisonment. He was captured on July 8 1944, and more than a month passed before his mother received a telegram from the government informing her that her son was "missing in action" since July 12, 1944, somewhere in France.

A personal letter from the Adjutant General followed several days later and confirmed the content of the telegram and he apologized for the "added distress caused by the military's failure to receive more information or details." The AG explained that the term "missing in action" indicated only that the whereabouts or status of an individual was unknown. It is not intended to convey the impression that the case was closed and emphasized that every effort is being made to clear up the status of missing loved ones, but explained how difficult a task that was under war conditions. The War Department was helpless to expedite such reports, since countries, with which we were at war, furnished this information to us. Dick's family took some solace from the fact that many soldiers initially reported missing in action were later found to be prisoners of war.

At times, the German government would broadcast the name, address, serial number, and age of Americans captured during the hostilities and requested listeners to notify the families. Often, it was the first notification a family received that a loved one might be safe and well, or wounded and receiving care. The *Dad MacMannis Listening Post* in West Palm Beach, Florida, was a free, humanitarian service that monitored information on short-wave radio regarding prisoners of war. Upon hearing a name, they immediately mailed a printed postcard to the families with news of their loved one's status. Often, families received notice of the broadcast from other people all over the United States and Canada who had also heard the message. Almost forty people who had heard about Richard's situation contacted the Mulcahys.

It was not until August 22, 1944, that Mrs. Mulcahy received official notice that the International Red Cross had reported that Corporal Richard V. Mulcahy was a prisoner of war of the German government. The family breathed a sigh of relief that he was alive. The next day, his dad wrote an eight-page letter expressing the family's anxiety during the past two months and telling Richard how grateful they were to learn that he was alive and well. The letter was mailed to his son's last-known overseas address in the hope that it would somehow be forwarded to him. It was "returned to sender" by a censor with a note, "Former military units of members of armed forces who are now Prisoners of War are objectionable in mail destined for enemy territory." When he returned home in May 1945, Richard finally read the letter.

Richard V. Mulcahy received his honorable discharge on November 22, 1945 at the rank of Sergeant. He was twenty-one years old. He was awarded the Combat Infantryman Badge; Bronze Star Medal; POW Medal; WW II Victory Medal; American Campaign Medal; European, African, Middle-Eastern Campaign Medal; and the Good Conduct Medal.

Dick & Esther Mulcahy

Combat Infantryman's Badge

NAZIS CLAIM THEIR CAPTURE — who surrendered during recent fights in This picture, of German origin, claims to the Allied Atlantic bridgehead strip," show a "group of American prisoners waiting removal to an internment camp.

NAZIS CLAIM THEIR CAPTURE – This picture, of German origin, claims to show a "group of American prisoners who surrendered during recent fights in the Allied Atlantic bridgehead strip," waiting removal to an internment camp.

Richard Mulcahy, standing, extreme left

257

William P. Booth
Port Lyantey 1951

WILLIAM P. BOOTH

"No one, but me, will know what
I went through and what
I suffered and
I'll continue to keep it that way!"

WILLIAM BOOTH'S STORY was the final narrative chronicled in the original collection. The position of his story was not meant to diminish his deeds or the sacrifices he made in behalf of his country. He saw his duty and did it to the best of his ability. Like so many others, he went through unimaginable hell. He faced the anxiety and fear of combat, had his plane destroyed by enemy fire, jumped into the unknown and suffered the indignity and deprivation of being a prisoner of war. He experienced the misery of one of the great atrocities perpetrated against American POWs during World War II, the incredible forced march across Germany; a journey that would stretch for hundreds of miles and last for three months during one of the cruelest German winters on record. Many of the survivors suffered injuries and illnesses that would plague them for the rest of their lives. Memories of the outrageous cruelties and deprivations are so vivid that they continue to burn in the consciousness of many of the survivors, even now, more than sixty years later.

William P. Booth, like all those who gave up their freedom in service to their country, was a hero for his deeds and sacrifices, and his story and the others' should be chronicled in the hall of heroes. They are the men and women who saved the world. Can any of us imagine what life would be like today if the Nazis and Japanese had prevailed during World War II?

His story is similar to the other Airmen's stories in this collection. He is unique in that after serving during the Second World War and surviving capture by the Germans, he had the courage to enlist in the United States Navy and serve his country again in the Korean War. The following events will chronicle only his WWII experience.

His home was Philadelphia, Pennsylvania, when inducted and assigned to the Army Air Corps. He took basic training in Miami Beach and went to gunnery school at Tyndall Field, in Florida. Crew assignment-transition was at Westover Field in Chicopee Falls, Massachusetts. In May 1944, he embarked from Mitchel Field, Long Island, New York, on a B-24 to a place called Nutts Corner, Northern Ireland and assigned to the 446 Bomb Group and 705 Bomb Squad.

William went into combat immediately. He flew a total of twenty-nine missions, and on his twenty-ninth mission, his plane was hit by enemy flak. Engines number one and number four were lost when they took a direct hit in the bomb bay cutting off fuel to the other engines and he and the crew bailed out.

This is William Booth's story:

On September 26, 1944, we were flying a B-24J *Temptation* and our crew that day consisted of Lt. John E. Mullery, pilot; Lt. Robert F. Kallstrom, co-pilot; Lt. Aubrey E. Jones, navigator; and Lt. John A. Watt bombardier; Lt. Isaac H. Lingual, Jr. nose turret gunner and lead bombardier. Also, T/Sgt. Herbert S. Gold, top turret gunner; S/Sgt. Robert L. Cochran, ball turret gunner; S/Sgt. John T. Bush waist gunner; S/Sgt.

Richard E. Cotton, waist gunner; S/Sgt. James Haugen, tail gunner; and I was the radio operator.

This was to be the crews' final mission before rotating to the States. The marshaling yards at Hamm, located only ninety miles inside the German lines was the target. None of us wanted to pass up this milk run, as short sorties were called.

Everything was going great that day. As we approached the target, we had not seen flak or enemy fighters, but this was soon to change. At 1430, we turned on the bomb run. The navigator notified the crew when we approached the Initial Point (IP), and the pilot turned the controls over to the bombardier who was then responsible for pinpointing or toggling. My job as the radio operator was to open the bomb bay doors and to hold the doors open until the bombs were released, since I had no gun to operate. I crawled down into the well just next to the bomb bay doors and, on orders, opened them at the IP and held them open. There was plenty of flak all around us and under us and it was so violent that the pilot was assisting the autopilot to keep the ship on a straight course. Down in the hole, I kept watching the flak come higher and higher, and then it hit! You might ask what you do in a situation like this. Well, you continue to do your job, but you also toss in a few prayers. In fact, there were three direct hits; one hit in the bomb bay, one took out the No.1 engine, and one took out the No.2 engine. We continued on the run and after releasing the bombs, I closed the doors to stop any drag. The pilot called for a damage assessment. I advised him of the damage in the bomb bay and the gas tank for the inboard engines was spewing fuel. He told me to reopen the bomb bay doors, which I did, and luckily so because the hydraulic lines had been damaged by flak and were also leaking fuel. The pilot then gave the command to bail out.

One of our waist gunners, T/Sgt. John T. Bush had taken a shot in the arm and needed help putting on his chute, and then he was pushed out of the plane because of his wound.

I was not happy about jumping. I put one foot out as you would to test the temperature of the water at the beach. The fellow behind me gave me a kick in the rear and out I went, saying a prayer. As I was floating down a dozen or more people on the ground were clearly visible and they watched me descend. I had a brief communication with God thanking him for my life and asking for additional protection. As soon as I landed, I heard people yelling and immediately looked for a place to hide. Wearing a heavy flying suit, heavy boots and goggles, I was rather conspicuous. A haystack looked like a safe haven and I tried to burrow under it, but the weight of the hay would not permit me to do so. A group of young children chased me, hitting me with sticks. German soldiers arrived and with their weapons aimed directly at me, I raised my hands and uttered "Comrade."

With my hands still in the air, they directed me to a waiting vehicle much like our jeep. Direction was given in words I did not understand plus a couple of jostles that I did understand. They took me to a convent that had a Red Cross painted on the roof, which the military occupied. During a brief interrogation, there was not the expected reprisal when I gave only my name, rank and serial number. They then turned me over to a young German soldier who threw a round in his gun, and marched me out to the convent wall. I thought I was about to be shot. However, he took me through the gate and we boarded a public bus that took us to Munster airfield. They put me in a cell, with nothing to eat. A mattress filled with straw covered a bunk with widely separated slats. Each man was in a separate cell with a window that was up about eight feet. We could not look out, but we yelled to find out whom the other prisoners were. Everyone except Cotton and Cochran was there. We were fed barley soup, bloodwurst that was terrible, a cup of ersatz coffee made from acorns and tree bark, and a piece of black bread so hard that you could not eat it.

We boarded a train and arrived at Frankfurt am Main. The station was a mass of twisted steel beams and broken concrete. The interrogation center was located on the outskirts of town. After a brisk march, we were taken in and separated. I was placed in a single cell in a long cellblock, and occasionally removed to be searched, have my picture taken, interviewed, and other functions such as eating and going to the lavatory. Time passed so slowly and lack of companionship made it very boring and tiring. I do not recall exactly, but I think we were there three or four days. This was also the place that I was the most frightened. Four different officers, all of whom spoke very good English, interviewed me at least four different times. They knew more about each crew member than what any one of us could have revealed.

At the Interrogation Center I was reunited with Cochran and Cotton who had been captured the second day. I had not seen any of the officers of our crew since our arrival and now we were leaving without knowing their whereabouts. We learned that they were going to Stalag Luft I, a camp for officers, and that Stalag Luft IV, a camp for Air Forces enlisted personnel, was to be our new home. Next, they transported us to Wetzlar, Germany. This was Dulag Luft where we had our first shower, shave and sit-down meal since we left England. The shower was beautiful, one minute of water, one minute to lather and one minute to rinse.

We received new clothes from the inside out, quite a change. This place was a transit point from which we would be shipped to a permanent camp. It was here that we received a postcard to address to our families to let them know our whereabouts and condition. They also let us write our first letter and both were mailed from there.

At Dulag Luft we boarded a train and crammed into passenger cars for transfer to our permanent camp. As I recall, there were about ten or more in compartments designed for six and we took turns sitting on the benches. There were no facilities to relieve ourselves. Our train stopped in the Berlin railroad yards, and it was here that I witnessed my first air raid from ground level and at night. German spotlights lit up the area, and we watched as they picked up British aircraft and tracked them across the sky.

Flak burst throughout the sky and if it weren't for where I was, I would have thought it was a 4th of July firework display. We could hear bombs exploding and see ground flashes, but none were near us. Our train remained stationary until an all clear was sounded and we proceeded towards our destination once again.

The next morning the train pulled into a small station where we were met by a detachment of guards and their dogs. The name on the passenger shelter was Kiefheide. The address of the camp was Grosstychow, which is the major city in the area, so the train stop at Kiefheide must have been on a spur. We all disembarked and lined up for a march to somewhere. The guards started us out on an easy pace, but gradually increased the speed by prodding those POWs on the outside ranks with their bayonets and letting the dogs snip and snap at their legs. There were many injured POWs who should have been conveyed, but that was not to be. This march took only about fifteen minutes, but it was enough to make everyone very uncomfortable, especially those who received bayonet cuts and dog bites. At the camp, we went to a large auditorium where we disrobed and were searched.

We dressed and had more pictures taken and filled out more questionnaires. We had been trained not to talk to anyone about the mission or any other details if captured, until we were properly indoctrinated into the camp. A number of Germans, who had previously lived in America and returned to Germany to join the Nazi cause, now infiltrated POW camps to gather intelligence.

I was assigned to Room 7, Barrack 10, and Compound C. The room had one table that seated five men on each side, a small round stove, and straw on each side of the room covered with blankets. This was the living quarters for thirty-two men; sixteen men slept on each side of the room and we all slept quite uncomfortably. When one person moved the others would have to move; therefore, it was necessary that we slept as still as possible, which was very difficult. A few of the men had bad dreams about their experiences, some were the sole survivors of their aircraft, and others had lost one or more of their crew with whom they had been close friends. It took some doing to become accustomed to this arrangement, but it was only to last until November when they sent in some carpenters to make bunks. They built double-decked bunks that slept four on the top and four on the bottom. There were four bunks (for eight men each) built in each room.

On my second day of confinement, I was asked to be the room chief, which after a little coaxing, I accepted. It was not a tough job. All I had to do was to assure that each of us received the same rations as the others in the barracks, slice the bread equally, arbitrate disputes, and act as a go between for the men in the room and the barracks chief and all other room chiefs.

I was at Stalag Luft IV from September 1944 to February 1945. One day we were told to prepare to evacuate the next morning. We did not know where we were going, nor did we have knapsacks or anything else to carry our meager possessions. We did not have much, but we had an overcoat, extra pants and a shirt, a blanket and any foodstuffs we may have saved. I took a shirt, sewed the bottom closed, sewed the sleeves to the bottom and filled it to sling over my back. On the way out, on February 2, we each received a Red Cross parcel that weighed ten pounds. It may not seem like much, but in my condition, it felt mighty heavy.

We started our march with no idea of where we were going; we just plodded along. On the first day we walked thirty-two kilometers and ended at a barn where we were given a hat-full of potatoes. We did not have any mess gear, so we managed as best we could. After a while, we wised up and used an empty klim (milk) can for both food and water when available. After having the potatoes we were directed to a barn, where there was a mad dash for sleeping space in the hay, both in the loft and below. A slit trench was dug outside for our convenience, but to get to it necessitated crawling over your fellow POWs and since they weren't very pleasant about it, we just made a hole in the hay, relieved ourselves, covered it and went back to sleep. Each day was worse than the day before. We had dysentery and scabies. The lice were horrendous. We drank water from ditches and any other source available. We received three potatoes a day, no morning ersatz, no afternoon beverage, but a great many anxious moments. We even tried to dry out horse manure hoping we could smoke it.

We slept in fields in snow and rain and we were not permitted to build fires. Imagine walking along with wet pants chafing your legs, a water-soaked Army overcoat, a water-soaked blanket and wet feet in shoes and socks that had not been removed since you could not remember when. We picked lice from our clothing for days. As for the scabies, we brought them home with us.

We walked back and forth across Germany for three months not knowing what day it was.

At times, we were given small farm wagons to carry our sick. There were seldom horses available so teams of POWs pulled the wagons. The most we were ever able to accommodate was thirty-five men, but hundreds of men were on the verge of collapse. It was our practice to load the wagon and as a man collapsed, he would replace another man who was not quite so ill. Whenever our column came close to a permanent POW camp, we would send our most sickly men to that camp and the rest of our column marched on. We continued to drag ourselves along in spite of pain and immense suffering until our rescue and return to American Army control.

William P. Booth returned to the United States in May 1945 and received his honorable discharge from the Army Air Forces in October 1945 at the rank of Staff Sergeant. He was awarded the Air Medal; POW Medal; WW II Victory Medal; American Theatre Medal; European, African, Middle-Eastern Campaign Medal with Four Battle Stars; and the Good Conduct Medal.

In Conclusion:
During his incarceration, Bill suffered enormously at the hands of his captors and he believes he was wounded mentally as well as physically. His body weight dropped sixty pounds. He pointed out, "No one, but me, will know what I went through and what I suffered and I will continue to keep it that way." He is partially right. The other men at his side who lived through his nightmare know what he suffered, because they lived and suffered through it themselves. Others are trying to understand and more fully appreciate the hardships, cruelty, and agony that former American prisoners of war went

through. We respect them and pay honor to those who sacrificed so much in our behalf.

Many of the survivors suffered injuries and illnesses that would plague them for the rest of their lives. William Booth suggests, "If one prisoner in my camp received 100% disability, then everyone should get 100%." He could be right. We may never know the mental anguish he and the other POWs suffered and continue to suffer. We are trying to understand, and we thank them.

Top: E J. Mullery, pilot; R. F. Kallstrom, co-pilot;
A. E. Jones, navigator; J. A. Watt, bombardier
Kneeling: H. S. Gold, engineer; R. L. Cochran, tail gunner;
V. T. Bush, waist gunner; W. P. Booth, radio operator;
A. J. Charrou, asst., radio operator; J. Haugen, gunner

William Booth relaxing at home, 1999

Leonard Greig

LEONARD C. GREIG, JR.

"Our common goal was the total defeat
of the enemy so that we may return
to our families, our homes,
and our normal way of living."

LEONARD GREIG was eighty years old when he returned to his former high school in Meyersdale, Pennsylvania. He was pleased to have received an invitation to address the students and share with them his experiences as a former airman and prisoner of war. As he walked toward the podium, he looked out at the anxious faces of the young boys and girls who had gathered to hear his talk. There were sixty, seventy, or maybe more. It was hard to count and he did not try. They were friendly faces – many were the grandchildren of his brothers and sisters. Leonard was the oldest of his parents' twelve children and his family was well represented in the audience. He was very proud; family values were always important to him. As he stood before the group, his memory flashed back to the horrors he had endured so long ago. It was his love, he recalled, for his wife, his baby daughter born while he was a captive, his parents and brothers and sisters all who gave him the strength and courage to survive.

He smiled at the group with his endearing smile that wins people over immediately. The audience warmed to him at once. He began by saying, "The impact of having your freedom taken away is hard to describe. As you might have heard before, "You don't miss the water until the well runs dry." Or, "Freedom is like the air you breathe. You don't really think about it until you lose it."

Then he began his story:

More than sixty years ago, I sat where you now sit. Life was quite different then. I was only seven years old when the Great Depression struck our country and the world. The economy collapsed, and quite simply, jobs were very hard to find. They were years of sacrifice, deprivation, and despair. Those hard times helped mold the character of my generation. After graduation from high school, there was little work available in Meyersdale and, as many of you know, I came from a very large family. My parents needed help. Approximately one hundred miles south was the city of Baltimore, and with its steel mills, shipyards, and aircraft factories, it offered opportunities that were just not available at home. As a result, at eighteen years of age, I kissed my Mom goodbye, boarded a bus for Baltimore. There I found a room at a boarding house, obtained employment with the giant Glen L. Martin Aircraft Company, and began to mature.

War had broken out in both Europe and Asia. Nazi Germany had invaded and conquered its neighboring states and Japan was doing the same in the East. In Europe, Great Britain held firm against oppression. Our government began drafting young men into their military services but there was strong sentiment that our country should avoid involvement in another foreign war. Suddenly, on December 7, 1941, Japan attacked the United States naval base at Pearl Harbor in the Hawaiian Islands and caused considerable damage to our Pacific fleet. The U. S. declared war on Japan and pledged support to our allies in Great Britain. Nazi Germany declared war on America and the world was plunged into war. I knew that it would not be very long before I was called to serve my country.

It was during these uncertain times that I met and fell in love with Mae Theresa Wichert. She was, and is still today, as pretty as a picture. We both knew that I would leave soon and we debated the wisdom of marrying at the time. Convinced that our love was so strong that it could withstand whatever the future would bring, we married.

In September 1943, at the age of twenty, I received my draft notice. Today, many twenty-year old men and women are pursuing a college degree or embarking upon a career. I was called to put my life on the line and fight in the most brutal and devastating war in the history of mankind. Perhaps it was the experience gained working in an aircraft factory or above-average test scores, but I was selected for the Army Air Corps and was excited about the prospect of flying. Today's Air Force was a branch of the U.S. Army at that time. I went to Greensboro, North Carolina for basic training and then to gunnery school at Kingman, Arizona. If you liked to fly and shoot at moving targets, it was the place to be. I liked it, qualified, received my aerial gunner wings, and a promotion to sergeant. The pay was not all that much but the promotion nearly doubled my salary. My wife liked that. Next, I joined my crew at Hunter Field outside of Savanna, Georgia where we were assigned to a brand-new B-17 bomber. The crew came from all over the country. Our pilot was Harold Farthing; co-pilot, Frank Page; navigator, Jim George; bombardier, Jack Carson; engineer, Bill Sweetie; radio operator, Frank Pestles; ball turret gunner, Ernie Viles; tail gunner, Joe Melnyk; Joseph Riffle and I were the two waist gunners. Joe Riffle was wounded on our first mission and did not fly the day we were shot down. All the others became prisoners of war and Frank Page was injured that day and later died in a prison camp but I don't want to get too far ahead of my story.

Let me tell you a little about the Boeing B-17 Flying Fortress. It had a wingspan of 104 feet; it was 68 feet long, powered by four 1200 hp engines, and weighed 46,650 pounds fully loaded with crew, bombs and ammunition. Its maximum speed was 325 miles per hour at 25,000 feet and it carried a bomb load up to 8,800 pounds. For protection, it was equipped with six .50-inch caliber and one .30-inch caliber Browning machine-guns mounted in power-operated gun turrets. Electrically heated flying suits permitted crews to fly for long periods at extreme altitudes and would protect in temperature as low as minus 40 degrees Fahrenheit. Although the Fortress is a very large plane, our conditions were very cramped and often we flew in a fetal position. Although flying was considered glamorous, long flights were really quite boring.

From Savannah, we flew to Gander Newfoundland, then on to Prestwick, Scotland. From there, we flew to our new home base in Molesworth, England and were assigned to the 8th Air Force, 303rd Bomb Group affectionately known as "Hell's Angels" and the 360th Squadron. As the war progressed, both of these units were recognized for their significant contributions to the war efforts. The first few weeks at Molesworth we flew training missions to sharpen our individual skills and develop the teamwork necessary to make us combat ready. Our first combat mission was June 21, 1944. As we gathered in the briefing room that morning, we were told "Gentlemen, we are going to Berlin." You could hear lots of "Oh my God!" This was to be a record raid by heavy bombers and the first since the Allied invasion of the French Coast. More than 2,000 American warplanes, the mightiest air armada ever assembled, flew toward the German capital. Shepherded by an estimated force of 1,000 fighter planes, more than 1,000 B-17

Flying Fortresses and B-24 Liberators showered 3000 tons of explosives on targets in Berlin that day.

There is a saying about "safety in numbers." The armada stretched many miles and we may have become complacent snuggled somewhere in the middle of this great force, but as soon as we crossed into France, German fighters attacked us. Even with 1,000 American fighter planes flying support, the German pilots were able to break through and peppered the bombers. Our fighters chased them away and our formations tightened up and lumbered on. Over the target, flak was heavy. There was so much black smoke; it was like flying into the darkest cloud. We watched anxiously as anti-aircraft shells exploded all around us. Suddenly, the plane shook convulsively. Our number 3 engine took a hit but was not on fire. Out my waist gunner's window, I watched other bombers going down and men bailing out. We tried to count the number of parachutes that blossomed. Then our plane rocked again. I looked at the other waist gunner. Blood streamed from his arm. I got him to the first-aid station in the radio room. The plane rocked again. A third hit! Fragments of bursting shells cut through my window and out the roof of the plane. Had I been at my station, I would have been decapitated. Finally, we dropped our bomb load on target, reached the rally point and made our turn for the trip home, as we used to say then, "On a wing and a prayer." Our badly damaged plane became a "hanger queen" and salvaged for spare parts. This was my baptism under fire as an aerial gunner. Was I scared? You bet I was and I never wanted to go back.

The Air Force had different ideas. The next morning at 2 a.m., there were eggs anyway you wanted them, and then on to the briefing where we learned our target for that day was the V-2 rocket installations at Pas de Calais, just across the Channel. These pilotless flying bombs had been causing havoc over Southern England, particularly London for several months. Our assembled task force for this mission consisted of 250 Fortresses and Liberators. Not one enemy aircraft rose to protect the rocket launching pads. Apparently, they were preoccupied fighting the battle that was raging in Normandy, just south of Calais. Although every type of Allied plane had battered the launching pads night and day, the ground defense was still strong and flak was heavy. We watched another bomber go down as an exploding shell severely damaged our plane.

Following two missions in two days and two near-death experiences, tension built and anxiety was beginning to take its toll. Heavy losses affected morale and the signs began to manifest themselves. Mental stress led to serious psychological disorders. The tail gunner refused to fly the next day's mission and had to be persuaded. The target was the sub pen at Le Havre, another heavily defended area. There were no easy targets. We were still without a second waist gunner who was hospitalized from the wounds received on the first mission.

On this mission, exploding shells fired by antiaircraft ground forces struck our plane knocking off our stabilizer and damaging our rudder. Only good piloting brought us home that day. Anxiety increased as the men realized it was only a matter of time before they were theoretically wiped out. Despite the emotional breakdowns, the next day we returned to LeHavre, where the target was the marshaling yards. Once more, antiaircraft weapons filled the air with exploding cannon fire and we returned with another damaged aircraft. On each of the four missions, our planes were so severely damaged that they could not fly until repaired.

Our fifth mission in five days was on June 24, 1944. At the briefing, the briefing officer stretched the ribbon from our base toward the target for that day, Bremen, another heavily defended city. The 'Oh, Gods!' again rang throughout the briefing room. As we climbed into formation, we began to have trouble with one of our engines. Eventually, the engine was shut down and the props feathered; that is, the props were turned to decrease wind resistance when the engine was not operating. We straggled most of the way and eventually fell completely out of formation. A single bomber flying out of formation is like a sitting duck for enemy fighters. We came under attack. The tail gunner called for evasive action. We fought back and continued on three engines toward the target. As we approached their defensive zone, the German fighters begged off seeking new targets. Just before reaching the Initial Point, a shell struck the bomb bay. The entire bay was a mess with the bombs turned sideways. The doors hung open but we could not release our bomb load. Hydraulic fuel was spraying everywhere. There was simply no way to salvage the plane. The pilot ordered us to bail out. I left our plane through the waist door.

With all the training the Air Force had provided, we did not get a practice jump. During classroom sessions on how to bail out, we were instructed to delay pulling the ripcord until we could recognize objects on the ground. This maneuver would give the people watching below less opportunity to track us and increase our chances for evasion and possible escape. When you make a parachute jump for the first time and it occurs while under violent attack, your main concern is, "Will the chute open?" Despite the training, I pulled the cord sooner than instructed and nothing happened. Panic set in quickly. Imagine free falling from 30,000 feet with a parachute that will not open. I gripped the cord with both hands and pulled. The chute blossomed and I breathed a sigh of relief. Descending I saw high-tension electrical power lines on the ground directly in my path. I avoided them by maneuvering the chute and landed safely in a barley field. While gathering my chute, I heard civilians calling to each other as they came closer. Afraid it could be used against me, I tossed my 45 automatic pistol.

Less than a half-hour after hitting the ground, a shotgun was shoved in my face and I was marched out of the field to a violent crowd seething with anger. To them, we were the gangsters of the allied air forces who bombed their homes and killed their families. Someone struck with a shovel, and another tried to poke me with a pitchfork while others beat me with their fists and the handles of rakes and hoes. Not soon enough, German soldiers arrived in a large truck and rescued me from the crazed mob. I felt lucky to be alive. Several members of my crew were already in the truck. We picked up others along the way and they transported us to the local jail and put us into separate cells.

A few days later, a German army truck carried us to the interrogation center at Obereusel near Frankfurt where we were placed in individual cells with no windows or light. It was eerie sitting there in the dark, not knowing what was to happen next. The only sounds were the distinct tap of hobnailed boots walking on a cobblestone floor, and a door opening and then closing. Strange thoughts began to run through my mind.

After a day or two, it was my turn. At the interrogation room, a nattily dressed German officer and sergeant glared at me. They asked about our flight schedules, targets that we had bombed, the number of planes in our group, how many had been shot down and on and on. These interrogations occurred on a random schedule several times during my week in solitary confinement. One day, they informed me that three or four of my compatriots were scheduled for execution that day and they were sorry that they could not fit me in. "Perhaps tomorrow," the officer said snidely.

From the interrogation center, we marched to Wetzlar where we boarded a passenger train that transported us across Germany to Kiefheide, a rail stop in northeastern Germany located approximately two miles north of Stalag Luft IV. The trip took several days and while passing through Berlin at night, we watched a RAF air raid. As we left the train in Kiefheide, we got our first taste of what life as a prisoner of war was going to be like. German guards with fixed bayonets prodded us to move swiftly along. Several guards had leashed dogs that snarled and snapped at every movement. Every two prisoners were shackled together at the ankles and forced to move very quickly. Some had to run to keep up – not an easy task when your ankles are chained to another. If one tripped, usually both fell and they were bayoneted or bitten on the legs by the dogs. I fell and a bayonet punctured my leg. In addition to this wound, during the early months of captivity flak spurs would surface in various parts of my body and had to be removed. The Germans provided no medical assistance for these wounds.

My home for the next seven and one-half months was Stalag Luft IV, Lager A, Barrack 7, Room 3. Life in this prison camp was tolerable initially. The food was deplorable and although Red Cross packages arrived infrequently, they were lifesavers. Sometimes we had a whole parcel, other times it was shared with two, four or more men. We had shower facilities, albeit cold water, recreation facilities, and other amenities. Many men spent their day walking around the perimeter of the compound.

The Germans liked to play with your head. They would awaken us at 2 a.m. and make us fall out in whatever we were wearing and do a headcount. Then, they would come in the middle of the night, make us drop all our possessions on the floor, inspect them, and leave. To my knowledge, they never found whatever it was they were looking for, but the uncertainty of not knowing what they intended to do next was distressing.

Poor nutrition, boredom and the Germans' mind games led to the anxiety of not knowing how long we could last mentally and physically. Some men snapped. Others became sick and died. These events took their toll on the others. I had recovered from the beating I suffered when captured and my puncture and flak wounds were healing, but I began to experience other health problems caused by poor diet. Rations were primarily potatoes with little protein. They did not feed us enough to sustain our weight and I began to lose pounds. Others have suggested that the Germans' strategy was to limit caloric intake and thereby keep us focused on our next meal. As we grew more and more lethargic from lack of nutrition, we thought little about escape or anything else. However, we were able to keep abreast of the war's progress through newly captured prisoners and from the attitude of our guards. Knowing this ordeal would end someday gave us the mental fortitude to carry on.

On January 25, 1945, I received the biggest morale boost a POW can get. It was a telegram from the International Red Cross sent to me through the American Camp Leader, Sergeant Francis S. Paulas. It read "Margaret Mae arrived safely. Both send love. Anna Greig." After the good news regarding the birth of my daughter, things deteriorated rapidly.

Early in 1945, the Russian offensive threatened to engulf Stalag Luft IV. Upon learning that a prisoner of war camp of 10,000 allied airmen was in danger of being overrun by the Red Army, Hitler was outraged. He called it a disgraceful situation that might give the Russians 10,000 volunteer soldiers. Luftwaffe Head

Hermann Goering proposed that eighteen trains be made up for the evacuation of the camp. Hitler responded angrily. He said, "No! Strip them of their shoes and trousers and march them back through the January snow and mud and kill those who drop out!" Fortunately, these orders were not fully adhered to. We kept our shoes and trousers but little else.

On February 6, 1945, about 6,000 prisoners evacuated the camp on foot after only a few hours notice. The German authorities told us that we were going to a camp near Berlin, but we never reached another camp. For 87 days, in groups of about 250, a river of inadequately clad men flowed westward in bitter cold weather and subsisted on starvation rations. We lived in filth and slept in open fields or barns. Clothing, sanitary and medical facilities were nonexistent. Men suffered from dysentery, malnutrition, exposure, trench foot and other diseases. Our water sources were unsanitary surface water and well water of questionable quality. We ate snow, slept in barns or open fields, usually on straw or ground that was littered with the feces of dysenteric prisoners who had stayed there previously. Men dragged themselves onward in spite of intense suffering; others would collapse. The Germans gave us a few small farm wagons that we pulled along to carry our very sick. If a man collapsed, he would be put on the wagon and some other sick man would be taken off. If we passed another prison camp, our sickest men were left there. We never knew their fate. Men died along the way. On several occasions, I was selected for burial detail at a local graveyard.

After walking two months, we reached the town of Ebbsdorf, where we were jammed into boxcars at the rate of about sixty men to a car. It did not seem to matter any longer. We were too weak to protest as if that would do us any good. The train remained at the siding for two days. While it sat, we remained locked in this jammed position without food or water. The filth and resulting stench aggravated the misery of our confinement. The freight cars were not marked to indicate that helpless prisoners of war occupied them. There was considerable aerial activity in the area at the time, and we were fearful our own planes would strafe us. After several days, they removed us from the train and we started marching again. Our first march had been in a general westerly direction, since the Germans were then running from the Russians. This march was in a general easterly direction because the Germans were now running from American and British forces. As a result, we doubled back and covered a lot of the same territory we had come over just a month before. I estimate that we walked over 500 miles in 87 days before British forces liberated us near Luneburg, Germany.

The joy of being free and the realization that I had survived this nightmare are indescribable. I felt I was reborn. At the time, my thoughts were of food and going home to my family as quickly as I could. Horse-drawn wagons carried us to a British camp in the town of Luneburg where we received nourishment, medical attention, and a reintroduction to civilized life. From there we went to LeHavre and in June 1945, I boarded a troop ship and sailed for home.

My wife Mae met me at Fort Meade, and after being processed, I joined her for a bus ride to Baltimore where she and our daughter, Cindy lived with her parents. A few days later, we took a train to Meyersdale, where my family resided. A large group of family members that included my mother and father, sisters, brothers, aunts and uncles met us at the train station. Two of my brothers were still on active duty. My mother, a very emotional person, cried uncontrollably in my arms. She could barely speak. My sister Nancy later told me that for weeks after I was reported missing, mother would break down whenever my name was mentioned. When we think back of our ordeal, we have a tendency to overlook the very great impact our misfortune has on those people close to us. We just did not realize the pain they suffered while we were imprisoned.

Following my discharge, I became an apprentice tool and die maker. This required attending night classes at Baltimore's Maryland Institute. After four years of intensive study and work, I became a certified Tool and Die Maker, and worked in four different machine shops before becoming a manager.

Our daughter Cindy died in 1985. We are blessed with another daughter Judy and a son Leonard III. We now have five grandchildren and four great grandchildren. Mae and I celebrated our 60th Wedding Anniversary on March 19, 2004.

The 303rd Bomb Group "Hell's Angels" became the first heavy bomb group to complete 300 missions from American bases in England. Eventually the 303rd flew 360 missions and dropped more than 24,000 tons of bombs on German war plants and military facilities crippling their ability to wage war. In addition, despite the many enemy fighter attacks and strong ground defense, they never once stopped the 303rd from reaching its target. As part of this group, the 360th Squadron was responsible for leading some of the more outstanding and successful missions. Although I was a prisoner of war during part of this period, I still take pride in our group's accomplishments. I know that my crewmembers and all the men of the 360th Squadron were of the highest caliber. We all worked very hard under trying and adverse conditions. Our common goal was the total defeat of the enemy so that we may return to our families, our homes, and our normal way of living. I am proud to report, "Mission accomplished."

Anna Mae and Leonard Greig

Bill and Imogene Rutkowski interviewing Leonard

Leonard Greig

Jack Meyers, Rome 1944

JOHN H. MEYERS

*"Those men, who were there and knew the difficulties of
the assault and the strength of the German fortifications,
knew Cassino was an outstanding achievement."*

A S WE CELEBRATE the sixtieth anniversary of
the Second World War, we should pause and
reflect on the valor of the men and women who
sacrificed so much during this bloody conflict. Today
the survivors are all in their twilight years, basking in the
warm light of well-deserved honor and recognition that a
grateful nation casts upon them. Motion pictures such as
Saving Private Ryan portray them as heroes. Books refer
to them as *Citizen Soldiers, The Victors*, and Tom
Brokaw has named them *The Greatest Generation.*

For many years following their return home, many
veterans had little to say about the conflict, the terror
they faced and the cruelty and hardships they endured.
Perhaps the memories were too painful. For some, it
took the passing of years and medical treatment to cure
their wounds – both physical and mental. Most veterans
wanted simply to return to their family and their jobs.
Proud of their accomplishments, they quietly and
consistently pursued their goals for a new life and
contributed to a growing economy such as the world had
never seen.

Time passed and wounds healed. As significant
anniversaries bring the world's attention to the
accomplishments and failures of that bloody conflict,
more and more vets are willing to share the trials and
tribulations they had experienced. Today, as they prepare

to have their memoirs documented, so many have incredible records – diaries, scrapbooks and memorabilia that had been secreted away for more than sixty years. Some are so delicate with age they crumble when touched giving the feeling that you are holding something sacred. It is amazing to find the detail of the material accumulated and the vivid memories these documents awaken.

There is a sense among our veterans that our current generation is not fully aware of the struggle, the sacrifices made, and the disaster that nearly befell the world. Our veterans want their stories told. They want today's youth to glimpse at their experiences and come to the realization that freedom is not free and we must stand ready to oppose any foe who would attempt to destroy the freedoms gained by the blood of their fallen comrades.

Then, there are other veterans whose experiences were so brutal that they have spent a lifetime eradicating the horrors from their memory. Interviews became incomplete, inconclusive, and the author struggles to define details in order to tell their story. Histories and official records are bones to which we attempt to add the flesh of reality.

Jack Meyers is a good example of a man who really wants to tell his story and yet has trouble recalling specific events. He recently celebrated his 82nd birthday. When he was drafted into the U.S. Army in 1943, he was only nineteen years old. Following infantry training at Camp Croft, near Spartanburg, South Carolina, Jack arrived in North Africa only four months after his induction. The German and Italian forces had surrendered the previous month. All resistance had ceased and the African war had ended before he arrived. Jack was a replacement for a strong and confident team.

Planners began to look across the Mediterranean to Europe where a new land war would take place.

Jack's official records indicate that he entered Africa on June 21, 1943. He recalls Bone, Africa now named Annaba. It is a port city in Algeria, North Africa approximately 125 miles west of Tunis. Who today would know of Bone, Africa, unless they had been there?

During the African campaign in February 1943, the 168th Infantry Regiment was surrounded and cut to pieces with heavy losses near Kasserine. More than one-half of the regiment was killed, wounded or captured. Following the axis surrender, the 168th moved to Oran, Algeria, where replacements from the 3rd Infantry Division and new recruits from the United States brought the 168th back to fighting strength. Following his release from the hospital, Jack Meyers was assigned to the 34th Division, 168th Infantry Regiment, 3rd Battalion, Company L.

September 9, 1943 was D-Day for the invasion of the Italian mainland as the 36th Infantry established a beachhead at Salerno. The allied forces encountered heavy resistance. The Germans counter-attacked and their spearhead was so intense that only the weight and accuracy of naval gunfire tipped the balance. During the action at Salerno, the U.S. Navy delivered more than 11,000 tons of shells on this beachhead. Additional help arrived from the air as hundreds of Allied bombers blasted targets at key positions beyond the beachhead.

Reinforcements came pouring in. The 34th Division's 133rd, 135th and 168th Regiments went into Salerno to help restore the beachhead. The German Command, convinced that its attempts to smash the beachhead had failed, decided to swing north and occupy the high ground north of Salerno. During the nine days following the invasion, the Americans suffered 3,500 casualties – 500 killed, 1800 wounded, and 1200 reported missing in action. British casualties were even heavier – a total of 5,520 killed, wounded and missing in action.

Throughout the fighting in Italy, the terrain proved to be as formidable an enemy as the German defenders. The Italian Boot is about 750 miles long and varies from 85 to 120 miles wide. Running down the center is a dorsal of jagged mountains up to 6,000 feet in height that are usually topped with snow as early as October. The weather can be abysmal – rain, fog and freezing sleet in the winter and blinding heat in the summer. There is little room to deploy tanks. This is "foot-soldier" country and this is where Jack Meyers first experienced the agonizing pain of combat against a ghost-like foe.

Jack recalls the assault on Mt. Pantano. The men were exhausted, plagued by constant rain mixed with wind and cold and mud. Their clothing was sodden and boots were soaked through. Trench foot was almost impossible to avoid.

As they advanced, the Germans fired heavy artillery and mortar fire. It was impossible to dig a foxhole so the GIs had to pile boulders around themselves for protection from the exploding shells. After two weeks of constant shelling, the 168th held only one of four peaks on the top of Mount Pantano.

Casualties had been severe. Suffering from battle fatigue, frostbite, trench foot and pure exhaustion, the men appeared to become zombies with blank stares from expressionless eyes. Relief finally came on the 8th of December as the 2nd Moroccan Division passed through and relieved the 34th Division. The regiments withdrew to the rear for rest and reorganization. Christmas 1943 was spent at San Angelo. The men had hot food, showers, and were issued clean clothes. Replacements were absorbed. Christmas dinner had scarcely been eaten before the first units returned to the line.

The Germans' defenses beyond the Volturno River consisted of three different lines, each progressively tougher than the one before. The most intensely fortified position was referred to as the Gustav Line.

This line was anchored on a superb natural fortress, Monte Cassino, the centuries-old monastery founded by St. Benedict. There were only two main roads between Naples and Rome. One was the ancient Appian Way, known as Highway 7, which approached Rome by way of the coast. The second road, Highway 6, threaded its way through the mountains about 35 miles inland from the coast. Once the road passed Cassino, it led into a wide valley that was the gateway to Rome. Knowing full well the route that the Allies would take, the Germans concentrated their strongest defenses to block it.

Mine fields and barbed wire laid at the base of the mountain prevented passage of tanks or foot troops. Reinforced concrete bunkers had been blasted out from the rock of the Cassino hills. On January 21, 1944, the 36th Infantry Division attempted to cross the Rapido River south of Cassino and was repulsed with much blood shed. Three days later it was the 34th Division's turn. The 168th Regiment attempted to storm the north side. They faced intense enemy fire, heavy minefields, and barbed wire. A bridgehead at the base of the mountain was established and two small hills were attacked and captured.

Three days previously, an Allied amphibious force had successfully established a second beachhead at Anzio, north of Salerno. The plan was to bypass Cassino but because of the priority given to the preparations for the invasion of France, not enough resources were available for a breakout from the Anzio beachhead. Meanwhile, the mountain fighting remained stubborn and progress was slow. Casualties on both sides were heavy. Evacuating casualties down the shell-swept mountain trails became a very treacherous job. The 168th managed to reach the northern slopes of Monastery Hill but furious enemy counter attacks forced a withdrawal. The battle raged and the enemy reacted viciously. After three weeks of constant fire, repeated attacks and counter-attacks, seemingly endless nights on the bare rock of the mountain with little protection against the furies of rain, wind and snow, the men began to reach the limits of human endurance.

On February 14, 1944, the British 4th Indian Division took over the positions held by the 168th Infantry Regiment and the evacuation of the Americans began. Jack recalls some of the men had to be lifted bodily out of their holes and carried to waiting vehicles and he too was carried to a truck, because he was physically exhausted and disabled by trench foot. As I was being evacuated, I remember watching waves of American bombers demolish the monastery and I thought if the foot soldiers had any regret, it was only that the monastery had not been bombed earlier. After the abbey had been destroyed, the Allies learned that it had not been used for military purposes and the rubble now provided ideal lodgments for German mortar and machine-gun crews to repulse attacking allied forces.

I was taken to a field hospital where my combat boots had to be cut off and I was placed in a bed with a box placed at the foot of the bed so nothing would touch my feet. The slightest touching even a breeze caused considerable pain. After a few days of treatment, the doctor indicated that he wanted me to get up and begin walking to improve circulation. I responded, "Over my dead body!" The doctor explained that if I did not begin to walk soon, I would have to have both feet amputated. Fear of losing my feet gave me the resolve to begin therapy, but each step was so painful that I would scream as weight was placed on either foot. I struggled through that torment and eventually my feet healed.

In the *Story of the 34th Infantry Division* the author indicates, "The battle of Cassino was a failure. The Division had failed to take its objectives. The German paratroopers had succeeded in blocking the best effort of our troops to advance. Yet, for those who were there and who knew the difficulties of the assault, the tremendous strength of the German fortifications – to those men, Cassino was the outstanding achievement in the Division's history."

Little could be done for the decimated 168th regiment except to rest and recover the strength they had lost on the Cassino hills. Although large numbers of replacements were received the Regiments were still under strength and again faced a formidable task. Between March 17 and 25, 1944, LSTs made a journey each night from Naples carrying the 34th Infantry to the beachhead that had been established at Anzio, forty miles south of Rome.

At Anzio, the invasion had stalled and for the men of the 34th the warfare had now changed from assault to a routine of manning defensive positions, posting guards, and constant raiding parties to secure information on enemy units, their tactics and their defensive positions. Soon after my arrival at Anzio, while on information-seeking patrol at dusk, my squad was following a canal when we stopped breathlessly as we heard the sounds of weapons being readied. Looking around we could see all around us the silhouettes of German soldiers with their weapons ready. A voice ordered, "Surrender! Hands up!" We looked at each other only for a moment and quickly realized our situation was hopeless. We had two choices – surrender or die. We laid down our weapons.

We were marched back to what I believed to be their company headquarters. Our men were separated and I was taken to a tent where several German officers interrogated me. They spoke English well enough for me to understand their questions. As scared as I was, I would only state my name, rank, and serial number. After a short period, one of the officers stated the name of my unit and explained that they already knew the strength, positions, and plan of attack. Not knowing what to say or do, I remained stoic. In retrospect, I don't think I was ever so scared in my life. With all the death and destruction on both sides that I had witnessed in Italy, I began thinking what a burden I was to the Germans. If they shot me, they would not have to house me, feed me or guard me. But the Germans honored the Geneva Convention, and my buddies and I were placed in what I would describe as a scout car. We followed the road to Rome and then onto a holding camp somewhere near Florence, but I am not exactly sure where.

There, after enough prisoners were collected, they were placed on trains and transported to POW camps in Germany or Eastern Europe. The building in which we were kept was lined with fiberglass. The floor was covered with lice-infested straw. I recall being given brown bread when the Germans had any to spare. It was not unusual to go several days without food. We were also fed soup made of young shoots of nettle plants about every other day. It reminded me of spinach soup. I recalled as a child my mother putting food on my plate and I would not eat because I did not like the taste. My mother would shake her finger and say, "Someday you will be glad to have this food." Every day while in captivity, I remembered my mother's words and shaking her finger at me.

The Germans kept us occupied. Each day we went on road-repair projects. Life was miserable. We were hungry, dirty, lice-infested and sleep deprived. If we did not respond quickly to an order, we could expect the butt of a rifle in our legs. Since this was only a holding camp, escapes occurred. Following an escape, we stood for headcount for hours. Our captors played mental games with us pretending to execute a prisoner. We played our own games with them. I sometimes think survival depended upon an individual's sense of humor. We would do various things to screw up their headcount but in the end all we ever accomplished was to stand in formation longer than necessary. Yet, it was a form of satisfaction and relief from our situation. We were all hopeful that we would be rescued before being transported to Germany. The attitude of our guards would tell us how things were going at the front.

One evening at dusk, the guards ordered us to fall out and line up in columns of four. No one knew what was going on. Eventually we started marching toward the railroad station. The road was narrow and a German soldier was positioned about every twenty feet. We were on the road about an hour when darkness set in. As we approached a narrow bridge, the column was reduced to two. The bridge was about fifteen feet above a small stream. It was difficult to see, but I felt that I could jump safely. I think I was more afraid than brave. The thought of being sent to a prison camp really frightened me. My adrenaline began to flow and at that moment there was an opening in the rail. I stepped off the bridge and maintained my balance as I hit the water feet first and fell backward. I lay partially covered by the flowing water expecting excitement from the guards above. Nothing! I wasn't missed. I lay there silently until the columns passed and then I crawled to the bank. I began running away from the direction in which the troops were marching and had no idea where I was or where I was going, but I knew I had to get as far away as possible. Exhausted physically and emotionally, I found my way to some tall grass and passed out.

Awakened by the light of the next morning, I tried to get my bearings from the direction of the sound of cannon fire. I walked under the cover of a wooded area, and by mid-day, my lips were parched and I began to feel the pangs of hunger. I saw a farmer working in his fields. Unsure as to what to do, but I needed help. I called to him, "Signore, scusa!" He was frightened but came to the edge of the road. I did the best I could to convince him I was an 'Americano.'

With hand gestures and the little Italian I had learned, explained that I was thirsty and hungry. He invited me to accompany him, but I was fearful that he might turn me in for reward money. He acknowledged that he understood and left. I moved to a different position so that I could get away if he returned with soldiers or others. Fortunately, he returned alone and brought a loaf of bread, olive oil and a jug of water. Never before or since has anything tasted so good. He pointed to the direction I should take to make good my escape. I stayed within the woods as much as possible.

As I made my way, I encountered a group of Italian partisans. They were armed with weapons captured from the Germans or had been dropped by allied aircraft. Following Mussolini's depose in July 1943, the partisans had become more emboldened and began to run amok without restraint. They suspected that I might be a German plant disguised as an American. Despite my protests, they locked me in a makeshift cell until an English-speaking partisan arrived to interview me. After convincing him that I was an American soldier who had escaped from German captivity, the group now accepted me. Because I would have had to pass through German lines to return to the Allied sector, they suggested I remained with them for my own safety.

Their activities included cutting telephone wires, dynamiting bridges, culverts and railroad tracks. They did their work under the cover of darkness or fog, but never openly. The Germans detested their methods and every German soldier saw every Italian civilian as a fanatical assassin. For every German soldier killed or wounded by partisans, the Germans routinely executed ten civilians of military age.

The Germans were too close for comfort so I decided to leave. One of the partisans accompanied me for several days. He escorted me to the edge of the front lines. Under the cover of darkness, I inched my way south, always fearful that I may run into the enemy. As daylight approached, I lay motionless, listening. I heard voices and, thank God, they were speaking English. I had successfully crossed into friendly territory.

The British soldiers were cautious. They took me to their Command Post and a British officer interrogated me. Convinced that I was an American GI, they transported me to a British transition camp where I showered, shaved, received a haircut, given a British uniform and fed. There I met another American who had crossed into the compound several days earlier. We felt a great deal of pride and joy when told that Rome had fallen to Allied Forces on June 4, 1944.

The other GI and I wanted to get back to our outfits so we decided to make our way to Rome and from there attempt to reconnect. We walked out of the encampment and hitched a ride to Rome. After being dropped off, we approached an MP and explained our situation. He directed us to a supply depot where we could get out of the British and back into American uniforms. We had a bit of a hassle with the GI in the supply room who suspected we were German soldiers looking for American uniforms. We did everything we could to convince him otherwise but he still refused. We then went to a corner of the room and removed our clothing explaining we were not going to wear those woolen British uniforms one more minute and would stand where we were until he supplied us with American uniforms. Not knowing what to do, he left and returned with a supply officer who wanted to know what the hell we were doing. After much explaining and pleading we were given new uniforms. He said we must be GIs because no one else but a GI would ever pull a crazy stunt like that.

MPs accompanied us to their Headquarters where several officers debriefed us. After a million questions, we were released and MPs escorted us back to the same British transition camp that we had left earlier that day. This camp housed and processed Allied soldiers who were being returned to their home country. Many had serious wounds; others had acquired enough 'combat points" to rotate home. I never was sure why they selected me to return to the U.S. Maybe, they were just happy to get rid of me. Afterward, someone advised that because I was an escaped prisoner of war, the Geneva Convention prevented my return to a combat unit in the same Theatre from which I had escaped. Whatever the reason, I was happy to leave Italy. I had had enough. The ship *Kykladis,* manned by the British Navy departed Naples on August 25, 1944. Returnees were mostly Purple Hearts recipients.

I returned to Camp Kilmer, New Jersey still wearing the one and only uniform issued in Rome. By this time, it was quite soiled. I pleaded for clean clothes but instructed to report to Fort Meade, Maryland, where new uniforms and whatever else needed would be issued. Therefore, looking like a tramp, I left Camp Kilmer by train and as I made my way MPs stopped and questioned my appearance. When we arrived at Penn Station in Baltimore, I borrowed money from an MP to make a call home. I called my sister and asked her to come get me, as I did not want my folks to see me looking so disheveled. My sister and her husband arrived and informed me that my mother was seriously ill. Despite my appearance, we went directly to my parents' home. When my father opened the door, he stood there not believing his eyes. I went into the bedroom and my mother began to laugh and cry together. After a short visit my Dad drove me to Fort Meade. The next day I was processed, issued new uniforms and equipment and given a 30-day leave.

I was next assigned to the Quartermaster Corps and my Military Occupation Specialty (MOS) was changed from Rifleman to Foreman Warehouse, and I was assigned to the Quartermaster Depot at Greensburg, Pennsylvania where I spent my time waiting to be shipped to the Pacific Theatre. On March 27, 1945, I embarked from San Francisco for the Philippines and on the way, VE Day occurred in Europe. I was assigned to the 4172nd Quartermaster Depot Company. American forces recaptured Luzon in January 1945, and continuous bombing of Japan had begun shortly thereafter.

After all the hell I had gone through in Italy, I felt that I had landed a cushy job, but the U.S. was mobilizing for invasion of Japan. We were all concerned about our future if land forces invaded the Japanese homeland. Some of Japan's leaders vowed to fight to the death. Following the nuclear bombing of the cities of Hiroshima and Nagasaki, the Emperor wisely capitulated and on August 14, 1945, the Great War was over. I remained in Luzon until December 8 and returned to the good old U.S.A. four days before Christmas, 1945.

When my dad received the telegram advising that I was missing in action, he withheld the information from my mother. He was afraid the news might be too much of a shock for her. Besides, he was confident that I would be found and be O.K. Eventually, he shared the news with my Mom. There were tears and prayers, but Mom and Dad consoled each other through their mutual belief that I was alive and would return to their love. Following my escape and return to safety, things happened so quickly that I was unable to notify them that I was on my way home. So, one can imagine the shock my Dad must have felt when he opened the door and saw his soldier son standing on his doorstep. In retrospect, it was my faith in God instilled in me by my parents that kept me going through those terrible times."

Sergeant John H. Meyers received his honorable discharge from the military service of the United States of America on January 8, 1946. His awards include the Combat Infantryman's Badge, World War II Victory Ribbon, European African Middle Eastern Service Ribbon, Asiatic Pacific Theatre Ribbon, Philippine Liberation Ribbon, American Theatre Service Ribbon, Good Conduct Medal, and the Bronze Star awarded to all combat infantrymen in WWII and the POW Medal.

In civilian life, he was employed by the Domino Sugar Corporation for 32 years as a Quality Control Supervisor. He became active in the American Ex-Prisoners of War organization and was elected Maryland State Commander in 1990, a position he continues to hold. He is a member of the Maryland Veterans Commission and serves as a military advisor to Maryland U.S. Senator Barbara Mikulski.

Jack Meyers, November 2004

Stacy Wiitala, Fort Meade, December 1942

EINO "STACY" WIITALA

"You men carried the ball for us and
We will not forget it."
- General Dwight D. Eisenhower

THE GREAT DEPRESSION in the 1930s was
America's most devastating disaster since the
Civil War. Times were hard and sixteen million
people were looking for work. With the outbreak of
hostilities in Europe in 1939, the U.S. economy began to
improve. Stacy Wiitala was employed as a coal-miner
for the PGH Coal Company in western Pennsylvania. As
the sole support of his family, he was deferred from the
"peace time" draft that our government had introduced
in September 1940. When America was forced into war
against Japan and Germany, the military's demand for
manpower increased significantly, and Stacy was
twenty-five years old when he was drafted in December
1942.

His initial processing and testing took place at Camp
Meade, Maryland, and Stacy qualified for assignment to
the Army Air Forces, who were seeking skilled
personnel in more than 500 disciplines. Following
twelve days of basic training at Jefferson Barracks,
Missouri, he was transferred to Randolph Field in San
Antonio, Texas to attend welding school. As a civilian
he had had welding experience, and the Air Forces
provided advanced training in electric arc welding and
blacksmithing.

Following completion of this training, he was selected for the aviation cadet training, at Randolph Air Base.

Stacy completed pre-flight training and advanced to primary flight training at Coleman, Texas, where ninety-two hours were devoted to academic work in ground school along with fifty-four hours of military training. His progress was good. He flew seventeen hours of pre-solo and three and one-half hours of solo flight developing proficiency in landing techniques, and recovery from stalls and spins. However, the requirements to become a pilot were extremely rigid and by failing to advance to the next phase of flight training, Stacy transferred to aerial gunnery school at Harlingen, Texas, to begin training as a career gunner.

Next, he joined a group of ten airmen and officers for unit and crew training on a B-24 bomber. The crew ferried their B-24 from Topeka, Kansas to Wales in the British Isles and arrived at their station on May 16, 1944. They became part of the 44th Bomb Group, 506th Bomb Squadron named *The Green-Nosed Flying Eight Balls*. Stacy's baptism under fire came just three days later on May 19, 1944, and one can hardly imagine a more frightening introduction to war. The target that day was the industrial complex at Brunswick, Germany, about 150 miles west of Berlin.

Stacy Wiitala's Story:
The formation for the May 19, 1944 raid consisted of 26 ships from the 44th BG. Nine of these aircraft were from the 506th squadron. This was my first combat mission. I was the nose gunner on Lt. Irving Gurman's B-24 and had an exceptional view of the entire operation. There was plenty of flak and the sky was covered with planes. Approximately 200 enemy fighters outnumbered our fighters by about four-to-one and they

began taking a good toll of our B-24s. As we neared the target, a storm of flak rocked our plane sending fragments through her metal skin. We held steady and, as we continued on the bombing run, I could see other planes being hit by flak and several went down. Parachutes blossomed. It was very rough going but we made it to the target, dropped our bomb load and headed back to base. It was a costly strike; one crew counted fifteen B-24s going down, and later photos showed only fair hits on the target.

After that terrifying mission, I began to worry about what the future held for me. Heavy losses always had a negative affect on morale, particularly on your first mission, but we had a job to do and that was to get bombs accurately on target. In order to cope, I developed this fatalistic attitude, "If I get it, I get it. There isn't a helluva lot I can do about it!" On the positive side, I reasoned one mission was now over and I had twenty-four more to go before rotating home.

Four days later, on May 23, 1944 we were up at 0100 for a 0445 takeoff to a German-held airfield about sixty miles south of Paris. It was extremely cold with a free air temperature at 29 degrees below zero. The flak over the target was light and the bombing results were very good. A real milk run, and strike photos showed excellent results. Colonel Gibson led the Division on this mission and reportedly stated that the bombing was the best that the Group had ever achieved.

The next day, May 24, our target was the French town of Melun, about 25 miles south of Paris. The 44th Bomb Group sent thirty-six ships on this mission. Our crew was one of eleven aircraft from the 506th. The flak was medium but accurate and several ships were hit, but none were downed. The bombing results were fair.

The target for May 25 was the marshaling yards at Belfort, France about ten miles northwest of the Swiss border. The rail line was a main transportation route into southern Germany. Although smoke obscured the target, bombing results were good. We had no casualties. After releasing our bombs, we turned for the "long run" home.

May 28, 1944 was my fifth mission in ten days. The target was a large synthetic oil refinery at Zeitz, located 120 miles south of Berlin. That morning everything seemed to go wrong. Our bombardier, Morton Bouman, was sick and could not fly. Then, when we were all set to take off, the plane did not check out on the final check. We taxied back for another plane and moved our guns and other equipment to *The Banana Barge*, and finally made it off. It was about an eight-hour flight. Before we reached the target, we were in the heaviest flak I had ever seen. It seemed to swallow up the bomber formations as they moved into it. We took a hit and lost an engine. Then another hit and another engine lost. Flak was everywhere and the next hit cut the fuel lines to the other engines and fuel began spilling into the plane. I was covered with it. The plane was completely disabled and the pilot could not keep it flying. He ordered us to bail out immediately. I went out through the nose wheel opening.

Looking up, I could see parachutes floating down. Looking down, I could see a German farmer with a weapon, either a rifle or shotgun, tracking me. As I hit the ground, he hurried toward me and I quickly got out of my harness and ran toward the woods. German soldiers were on that side. A shot rang out and struck me in my rear. The German soldiers closed in and quickly took charge. Fortunately, the bullet had deflected off my escape pack before striking me. One of the soldiers was able to remove the bullet from the cheek of my butt. Many years later, 1958, I received the Purple Heart for this wound.

Eventually, our entire crew was captured. Lt. Irving S. Gurman, was the pilot, Lt. Robert F. Jipson, co-pilot, and Lt. Andrew J. Kaulbach, Jr., the navigator. S/Sgt. George B. Costello was top turret gunner, and S/Sgt. Joseph Carson, the radio operator. Sgt. James H. McMaster was the ball turret gunner, Sgt. Theodore D.Willis, was the waist gunner, Sgt. Charles D. Williams, tail gunner, and I was the nose gunner.

We were loaded onto a truck and taken to the interrogation center near Frankfurt. They questioned us about the plane, the type of bombs we carried, number and types of armaments, the flight group, where we were based and on and on. All I ever gave them was my name, rank, and serial number. Alone in a cell without lights, they would fill it with steam at night. After several days of this routine, the interrogator offered to let me go back with my buddies if I would give him the answer to only one question, "What is your mother's maiden name?" Bewildered, I asked myself, "Why would he want to know that?" I continued to refuse to answer. They returned me to my cell and again turned on the steam. The next day, they again asked the same question. Refusing to answer, they forced me to strip and stand naked in a corner while they questioned other prisoners. At night, they would awaken me and again ask the same question. It was tortuous and it became a battle of wills. I never gave them the satisfaction of an answer.

This questioning has always mystified me. At the Stalag, I talked with fellow prisoners about it. Someone suggested that perhaps a high-ranking Nazi had married a Finnish woman whose sister or someone else had married a man named Wiitala and he was trying to determine if this other woman was my mother. It is a rational theory that may or may not be valid. Even today, I wish I knew the reason for their question.

After several days, the American POWs were marched from the interrogation center to the rail station in Frankfurt. The Germans guarding us had bayonets fixed to their rifles and if we walked too slowly or stepped out of line, they would jab us with the point of their bayonets. German citizens along the route screamed at us, threw things and spat on us. It was a very scary experience. At the station, we were loaded onto boxcars and transported to Stalag Luft IV in northeastern Germany. Fifty-six men were crammed into my car leaving barely enough room to stand or sit. We arrived at Keifheide on D-Day, June 6, 1944. If I had known then that the invasion of Europe was taking place, I would have been less anxious about my situation.

From June 6, 1944 to February 6, 1945, I lived in Barracks 2, Room 5 at Stalag Luft IV. Life as a prisoner of war was boring and tedious. We kept ourselves occupied by playing cards that were provided by the American Red Cross, and reading the few books that were available. We had a softball bat and organized a barracks team that competed against other barracks' teams. Periodically, there would be a discussion about escaping. Because of my coal mining experience, I was enlisted to help build a tunnel, but the area where the camp was located was so remote that I don't think any of us could have made it back successfully.

I was a POW for almost eleven months, and during that entire period, I received only one letter – notifying me of my father's death. They allowed us to send out two letters plus four postcards a month. We kept informed of the progress of the war because someone had been able to rig a crystal radio while we were in camp.

Overall, the quality of our food was very poor and barely enough to keep us alive. It was primarily barley, carrots and dehydrated bullion made into soup. The bread was hard and mixed with sawdust. We were always hungry. The Red Cross parcels really helped. We never knew when we might get one and we always had to share a parcel with one or more of the other men. At the time of my capture, I weighed 165 pounds, but by the time I was liberated my weight had dropped to 115 pounds. Much of that weight loss occurred after we had evacuated Stalag Luft IV.

Because the Russians were approaching from the east, we were forced to evacuate our camp and marched across Germany during one of the cruelest winters on record. We lived like animals, sleeping in the open, foraging for potatoes or anything else we could scrounge from the fields, never changing clothes, much less bathing. We were all lice infested. The weather was bone-freezing cold and we would huddle together at night under a thin blanket to try to stay warm. We wandered aimlessly, seemingly without a destination, always hoping that tomorrow we would reach another camp. Another camp never came. Then, during the night of May 2, 1945, our German guards took off while we slept in a farm field. Unescorted, we continued to walk west for two more days until we finally reached the lines of the British 2nd Army. We must have been quite a sight to behold – starved, exhausted, filthy, and infested with lice. Our tattered clothes were incinerated; we were deloused, had a hot shower, and issued new clothing. I contentedly ate my first full meal in almost a year. My ordeal was finally over.

At St. Valery, France, while I was awaiting shipment home, General Eisenhower came to visit. About 40,000 former prisoners assembled to hear him speak. He stood on a flatbed truck that was equipped with a public address system and told us that he was personally doing everything he could to get us home as soon as possible.

He said he had issued orders for American-bound ships carrying liberated POWs to be loaded to capacity, even to the extent of asking men to share individual beds and to sleep in shifts in order to fulfill their wishes of getting home soon, "even if we have to swim." He reminded us that the war was still being waged against Japan and said, "We can't supply all the shipping needed for you immediately because we must also think of your fellow soldiers fighting in the Pacific." He expressed his gratitude to all of us for helping to defeat Germany saying, "You men carried the ball for us and we will not forget it." Later, he walked among the men and spoke personally to about one hundred individuals. I had the privilege of being one of them. Somehow, that made the memories of my ordeal a little more bearable.

Personal Message

As I look back over the years, I have come to realize that the sacrifices made during that terrible war were small in comparison with the many blessings I have received since then. I have been married to my loving wife Ethel Guffrey for fifty-eight years. Together we have two wonderful children, six grandchildren and one great-grandson. As a token of my love, I dedicate this story to my children – son, Alan and his wife Karen and their children, Chrissy and Holly; and great-grandson, Dakota Fleck; and daughter Beth and her husband, John Williams and their children, Marc, Betsy, Jono and Lucas.

Eino J. 'Stacy' Wiitala received his honorable discharge from the Army Air Forces at the rank of Staff Sergeant on January 9, 1946, at Mitchell Field, Long Island, New York. He was twenty-eight years old. He was awarded the Purple Heart Medal; POW Medal; European, African, Middle-Eastern Campaign Medal; World War II Victory Medal; American Theatre Medal; and Good Conduct Medal.

STALAG LUFT IV, LAGER A

Fire Pool
In A & B

Outdoor
Washroom

Mess Hall

Night Latrine

Room 10

Indoor Washroom
Room 5, Barracks 2

B Lager under construction

Potato Cellar

Guard Rail

Cemetery

Guard Tower

D Lager

Stacy Wiitala lived in Room 5, Barracks 2 (extreme left) from 6/6/44-2/6/45

311

Walter & Florence Kehs

WALTER J. KEHS

"Following Allied bombing raids, the
POWs were taken to the bombed sites and made
to dig through the rubble and recover the
bodies of dead German civilians."

AFTER GRADUATING from Baltimore's
Thomas Edison Vocational High School,
Walter Kehs worked as an electrician out of
Union Local 24. He was drafted in June 1941, but he
sustained a serious hand injury and, as a result, was
medically discharged. Once the injury healed
sufficiently, he was again drafted in June 1942.
Following basic training at Camp Lee, Virginia, he
attended radio operator school at Camp Hood, Texas.
Next, he was assigned to the 7th Armored Division at
Camp Polk, Louisiana, where he became a radio
sergeant in the 814th Tank Destroyer Battalion's
Reconnaissance Company. In February 1944, the
Division sailed aboard the unescorted *Ile de France* from
Halifax, Nova Scotia to Greenock, Scotland, a ten-day
journey. Walter trained for combat on the moors at
Greenock and later at a base outside Coventry, England.
The 7th Armored Division entered France on August 8,
1944, and immediately went into combat with Patton's
3rd Army.

Following the Germans defeat in Normandy, the 7th
Armored Division was positioned near Aachen on the
Dutch-German border. Walter was the radio operator on
an M-20 utility carrier, an armored combat vehicle. He
was part of a unit whose job it was to scout the terrain to

locate enemy tanks, and radio this information back to the battalion's tank destroyers' crews who would then move forward to engage the enemy. This was high-risk business. It had some side benefits. On one occasion, a single-engine German reconnaissance plane flew low over the area and Walter opened fire with the .50-inch caliber machine-gun mounted on the M-20, and shot down the plane and he and the crew captured the German pilot.

The Allied forces had been so successful in destroying French railway bridges, rail lines and rolling stock during the Normandy battle that when their armies broke out of their bridgehead in August, rail transportation was almost non-existent and they were supplied by truck over the roads from Normandy. The constant stream of vehicles supplying the front became known as the "Red Ball Express." The Allied forces needed 700 tons of material per day simply to sustain their armies and more to support a major offensive. Without available ports along the channel, their advance ground to halt. The superb port of Antwerp was essential to supply an offensive into Germany.

Hitler reasoned that if the Allies were denied the use of the port at Antwerp, then their offensive into Germany would be delayed for months. He also believed that if the German army took the offensive, it could cut off the British 2nd and Canadian 1st Armies from the Americans, encircle and destroy them. He dreamed of another Dunkirk. Once that was accomplished, he planned to strike at strategic Russian positions on the eastern border. Meanwhile, his V-2 rockets would inflict increasing damages on London and so demoralize the English people they would pressure their government to end the war. Hitler knew Germany could not win the war, but if his plan was successful, he intended to sue for peace hoping to retain Germany's 1939 territory conquests, and the Nazi regime would remain intact.

When the German counter-offensive popularly known as the "Battle of the Bulge" was launched in the Ardennes on December 16, 1944, only four American divisions – the 28th, 106th, and 4th Infantry Divisions and the 9th Armored Division – were spread across the 90-mile front guarding the major area of attack.

The 28th Division was a veteran outfit having arrived in Normandy in July 1944. They had fought at Saint-Lo and the Huertgen Forrest where they had been so decimated that they were now in the Ardennes to be refurbished. North of them was the 106th Infantry Division, the greenest of the American Divisions, having arrived in France on December 4, 1944. These two divisions would face the German 5th Panzer Army.

The 4th Infantry Division was another veteran outfit, having fought in Normandy and Northern France and having entered Paris with French units. They, too, had suffered severe losses in the Huertgen Forest and after being relieved, repaired to Luxembourg. The 9th Armored Division, another inexperienced outfit, had arrived in France on October 3, 1944. These two divisions would oppose the German 7th Army.

Allied Commanders welcomed the opportunity to get the Germans out of their defensive positions so that their armies could be engaged and destroyed, but they sorely underestimated the strength and severity of the German counter-offensive.

Saint-Vith was one of two towns with key road junctions that were critical to the German's success the other was Bastogne. Saint-Vith's defenders initially consisted of a lone combat engineer battalion supported by a handful of infantry and a few antitank guns, but it was critical that the enemy advance be delayed until reinforcements could be brought in. Although German personnel and firepower overwhelmed the Americans, they put up a remarkable defense and prevented the Germans from advancing. When the Germans began their attack on December 16, 1944, the US 7th Armored Division was in the Aachen area one hundred kilometers away from Saint-Vith and they began their move immediately. They entered into the battle the evening of December 17, 1944. When Saint-Vith finally fell on December 23, 1944, it was a hollow victory, because the Germans had frittered away five precious days battling for Saint-Vith when they should have been racing to the Meuse River, and then northwest to their principal objective, Antwerp. December 23, 1944, was also the day Walter Kehs became one of more than 15,000 Americans taken prisoner of war during the Battle of the Bulge.

For 125 days from the day of his capture to the time he was liberated, Walter Kehs kept a diary of his odyssey as a prisoner of war. He focused his brief entries on his journey, location and what he was fed each day. It began with his capture on December 23, 1944, at 2200 hours at Saint-Vith, Belgium.

Walter tells his story:
The 7th Armored Division was on the Dutch-German border when the German counter offensive through the Ardennes began on December 16, 1944. We were ordered to move immediately. Two regiments of the 106th Infantry Division were trapped on a high ridge known as the Schnee-Eifel. They were surrounded, cut off and running out of ammunition. Our orders were to get to the area as soon as possible and punch a hole in the German's line and open an escape route for the two regiments. As we rumbled east, we became tied up in one immense traffic jam after another all caused by retreating American troops. Several times, out of

frustration, we used our tanks to push vehicles off the road that were blocking our way. Because of the delays, our lead units did not reach Saint-Vith until nightfall on December 17, and the rest of the division came in the next morning, too late to save the men of the 106th.

The route through Saint-Vith led to a massive American supply dump that the Germans counted on capturing to fuel their attack. Our mission now was to defend Saint-Vith and delay the enemy's advance until more reinforcements could be brought into the area. The 5th Panzer Army also arrived outside of Saint-Vith on December 17, 1944. We stood as one American armored division against the entire German 5th Panzer Army. Although they had superior numbers, the roads were icy and they were experiencing the kind of traffic jams that earlier had delayed our race to the town. As the Germans tried to coordinate an attack, our tanks' constant spearheads into their flanks tied up their army for nearly a week, disrupting their timetable and blocking their supply routes. The fighting was fierce but we were completely outnumbered and becoming encircled. Now, we faced the possibility of being surrounded and cut off. Only a narrow escape corridor remained open and a pullout was ordered for December 23, 1944.

I was one of two radio operators on a fifteen-man reconnaissance team in two M-20 armored utility carriers and two jeeps. The Germans had just blown a bridge partially blocking the escape route. Our orders were to locate their tanks and troop concentrations and radio this information back to help effect the retreat. Germans seemed to be everywhere. We came to a road junction, and being unfamiliar with the terrain, we radioed our position. Some unknown Colonel ordered us to take the left fork and proceed for another mile and report back. This was a suicide mission because we knew a major enemy force was moving toward us and we would run into heavy pockets of fire. Even to this day, I believe we were set up as decoys to give the rest of the unit time to escape. But orders were orders.

We had not proceeded very far when we ran into the enemy who began firing. We drove on at full throttle. As our four vehicles raced at breakneck speed on the ice-covered road, we fired furiously at the many German soldiers amassed along both sides of the road, catching many by surprise. They were so close we could see their faces and many were hit and fell. We rounded an S-turn and flew past a German Panzer. On a second S-turn, we skidded on the ice, slid head-on into another German tank and crashed into it just below its gun turret. An ammunition box in our carrier fell and crushed my big toe. Our other three vehicles slid to a halt. German soldiers quickly surrounded us and pointed their weapons directly at us. We could do nothing but surrender. At that point, all fifteen men were captured.

We were quickly loaded onto a truck and taken several miles behind the lines to a building where German officers interrogated us. These battle-hardened veterans were hungry for intelligence and short on patience. They wanted to know the name of our outfit, our troop strength, their location, and other related information. They threatened us with our lives when we did not respond. It was a nightmare experience. They relieved us of our watches and rings, and I had to remove my boots and exchange them for a German soldier's shoes that had wooden slats on the soles. I wore new parachute jump boots and the German soldier's shoes were two sizes too small for me, which aggravated my crushed toe. My protests were to no avail.

We were then forced to march the first leg of a forty-four mile, three-day journey to the German town of Gerolstien. I spent Christmas Day walking ten miles in unbearable agony and I had to use my first sergeant as a crutch. He literally carried me the last several miles. My only wish was that American paratroopers would capture the Nazi bastard who was wearing my boots. They had a special form of retribution for Krauts captured wearing American paratrooper boots.

We arrived at Gerolstien on December 28, after walking the final twenty-four mile leg that day. My foot still ached, but the pain was becoming tolerable. Gerolstien was not a prison camp, but there were about three hundred POWs housed in a large two-story barn. We were made to work around the clock everyday with a pick and shovel removing debris and filling in bomb craters. It is hard to say no when a rifle is pointed at your chest. We worked in eight-hour shifts and upon completion of a shift, I would return to the barn only to be selected again. I tried to explain but I could not speak German and they could not understand English. Several times I worked twenty-four consecutive hours, until I finally learned to stay outside until the next detail had been selected. I remained at Gerolstien for twenty days, worked every day and fed only one meal a day, usually soup and hard tack or bread.

On January 17, 1945, we drew rations and began a three-day walk in bitter cold weather to Mayen, and loaded into boxcars. After spending two freezing days and nights in the boxcars, we arrived at Stalag XIIA in Limburg on January 22, 1945. It was another bitter cold night with temperatures well blow freezing, and we were housed in barracks without any heat. The next day, I shaved for the first time in thirty-seven days. The cold water made the shave uncomfortable but it still felt good.

On January 26, we left Limburg by train with almost seventy men packed like sardines into each boxcar, and there we stayed for two more wretched days and nights. Our destination was Hammelburg and after arriving, we walked 2.5 miles to Stalag XIIIC. For the first time in months, I slept in a heated barracks. When you have been so cold for so long, it's hard to describe a simple pleasure like being warm. I took my first shower in forty-eight days. Although brief, it felt great. About a week later, I acquired a pair of boots that fit when one of the prisoners died, and on February 6, 1945, I had my hair cut for the first time in at least two months. Rations continued to be adequate but never enough.

Following Allied bombing raids, they took us to the bombed sites and forced us to dig through the rubble to recover the bodies of dead German civilians. Although it was a gruesome task, it had some rewards because we always searched for food and often found canned tins of food in the rubble that we were able to hide on our person and sneak into the barracks.

On March 31, we were on the move again, this time by freight train from Hammelburg to Nuremberg. While on this move, American fighters strafed the train and I am told that an American GI was killed and another wounded. Our stay at Nuremberg was short. We remained for only three days before beginning a sixteen-day march, in groups of one hundred, to Stalag VIIA at Moosburg. Food and shelter were scarce and we slept in barns when they were available or out in the open fields and scrounged the fields for potatoes, beets or anything edible. The camp at Moosburg was severely overcrowded but they accommodated us. As part of the camp's de-lousing program, we showered and our clothing was dusted with DDT. For the next twenty tedious days, the only notations in my diary reflected my focus on food – we thought about nothing else.

One day, all the guards walked away and we were overcome with joy when GIs from Patton's 3rd Army arrived at the camp's gates. One of the most emotional moments I have ever experienced was when they raised the American flag over the camp. I cried like a baby. My nightmare was finally over.

After leaving Moosburg, I traveled by truck to Ingolstadt, and then was transported by a cargo plane to Reims, France, and then by train through France to Camp Lucky Strike near LeHavre. I had lost thirty-five pounds during my four plus months of captivity, so for fourteen days I was fed gradually. I patiently endured the army's agonizingly slow processing procedures necessary before returning to the USA. Finally, on May 27, 1945, I left LeHavre for my return trip home aboard a liberty ship. After a brief leave at home, I went to Miami Beach, Florida for 14 days rest and recuperation.

During my 125 days of captivity, I was allowed to send only three postcards to my family, and I never received any mail from home. My wife and parents had to have been frantic with worry, not knowing if I was dead or alive. I believe their anguish was as difficult for them as my deprivations and hardships were to me.

Walter J. Kehs received his honorable discharge at the rank of Staff Sergeant on October 23, 1945. He was awarded the Purple Heart; POW Medal; American Defense Service Medal; American Campaign Medal; European, African, Middle-Eastern Campaign Medal with Three Battle Stars; World War II Victory Medal; Good Conduct Medal; and Marksman Badge – Army Pistol.